I0188494

A Philosopher Looks at Jesus

A Philosopher Looks at Jesus

Gleanings from a Life of Faith, Doubt, and Reason

Edward J. Machle

RESOURCE *Publications* · Eugene, Oregon

A PHILOSOPHER LOOKS AT JESUS
Gleanings from a Life of Faith, Doubt, and Reason

Copyright © 2008 Edward J. Machle. All rights reserved. Except for brief quotations in critical publications or reviews, no part of this book may be reproduced in any manner without prior written permission from the publisher. Write: Permissions, Wipf and Stock, 199 W. 8th Ave., Suite 3, Eugene, OR 97401.

www.wipfandstock.com

ISBN 13: 978-1-49825-060-3

Unless otherwise noted, all New Testament passages quoted are from the Revised Standard Version, copyright © 1946. Thanks is also given to University of Chicago Press for a quote from its "The Bible, an American Translation" and to James Clark for a quote from Weymouth's New Testament in Modern Speech. Old Testament quotations are from Jewish Publication Society's Tanakh, 1999.

Manufactured in the U.S.A.

Contents

Contents

Preface

> Men today are divided between those who have kept their
> spiritual roots and lost their contact with the existing order of
> society, and those who have preserved their social contacts and
> lost their spiritual roots.
>
> —Christopher Dawson[1]

T HIS BOOK IS NOT primarily a philosophy book. Nor is it a theology
book. Nor is it another attempt at writing the "life of Jesus." It is the
outcome of the long life of a young minister whose doubts and thinking
led him from the parish, to a Ph.D. in philosophy, to a career teaching
philosophy in a secular state university.

Now, as a professor emeritus for some years, I've had occasion to
reexamine where I am intellectually as a Christian. I don't pretend to be
a professional theologian or New Testament scholar. If the bibliography
and footnotes give some evidence of biblical or theological scholarship,
they also show my limits. But I have done a good amount of homework,
because a philosopher needs to have some confidence that he has actually
immersed himself in what he talks about.

So this book is several things: a response to questions put to me by
colleagues and students, an offering of conclusions I have reached concerning Jesus, and a reaction to a number of influences in recent academia.
My theology, therefore, appears more explicitly than my philosophy.

After two hundred years of trying, historians have been largely
forced to give up on writing historically accurate "lives of Jesus," because
so many intellectual problems have arisen out of the available records.
However, attempts to understand him can't avoid granting the adult Jesus
an influential boyhood and youth. Therefore this book contains some fiction, frankly acknowledged as such, but only fiction intended to give a

---

1. Quoted in Vidler, *The Church in an Age of Revolution*, 273.

presumptive background to judgments about his life. Besides such fiction, thinking about Jesus requires close attention to the records that tell us of him, and to the problems they pose—both as documents and as reports of events. And that demands thinking about our manners of thinking and the standards by which we ought to judge them.

Each one must read what is said as a personal kind of act. What Jesus means to one cannot be prescribed by another, no matter how extensive his information, how strenuous his disciplined thinking, or how deep his faith. I cannot prescribe belief for another. Do your own listening and responding. As Luther said, each must do his own believing, just as he must do his own dying.

Acknowledgments

A LIFETIME OF INTELLECTUAL and spiritual debts is too large to allow specific thanks to all of those who made significant contributions. Some of the multitudes of works that have affected my thinking through the past are listed in the bibliography. Others to be acknowledged in particular are my parents, who grounded me early in the Bible, the sciences, and critical thinking. A few scholars of importance to my development are mentioned in the text, some perhaps too frequently. I am beholden to them, along with many unnamed others.

Worthy of special mention are several of my philosophy professors, especially John H. Randall, Jr. and Herbert Schneider; and among theologians, Edward A. Wicher, Gurdon Oxtoby, and Paul Tillich. Nor can I pass over my philosophical colleagues, especially Walter Veazie, David Hawkins, William Sacksteder, and John Carnes. I alone am, of course, responsible for any wrong or foolish ideas presented.

Beyond this, I can only say a collective thanks to my parents, teachers, critics, pastors, and to the students, the good friends and family who have forced me to grow both by nurture and challenge. A special thanks is due to my careful copyeditor Nancy Shoptaw for her detailed concern with maintaining the integrity of the book. And what I owe to the love, patience, and common sense of my wife Mary Lou is beyond words.

Appreciation and thanks are due to publishers of copyrighted works quoted in the text. Journals include *Journal of the American Academy of Religion, Journal of Biblical Literature,* and *Studies in Religion/Sciences Religieuses.* For use of copyrighted material from books, I acknowledge and thank Abingdon Press, Atheneum Press, Bruce Publishers, Cornell Univ. Press, Crossroad Publishing, Doubleday, Wm. B. Eerdmanns, Fortress Press, Harper Collins, Holt, Rinehart, Oxford Univ. Press, Paulist Press, Pilgrim Press, Polebridge Press, Scholars Press, Scribner's, Trinity Press, and Westminster/John Knox Press.

1

Why Think about Jesus?

> Religion invites the scrutiny of philosophy, and philosophy
> may not neglect the problems of religion . . . We are sluggards
> or cowards if, pretending to be philosophic students and genu-
> ine seekers of truth, we do not attempt to do something with
> these questions. We are worse than cowards if, attempting to
> consider them, we do so otherwise than reverently, fearlessly,
> and honestly.
>
> —Josiah Royce[1]

WHY THINK ABOUT JESUS? Why, especially, should a *philosopher*
think about Jesus? And why in the world should one *write* about
Him? He may be important to popes, bishops, theologians, ministers, and
ordinary naive believers, all of who may have a stake in arguing about
him, or even meditating about Him. But philosophers? They want logical
arguments, not confessions of belief.

Thus, we philosophers generally don't have much of a problem with
the figure of Jesus of Nazareth. Especially so, if we take him as our fellow
scholars, the critical historians, may speak of him.[2] He did say some useful things often quoted in ethics classes; the stories about him—things
such as miracles—may raise questions. Beyond that, he seems to provide
nothing that might require serious critical thought. We philosophers, apparently, can easily dispense with him, and we usually do.

So we "thinkers" typically spend little time on Jesus, even as a moral
teacher. He wasn't, by our standards, a moral philosopher. His thinking
wasn't formally "logical." His teaching wasn't clear or well organized,

---

1. In Reardon, *Religious Thought*, 312.

2. "Critical" in this book usually means, "thinking carefully," not "criticizing" in the
popular sense.

though he was indeed "critical" of many of his contemporaries in one non-philosophical sense. No one can tell us of any well-worked-out theories he developed, nor any logical proofs he offered. He doesn't clarify his concepts; we have to clarify them, if we can. And his "method" is hardly definable.[3]

He puzzled and confused his closest associates. He forced his later followers to write a wide variety of interpretations of what it was he was doing and teaching—interpretations that are still being argued about nearly twenty centuries later. (One must admit that the same could be said of the greatest philosophers.)

So why should a philosopher think about Jesus? If he was raised in the church or went to Sunday School, philosophical training probably led him to consider Jesus, as many philosophers do, as no more than another ancient Jewish teacher, easy to set aside. Yet he might well find Jesus still lurking in the back of his mind, making some claims upon his thinking in at least some areas. And if he follows those claims out, he may do some further thinking about Jesus, and find him harder to set aside than he expected.

One without such a background might still find Jesus' effect in history too great to allow passing over, and wish to go further.

However, I became a philosopher because I grew up with a Bible in one hand and science books in the other. The tensions between them have stimulated my intellectual life for many years. I've discovered that even though thinking about Jesus may not be in itself philosophy, it not only leads one to philosophy but also conditions how one philosophizes, including how one philosophizes about some apparently unphilosophical things.

A philosopher who undertakes to think about Jesus may question at least the following:

1. Is our information about Jesus reliable? What are our sources, and what problems do they raise?

2. To understand Jesus, what do we have to assume about his early years, of which we have hardly any knowledge?

3. What can we believe of the stories about his birth, his miracles, and his ideas?

---

3. Some sixty years ago a book, *The Experimental Logic of Jesus*, appeared. I know of no philosopher who took it seriously.

4. Can one make sense of the resurrection and the reports about it?

5. What influence on his believers did Jesus have beyond just his moral teachings?

After dealing with these first five questions he may be ready to look at the current situation, namely:

6. What present-day difficulties interfere with taking Jesus seriously?

But, for the philosopher, there's another question:

7. What has theology to do with philosophy?

This book wrestles with all these questions, in more or less the above order, but with the last discussed early and returned to periodically.

If Jesus doesn't awe us as a first-century Jewish teacher, he will seem easy to set aside. But if a serious thinker really faces up to the awesome claim that Jesus was resurrected as the Lord Christ, rather than brushes it away, then things change. He finds that philosophy, as contemporaries largely do it, cannot treat Jesus as Christians do, as "the Risen Lord." There is simply no satisfactory philosophical analysis of the terms "resurrected," "Lord," and "Christ," as used among Christians. Indeed, they are *used*, and don't just merely *occur*.

Where does awe come in? Because Jesus poses the most basic of all philosophical and theological questions, the problem that underlies all other such questions: *What does it mean to be a human?*[4] He comes to us as "the son of man," perhaps the representative human. If so, he claims a role that we ourselves, being philosophers, covertly assume. But Jesus' answer to that question was his distinctive self, *in his situation*, not some general theory he held or implies about humans in the abstract.

Let us start with his impressiveness as the *concrete unique individual representative human*. That is what has been more historically influential than his "ordinary man-in-the-street-ness," his "Rabbi-ness," or his "Cynic-sage-ness," nor any of the many kinds of "moral sageliness" that have been claimed for him—even more than his "God-come-down-to-earth" role. It is his impact as one of us, in the midst of us, yet one set

---

4. "The animality of man we can grasp with a fair degree of clarity. The perplexity begins when we attempt to make clear what is meant by the *humanity* of man. . . . As a process man may be described biologically; as an event he can only be understood creatively, dramatically." Heschel, *Who Is Man?* 43–44.

above us, without being foreign to us, that is important. It was those who *knew* him who first called him "the resurrected Lord Christ."

When we philosophers try to use terms like "resurrection," "Lord," or "Christ" philosophically, rather than faith-fully, we make them either secular or meaningless—and often end up doing both. Yet far too many serious and thoughtful lives have shown those terms to be both meaningful and relevant, and at the same time profound.

Had there been no resurrection, Jesus would not have been important enough to justify the immense, conscientious, and detailed labors that have been expended toward clarifying and understanding his presence in history. Had there been no crucifixion, the resurrection would not have had the power or depth of meaning that it has demonstrated it does have. But both crucifixion and resurrection presume the figure, life, and teachings of that Galilean Israelite, Jesus of Nazareth. Crucifixion attests his humanity, but resurrection claims he was, though thoroughly human, not just another ordinary person. So he poses both the question and offers the answer. But we can perceive that answer only partially, or some of us, perhaps, not at all.

That is why Jesus is important. Jesus has been most influential intellectually in terms of his effect on our understanding of us as humans. But he lived long ago, in a different age, and a different culture. He spoke and thought in a different language, different not only from ours, but from the language of the records we have of him. He himself left no written records, and it is very doubtful that any of those who wrote of him had heard him firsthand.

What we do know is that *the life he lived was a human life*, and being human is something that is *learned*. We were all taught our humanity by our parents, culture, and experiences, including our self-criticism. So a prime problem in clearing up one's idea of Jesus is thinking about how he learned what the records show he had learned, and was perhaps still learning. How this happened we can only guess—since our records cover so little of his life—and do so only partially, though our guesses should stay as close to the records as possible.

Understanding Jesus, then, must include some idea of his life before he appears in the gospels as an adult. But we have very little information about that, and what we have we can't be sure of. Based on what we have about his later life and character, we have to imagine a part of his life that we have almost no information about.

Such stories are, of course, creatures of the imagination. There is nothing wrong with that. Every scientific theory started out as imagination. History also demands it. So does every meaningful life. But honesty disciplines imaginations by what facts we do have, even when those facts are traditional stories like the gospels, or archaeological or linguistic facts that at any time may become reinterpreted or even disproved.[5]

The only particular basis we have for such stories, beyond what general knowledge we can glean about the history and culture of his times, is tradition.[6] Its relation to new developments may be open or closed. Is such tradition reliable? Our modern world largely shaped itself by distrusting tradition. At the same time, it built upon it. So we have to admit there are traditions to be distrusted and ones to be trusted.

The materials for constructing a story of Jesus are stories that went through a traditioning process for some years before being recorded. Does this disprove them? Can they be trusted?

Old Testament scholar Brueggemann says something important about how records like those we have of Jesus came to us:

> The traditioning process is one of interpretive imagination, that is, the actualization of an alternative narrative account of reality . . . quite in contrast to what we normally and modernly term "history" . . . an attentive reading of the material must allow for "more or less" in varying dimensions . . . This endless interpretive tension, often contrasting church interpretation and academic interpretation . . . is in the end inescapable, precisely because the tension of "more or less" is readily evident in the final form of the text itself.[7]

What he says is relevant even though he's talking about the Old Testament, which contains stories that passed through an even longer course of traditionalizing than is true of the records we have of Jesus.

---

5. Atomic Nobel laureate De Broglie wrote, "we . . . must insist on the danger which always threatens theorists and which is due to the temptation to consider the present state of our knowledge as definitive. Almost instinctively the human mind tends to construct syntheses which it imagines complete, on the basis of knowledge which is, and no doubt always will remain, fragmentary . . . it is always necessary to avoid considering them as definitive and of attributing to them a permanence which they have not got." *Physics and Microphysics*, 174. This is just as true of biblical studies as of physics.

6. "A tradition consists essentially in the discourse that seeks to instruct practitioners regarding the correct form and purpose of a given practice that, precisely because it is established, has a history." Satlow, "Defining Judaism," 850.

7. Brueggemann, *An Introduction to the Old Testament*, 96–97.

Tradition is ambiguous as history is ambiguous, because life is ambiguous and communicating about life is ambiguous.

Traditionalizing does not automatically disqualify what it says, as if it had no historical value. Rather, tradition often gives us important dimensions of an event we couldn't get easily from a bare description. The full event the gospels are dealing with is "Jesus of Nazareth as the risen Lord Christ," something that escapes historical description but has had great historical impact. *The church's Christ is the historical Jesus*, but it may not be the "historical Jesus" of critical historians and workers in "Religious studies," a "Jesus" distinguishable from "the Risen Christ."[8] As Bonhoeffer put it half a century ago, "The New Testament can only be rightly interpreted *historically* when the presupposition that Jesus is already proclaimed Christ, as Lord, is taken seriously."[9] And that applies to the gospels quite as much as to the epistles.[10] Still, Brueggemann's "more or less" makes interpreting a problem. One must decide for themselves what is "more" and what is "less."

Anyone who has studied all four gospels, and used them as background for reading the rest of the New Testament, anyone who has delved into the arguments of historical critics and their several positions, knows that there are thorny problems in both the most simplistic Sunday-school accounts of Jesus and the most learned and penetrating critical studies by historical scholars.[11]

---

8. Workers in Religious Studies, such as the authors in Cameron and Miller's *Redescribing Christian Origins,* moved by honorable academic critical consciences, are under pressure to be as "scientific" as possible in writing about Jesus. But the history of biblical studies shows clearly that each generation's "valid methods" and "established critical conclusions" are likely to maintain their "validity" for only about fifty years before being replaced by some new procedural enthusiasm. This doesn't confirm my criticisms of such workers, my conclusions, or some kind of orthodoxy. It only means that all our results are simply temporary "best we can do's" in our present situation.

9. *Christ the Center*, 70.

10. Readers may ask if I am "evangelical." In the historical meaning of the term, I am, since I affirm the Reformation principles of *sola gratia, sola fide*, and *sola scriptura*, but I may understand them and apply them quite differently from the ways of many present-day self-styled "evangelicals."

11. And one is impressed how critics' views differ from one another, often on the basis of different methods of noticing, weighing, and interpreting what facts we have. These reflect different starting points, different preferences, and different aims. In other words, like the rest of us, critics are humans, seeing things in terms of what we bring to them ourselves.

In this book I can't deal with others' accounts except in passing. Instead, I can only give the results of my own musing. Theirs may be affected by their backgrounds and their experience; mine certainly is by the evangelical Calvinism in which I was raised, and the many ways that growth, study, doubting, and living have opened up new standards for thought, insights into the texts, and understandings.

The fictions about Jesus' youth offered in this book are, of course, not gospel, though they do depend on what we have through tradition. They can't be considered part of that tradition in any way. They are my own construction. But they assume that what the tradition indicates concerning the resurrection is fundamentally true, without reflecting it as the gospels do. After all, Jesus could not have been resurrected before being crucified, or crucified without making some kind of splash in his society, and he couldn't do that without being a human with some unique background.

The aim of the stories in this book is not to convince anyone that things must have happened as I present them. It is to offer my own suggestions, growing out of many years of study and thought, as to how some of the puzzling things in the records we do have can be understood and made to fit together.

After the fiction, and after the reader has read the gospel of Mark (or reread it), several essays appear on some of the problems frequently raised about the gospels.[12] The approach to these problems is critical but not technical, showing some of the arguments that have led to my conclusions.[13]

St. Augustine taught that an orator should teach, affect feelings, and delight. An author should do the same. As a teacher of philosophy, I learned that the best teaching is the raising of questions and alternatives, questions quite as much as answers. My discussions and narratives are meant as suggestions to stir up further thought on your part. You are encouraged to disagree honestly and criticize. Let your feelings run free

12. Though Miller's *The Complete Gospels* contains twelve "gospels," eight of them require that "gospel" be defined rather too broadly. The four canonical gospels are indeed different from the rest in ways other than merely being canonical.

13. Trying to think and write philosophically without falling into technical philosophical lingo has been difficult, but necessary for most readers, despite the impression it may give of intellectual slovenliness. However, that can occur even when many contemporary philosophical catchwords appear in a text. Though using technical theological words may give some an impression of obscure nebulosity, or even nonsense, there are no other ways of saying what they attempt, often unclearly, to communicate. This is only somewhat less true of philosophical jargon.

about the growing young Jesus, his career, and his meaning for us, and to enjoy what you meet here. Where you come out is up to you. Each one must reach their own understanding about a figure that has had such influence in so many lives and, undoubtedly, will continue to have.

As already remarked, underlying everything I write is the conviction that the orthodox tenet that Jesus was divine (whatever that means) must not obscure the fact that Jesus of Nazareth was just as human—totally, one hundred percent, unqualifiedly human—though unique in his calling.

We humans have to *learn* what it means to be human, and we understand other humans most deeply in terms of their responses to the five poles of expectation, pain, confusion, beauty, and love. In fact, the reader might treat my whole account as a commentary on these few verses in Hebrews:

> For we have not a high priest who is unable to sympathize with our weaknesses, but one who in every respect has been tempted[14] as we are, yet without sin. (4:15)

> Therefore he had to be made like his brethren in every respect . . . For because he himself has suffered and been tempted, he is able to help those who are tempted. (2:17–18)

> In the days of his flesh, he offered up prayers and supplications with loud cries and tears . . . Although he was a Son, he learned obedience through what he suffered. (5:7–8)

As already suggested, one can't read the records we have of Jesus with any imagination without putting together a story of one's own as to what he did before appearing as an adult of thirty or more, as the gospels present him to us.[15] We need to have some idea of the "lost years at Nazareth" (or somewhere else) to fill out our own knowledge of how Jesus, like any human, became an adult, the particular adult he turned out to be. Jesus "learned obedience through what he suffered," and to think about him as a whole human, and not just the embodiment of some theological doctrines, is to live a boyhood and young manhood along with him in our imaginations. Everyone constructs such an account, even if unconsciously. In giving my own account, I'm also giving an account of part of his impact upon me.

14. Or, "tested." The Greek word can mean either.

15. Chilton's *Rabbi Jesus* represents a different construction of Jesus' early life. He and I see the Jesus of the records differently. That is quite appropriate.

When a critical scholar asserts that something is "established as his-torical fact," he asserts only what the available evidence would make it un-reasonable, in his view, to deny. All else he labels "hypothetical," and what is "reasonable" is often disagreed upon. If, on the other hand, a believer is trying to organize his belief as responsibly as he can, the burden of proof is much less. He has leave to affirm anything to which his conscience and the available evidence grant both room and appropriate reason to believe. Though the historian must give his suspicions full weight, the believer may be much more suspicious of his suspicions. The outcome for both is most usually hypotheses, even guesswork, rather than "facts."[16]

The difference is important. The critical historian seeks guesses so de-fensible he can assert them as "assured results" over against the criticisms of his academic fellows. As philosopher Richard Rorty has been quoted as saying, "Truth is what I can get away with among my colleagues." The be-liever seeking understanding (like philosophers Augustine and Anselm), seeks guesses sufficiently permitted by facts, but ones also contributing to his understanding of himself, Jesus, history, and the cosmos, including the world of faith. Both, however, must take note of the same evidence, though the critic, for professional rather than solely intellectual reasons, must treat it more stringently and with more suspicion than must the questioning believer.[17]

The critic seeks a secular answer to the question, "What actually happened?" The cultural historian, the genuinely humanistic philosopher, and even more the theologian, must wrestle with the question, "What was really going on?" That requires attention to more than just common-sense "facts."

Therefore religious beliefs, history, and rituals use non-literal, often deeply charged, language that the philosopher is likely to try to reduce to literal statements. "Philosophy of religion" becomes questionable precisely

16. The believer seeking to understand may rely more generously on such rules as "absence of evidence is not evidence of absence" than may the critical historian. And it is not clear what evidence outside the gospels is really relevant to establishing that Jesus did in fact say or do something attributed to him. Just how he was unique and creative is part of the problem.

17. Kasemann, *Perspectives*, 13n 18 remarks: "Historical criticism undoubtedly ex-poses dogmatic prejudices and fallacies, but it remains sterile if it does not also make a person willing and able to form dogmatic judgments." "Dogmatic" here does not indi-cate an authoritarian attitude (as a common psychological use would imply), but rather "religious beliefs worth asserting."

at the point where it thinks that expressive stories can't be as true in their way as literal, commonsense language, and need to be translated into it.

Part of what you'll find here, then, is fiction, stories that deal with a part of his life about which we have almost no information. It is preceded by discussion of some problems about the texts we have to work from, and followed by discussions of some of the problems those texts pose. Honesty demands that we use those records very carefully, questioning them, and their authors, when they lead us to do so. These stories and discussions of ours are based, so far as could be, on the records themselves and what other few sources there are that merit attention, used critically rather than naively. A philosopher cannot do otherwise.

These essays and fiction have been written, as much as possible, to conform to our increased, though still incomplete, knowledge of first-century Palestine, and by the gospel records we do have, which were critically studied. Reasonable efforts have also been made to reconcile discrepancies, unify their testimony, and discern details of their message.

One thing the reader will not find in this book is any discussion of a favorite topic in school philosophy, the question of "the existence of 'God.'" That is no question for philosophy. God is prior to thought; otherwise "God" is not *God*.

Philosopher John H. Randall, Jr. told us in class, "God is to be *seen*. He is the last thing in the world to be believed in" (using "believe" the way philosophers do, which is to accept without adequate evidence). I would rather say, "God is to be heard, *hearkened to*." Then one either obediently says, "Here am I, Lord," or one doesn't.

From here on, what the reader will find presents four major sections, plus a suggestion for reading. First there comes a discussion of the relation between philosophy and theology, followed by discussions of sources we have to draw on for information about Jesus. There follows an introduction to two narratives giving a fictional, but possible, account of the background Jesus brought to the ministry that the gospels record, leading to the two narratives themselves.

Then the suggestion is made that one read at one sitting a gospel, Mark, before going on.

After that, one can go on to read the essays dealing with some questions that have puzzled many. These treatments are motivated by questions asked not only by my students, but also by some philosophical colleagues.

Out of pity for the reader, these are treated as I might answer ordinary students, not fellow philosophers.

Then come discussions of questions the records raise, then a summary. There are five appendices dealing with issues of only slight importance to many ordinary readers but probably of interest to scholars who may want further data or arguments.

I have also, with misgivings, included two personal poems, both confessions, one more philosophical and the other more pious than theological—but relevant in both ways.

2

Philosophy and Theology

A philosopher may set out on his philosophizing with theological motives which may be hidden even from himself and which destroy the freedom of his inquiry, while a theologian may be so intent on conforming his faith to a philosophy that he distorts his faith in the process.

—John Macquarrie[1]

HOW ARE PHILOSOPHY AND theology related? That is an important question, but is it a philosophical question or a theological one? Are we asking for a philosophical answer to what theology is or ought to be, or a theological answer to what philosophy is or should be? And are those questions themselves philosophical or theological? They are both, and are inescapable and also insoluble. They're inescapable because work in either field raises problems in the other, and insoluble because each discipline works on the basis of its own basic principles, which are inescapably arbitrary (as all basic principles are).[2]

Philosophy assumes that if both sorts of problems are to be solved, the answer must be found in our careful thinking as the humans we assume we are. They are problems for *us* to solve. Theology agrees to a degree, but adds that *we* are also part of the problem, not just as the thinkers we "know" ourselves to be, but also as a mystery in the midst of mystery.

Our part in the cosmos presents a mystery. So does our part in history. And who we ourselves, the thinkers, are is also a mystery. These call for more than thinking; they also demand *awe*, since mystery always points beyond the familiar, the prosaic, even the conceivable.

1. Macquarrie, *Twentieth Century*, 16.
2. J. R. Carnes' *Axiomatics and Dogmatics* presents some relevant discussion.

Something that creates awe presents itself as something quite out of the ordinary, in fact, something unique in an elevated way. And Jesus is believed in as unique.

That particular uniqueness is what present Christians refer to with words like "resurrection," "Lord," and "Christ." And uniqueness is perhaps the most difficult problem for a philosopher, one he meets whenever he wrestles with terms like "freedom," "beauty," "history," "goodness," and even "future," and other terms that escape nice, crisp, clear-and-distinct concepts. But fitting Jesus' historical uniqueness into the way we study and interpret history raises the questions already listed.

What we humans are is basically a theological question rather than a philosophical one. Thus Christian-talk about Jesus, as "resurrected Lord and Christ," is theological rather than philosophical. So thinking seriously about the testimony we have to Jesus confronts us immediately with the question, "How are theology and philosophy related?"[3]

The philosopher bases his thinking on his humanity. That is, by living it in his thinking, he embodies what he takes his humanness to consist in. For him, that may make theological statements just more statements that need philosophical analysis, clarification, and judgment. As long as they do not in any way challenge his idea of himself, or his idea about the possibilities and limits of human knowledge, they are just problems or puzzles, so he can treat them on the same basis as any other human claims, or he can ignore them.

The theologian, at least the Christian one, if he is genuinely theological, does have his humanity, and hence his sense of the scope of knowledge, challenged by "resurrection," "Lord," and "Christ," even though perhaps also affirmed by them. Thus he must take his humanity differently from the way the secular philosopher takes it. The importance of Jesus for him lies precisely in the way that dwelling on the significance of Jesus transforms his perception of himself, his fellows, human history, and the cosmos.

---

3. A colleague, Wm. Sacksteder, put the problem as follows: "When you ask a theologian a theoretical question, he will answer with a story; when you ask him about the story, he will answer with a theological theory." Quite true—because theological language tries to state in theoretical language (prose) what cannot be articulated without narrative (and hence somewhat poetical) language. Philosophy deals in concepts, theology with humans, and the indeterminacies of the human situation.

To put it another way: to be human is *learned* in ways that go far beyond science or most philosophy, since to be a unified human is to *live* in the world, unifying its many discordant aspects—cosmos, others, oneself. That cannot be done by merely *describing* the world as if outside it, representing its many-sided concrete confrontations by abstract concepts, as science and much philosophy do. Jesus, taken seriously, opens one to vistas not apparent through philosophy's window.

Concepts look toward control, but the total situation involved in living confronts us with dimensions we cannot control. So many such dimensions, in fact, that a deeper honesty than what we ordinarily call "intellectual honesty," honesty regarding conceivable relationships, is required. That is, an existential honesty of *living* and *dying*, in their challenges to our finitude.

Consider the frequent comment, often uttered as a cheap jibe, "Christians say 'humans are created in God's image,' when the truth is 'Humans have created God in their own image,'" said as if they were two contradictory statements. But not only the biblical account, but anthropology as well, recognize that the only alternatives to imaging God along the lines of us, is to create:

1. An image of an animal or some other sub-human part of the cosmos.
2. An image that is only a phantasm, a grotesque creature of our imagination.
3. A concept, a construction, a creature of our human language, experience, and thought.
4. A negation of all finite assertions, so as to end up a negation of all conceptual meaning.
5. An image somewhat like ourselves, but more—a more that points beyond any imagination or expression of ours.

If we do otherwise, "God" is just a bit of ritual mumbo-jumbo that has no real meaning at all.

Most atheists I have listened to carefully over the years deny the existence of a "god" who is either a childish image one of a rather sub-human "omnipotent 'man' upstairs," or a concept such as "first cause," a "transcendent, infinite something-or-other." Or, far too often, I am afraid, an obscure challenge to our own claim to be the highest of all existents. In any case, the idea is humanly invented. One of my colleagues told me, "I'm an atheist because every kind of 'god' I can think of isn't worth worshiping!"

Of course! Any idea of God is a humanly invented idea, because even if we claim to have received revelation, we end up interpreting it in terms of our own thoughts, our own experience, our own selves, in our own language, and within our own cultural patterns. Any idea of God is just another idea.

But to use the word "God" at all seriously, that is, worshipfully, is in itself an admission of the inadequacy of our idea of what we're talking about. It refers to what far exceeds description. Honesty requires us to admit that.

So what? Consider the word "Christ." Whatever it meant before Jesus' time, it now means *God created 'God' in human's image—so far as that is possible—so that we humans, who fall so far short in actually being 'images of God,' might be recreated as more truly human by becoming more genuinely God's image.*

What God is for us is reflected in our idea of being human. As Karl Barth once put it, "In the mirror of this humanity of Jesus Christ the humanity of God enclosed in His deity reveals itself."[4] Another Protestant theologian, D. J. Hall, offers, "The Christian gospel has more to do with the humanity of God than with the divinity of Jesus." And the Catholic Edward Schillebeeckx tells us, "God is more human than any human being." But clearly, all three of them are saying our ideas of what humanity is are therefore deficient. And so, of course, are our ideas of God.[5]

If Jesus and his resurrection do not change our ideas of both God and humans, we have not yet heard the gospel message.

The point is that Jesus is important because he shows us our humanity as falling far short of what humanity may be, and what humanity is to be, as *the image of the humanity of God.* Hence "to make God in man's image" can be a very new kind of thing, if that image, presented in the Christ, is, as millions have discovered, both a judgment on how far we fall short of real humanity and a promise of what real humanity should and will be.

This is theology, certainly, but theology at the level that is *basic* to philosophizing. And every philosopher has a theology, or an anti-theology,

---

4. Quoted in Scott, *Sources of Protestant Theology*, 319.

5. In *Jesus and Yahweh: The Names Divine*, Harold Bloom seems to miss this point entirely.

hidden in the basis of his thinking. Few now hold to Ritschl's theological answers, but the noted nineteenth-century theologian saw the problem clearly:

> The intermingling and collision of religion and philosophy always arises from the fact that the latter claims to produce in its own fashion a unified view of the world. This, however, betrays rather an impulse religious in its nature, which philosophers ought to have distinguished from the cognitive methods they follow.[6]

Political philosopher William E. Connolly, speaking of how he was jolted out of his earlier secularism, writes:

> Nietzsche's most significant amendment of Spinoza, whom he admired, was to acknowledge that his own "philosophical" grasp of the world contains a mixture of argument, evidence, and faith or, better, the blending of each into the other. As I engaged Augustine and Nietzsche together in seminars and writing, it became more palpable to me, as an erstwhile secularist, how every domain of intellectual life is inhabited by existential faith without being reducible to it. . . . I was slow to discern how every sentence we utter or write carries a trace of confession in it . . .[7]

In the quote that heads this chapter, theologian John Macquarrie observes that theology may invisibly underlie philosophy, and the latter may deflect the former. I deem the relationship even stronger: philosophizing always has, at bottom, theologically relevant underpinnings.[8] And the reverse is also true.

Jesus is philosophically important because the claim that Jesus is the "resurrected Lord Christ" can raise problems for the philosopher in a unique way. Philosophers are humans, and have to work from a view of what that means. As already pointed out, Jesus has been most influential intellectually in terms of his effect on our understanding of us as humans.

As already emphasized, the life Jesus lived was a human life. Christian orthodoxy has often been defined too narrowly in terms of

6. Reardon, *Religious Thought*, 146. True, even though the shadows of both Kant and Hegel fell darkly over Ritschl's idea of philosophy.

7. Connolly, *JAAR* 72,2 (2004), 509–10.

8. "Anthropology" was a branch of theology before it became one of philosophy, and of both before the term was co-opted by those social scientists who limited it to what is empirically observable, in order to make it a "science of man."

Jesus' "divinity." Actually, his humanity has just as basically and emphatically been affirmed. In Chalcedon, in 381, the Church Fathers officially decreed that Jesus was "complete in manhood . . . of one substance with us as regards his manhood . . . without change, without confusion . . ."[9] Since our modern ideas of both "substance" and "humanhood" differ from those of the fourth- and fifth-century theologians, we must, to be honest, try to understand their language in terms of our present insights, and hope that doing so may give us clues as to just what they intended in terms of theirs.

As already remarked, being human is something that is *learned*. We were all taught our humanity by our parents, culture, and experiences, including our self-criticism. So a prime problem in clearing up one's idea of Jesus is thinking about how he learned what the records show he had learned, and was perhaps still learning. How this happened we can only guess—since our records cover so little of his life—and do so only partially, though our guesses should be as much controlled by the records we have as we can manage.[10]

That is the reason for the stories we mentioned in the introduction. Fiction, of course, is neither philosophy nor theology but imaginative narrative. There is nothing wrong with that. Imagination is just as truly a part of our humanity as vision or logical thinking. Imagination is one of the things that distinguish us from the lower animals on one side and computers on the other.

Our culture's commitment to "reason" has treated imagination as contrary to straight thinking. But, to quote another distinguished professor,

> Bookish academics need to remember that when it comes to works regarded as sacred by vast numbers of people, sound scholarship is like the firmness of bones, while appreciation and sensitivity are like flesh and blood. Without the latter, the former is just an ugly skeleton: morbid and monstrous, lifeless and lamentable. With the latter, scholarship becomes robust and living.[11]

The philosopher makes a sharp distinction between "facts," which the available evidence would make it unreasonable to deny, and "hypoth-

---

9. Council of Chalcedon, Actio V. Trans., Bettenson, *Documents*, 73.

10. "The insatiable desire to know more about Jesus is met with an irrepressible urge to say more than we know." Beare, *Matthew*, 15.

11. Hawley, *JAAR* 72,2 (Jun 2004), 375n.

eses," anything for which evidence is insufficient. Just when the evidence is "sufficient" may be a point of disagreement. On the other hand, the theologian, a believer trying to organize his belief about the facts, has leave to affirm anything to which his conscience and the available evidence grant both room and appropriate reason to believe. It often is guesswork, but guesswork that seeks and listens to what evidence may raise doubts.

The theologian does seek an understanding in terms of the available facts, but also one that contributes to his understanding of himself, Jesus, history, and the cosmos. He must also, to be a theologian, accept as serious evidence things coming to him in a well and long-established tradition, which the philosopher is likely to exclude, as being "special pleading."

To the theologian, the philosopher may be guilty of special pleading himself, accepting a philosophical tradition that insists tradition cannot have any evidential value.

Here it must be added that the theologian's position entails a broader theory of language than the critical philosopher works with. His defense for that is the obvious one: the critic's theory of language is not self-evident, but presupposed in his discipline's beliefs about philosophical method. All such beliefs have their human limitations, which prevent any truly exhaustive scrutiny of the marvelously and bafflingly complex ways in which language, and hence thought, functions.

The philosopher who would think seriously about Jesus, then, must recognize the limits of what Kant called *blosse Vernunft*, or "mere reason." If he, in the interests of clarity, chooses to do his analyses within its strictures, he limits himself to what can be done when treating all "meaning" as clear and conceptual.[12] He then misses what is important about Jesus.

To sum up the argument: Philosophers who would deal with those "objective" fields of inquiry such as formal logic, mathematics, and philosophy of science may do their work quite successfully while treating language as properly made up of distinct concepts that can be treated as bearing only their literal definition. But philosophers who deal with self-involving areas of life, such as morality, self-knowledge, freedom, and beauty must sacrifice some of the clarity of "mere reason," even though

12. This has been true, unfortunately, of those past thinkers who have insisted that the meaning of any metaphor can be exhaustively translated into literal prose, and those more recent writers who have argued that "what is said" should be taken in its "simple literal meaning." Both appear to be insensitive toward how live people actually use language effectively.

their more formal colleagues may complain they have abandoned the proper disciplines of philosophy to an unacceptable degree.

Workers in more formal, less expressive fields like mathematics or philosophy of science may quite safely ignore their theological or anti-theological commitments. But the theologian, who deals with the most self-involving area of all, faith, and the depths faith points toward, must be constantly aware that his philosophy shapes the structure of his theological thought, even though it may supply little of its content. But he must be careful that though they only partially overlap, they do not conflict.

The philosophy underlying this book maintains that it is a gospel—good news of a new basis for living—that gives rise to faith, which, called forth in a particular culture (that may even mean a particular group of viable philosophies), gives rise to a religion.

This produces distinct ways of celebrating, living, organizing, and speaking. Theology then arises to codify, interpret, and reconcile these developments.[13] Thus, a theology arises in a particular culture from the impact of a particular gospel, and cannot properly be understood except in terms of both the culture and the gospel to which the culture responds.

This distinguishes world religions like Buddhism and Christianity from religions like Islam and Judaism, which can only partially be separated from the culture in which they originated. The former are possible because all cultures have some common basics, the latter are limited by being too closely defined by their culture of origin. (Hinduism is such a mélange of many things that attempts to make a world religion of it differ widely as to what Indian overtones, if any, are necessary).

Where the philosopher's task is to understand the problems in his culture in as broad a way as possible, the theologian's task is to understand the "good news" that resulted from Jesus' impact on his culture and its subsequent development in the somewhat different Hellenistic culture into which it spread, but in terms of our modern culture. Our specific task is to focus on Jesus himself. But Jesus comes to us through a particular literature, the New Testament, and even more particularly, the "Gospels." So they must be addressed first.

---

13. Devotees may confuse with their gospel much that is their culture, or their culture's response to their gospel. Workers in many faiths could echo U.S. Imam Abdul Rauf's "In our communities, the challenge is people who won't just let go of ideas that they think define Islam when in fact it just defines the culture in which they were born." Quoted in Peter, "Culture clash," *Christian Science Monitor*, 16.

MY DOG AND I

My dog
Understands sticks and stones
And bones.
She enjoys being a dog,
A special dog,
She.
And she worships me.

I understand sticks and stones
And logs and dogs.
I enjoy being human,
A special human,
Me.
And I worship God.

God understands sticks and stones
And logs and dogs
And me.
God enjoys being God.

My dog and I,
We live suspended between understanding
   and worship.
We enjoy being.

3

The Gospel and the Gospels

WHAT IS A GOSPEL?

A book about Jesus, a historical figure of the recent past, whom the writer wishes to introduce and commend to his readers, and he achieves this aim by telling the story of (part of) his life and death together with a selection of his teaching.

—W. T. France[1]

NEARLY EVERYBODY KNOWS THERE are four gospels[2] and they are called "Matthew," "Mark," "Luke," and "John."[3] Most know that those four are the only usable sources of information about Jesus.

Though Jesus is mentioned briefly by the later Jewish historian Josephus, by still later rabbinical writings, and apparently referred to by one or two Roman historians, none of these add anything significant about him. The rest of the New Testament tells us little about his career or teachings, though his life, death, and resurrection are assumed throughout. Who the authors were and just when and where they wrote, we have to guess, based on the clues they give us.

Not one of the gospels is a biography or a history, but each is a "narrative theology" or "narrative sermon" presenting the author's understanding of the significance of Jesus in the form of a story, or a collection of stories, about his ministry and death. "The author's understanding" must be assumed to be very like that of his own church, for whom he was

1. France, *The Gospel*, 5.

2. A different and more basic meaning of "gospel" refers to any "good news" that founds or leads to a religion. This meaning is used in the preceding and some later chapters.

3. Because the first three contain so much similar or identical material, they are referred to as "the Synoptics."

writing his gospel, though the intercommunication of the churches led to its circulation through the church as a whole.[4]

Jesus' deeds and sayings, though transmitted seriously, were not done so as we would expect legal testimony to be. The record was reshaped and passed down by those who were deeply involved in it. Responsible tradition does not come with verbatim accuracy. Mark added his own comments and details, with varying degrees of skill, and the trend continued through Luke to Matthew.

Each was affirming and organizing what was already largely accepted. If he added anything, he took it for granted his audience would accept it, and find it profitable to attend to. In fact, one who reads should be asking, "What did this author believe his audience needed to hear?" It may even be, "What did he believe they needed as readings in their meetings?"

In short, each gives us an interpretation of Jesus, rather than the strict details of what happened. He was preaching, not recording. He wrote for the edification of listeners or for use in worship, not to historical critics for their approving nods.

Because we may need to hear more or something other than their audiences did, questions arise for us. Their attempts to meet their own questions or those of their audiences do not always yield answers to our questions. Thus we must always be experimenting, improvising, criticizing where we are, in hope we will move closer to where we ought to be.

Other books titled or sometimes referred to as "gospels" were written, but of those we have, all show signs of having been written, or collected, much later (with the possible exception of the hypothetical "Q" discussed below). The so-called "gospel of Thomas," for instance, is just sayings collected at a later time, only some of which seem traceable back to Jesus. And its general tenor is hard to attribute to Jesus. That is true of nearly all of those later gospels.

We have no sources of knowledge about the gospel writers themselves—not even that they bore the names we are so familiar with. Those are later guesses. So we don't know whom they associated with, or how much of what they wrote they got firsthand, how much second- or third-hand, and how much of what they wrote they collected, or how much

4. Though originally local, their continued existence was due to widespread general acceptance and agreement. "The success of these traditions was due to their appeal to people living in different times, geographical areas, and social locations." Czachesz, "The Transmission of Early Christian Thought," 67.

they invented themselves, if any. Our guesses can only be based on what is in them, since no books from their time giving us any help have come down to us (except that Luke's second volume, Acts, does refer back to his first volume, Luke).

No sources tell us when, where, or how the gospels were written, so we have to figure—usually to guess—answers for such questions.[5] Trying to make intelligent guesses requires us to have a method for reaching answers, and the preferred methods tend to change every generation, as new scholars modify what earlier scholars taught.

Thus, there are problems in using them as our "sources." One must ask, "Do our copies of them say what the ancient gospels themselves did?" The answer is that writings about Jesus were translated, then copied, and recopied by hand, right up to the invention of printing. Thousands of these copies remain, though the oldest ones, written on papyrus and as old as the second century, may be quite tattered and even fragmentary.

Complete gospels in Greek exist from the fourth century on, and translations nearly as old in Latin, Coptic, Georgian, Armenian, Syriac,[6] and other languages. Together, they are a much larger body of direct evidence for the gospels (and the rest of the New Testament) than is available for any other ancient literature.

Ever since Erasmus in the sixteenth century, many scholars have labored intensely, carefully comparing documents and working toward a text of the gospels (and other books) that best reconstructs what the ancient authors actually wrote. Unless copies are found that are older and quite different, we can be sure that any responsible edition of the Greek gospels comes very close to the original wording.

Having four gospels that differ from one another seems at first a problem, but it at least provides us with an important insight into the variety of understandings of Jesus that were active in the first century church. Written by different authors, they show alternate views of Jesus and different reasons for writing about him. That some gospels copy others shows they were written at different times, so we can see part of how

---

5. The titles aren't "The gospel *by* Mark," etc., but "The (one) Gospel *according to* (from the viewpoint of) Mark," etc.

6. Coptic was the ancient language of Egypt; Georgia was a country at the east end of the Black Sea. Syriac was a dialect of Aramaic (the administrative language of the former Persian empire).

those various ideas and materials developed over time, and probably in different places and under different circumstances.

Also, each of the four gospels shows signs of concern with the tension between Christians and other sects, especially those representing differing degrees of separation from Jewish culture. Christianity was always a Jewish sect until its (often welcomed) exclusion from Judaism by the Pharisee reconstitution of Judaism. That established a gulf that has grown wider over the centuries. Then the wide variety of Christian sects and interpretations forced the church to work for several centuries at deciding just what "normal" Christianity was to be.

Each author was expounding and making a case for what he himself believed. If that hadn't been in close agreement with what was believed by those he wrote for, and in harmony with whatever well-established traditions and rituals they had received and celebrated, his work would likely never have survived (or *her* work—some have suggested that Luke was written by a woman).

That they used "traditions" doesn't necessarily falsify their reports. Tradition can bring out hidden meaning. Walter Brueggemann points out, "the later traditioning process that did a literary imposition may, in fact, have discerned what was going on in the narratives."[7]

In short, each author wrote for the edification of his readers or for use in their worship, not for the approving nods of historical critics.

I said the gospels were narrative sermons, rather than histories. In a sermon, stories are told to stimulate and emphasize thinking about life, beliefs or behaviors. Historians may sermonize and preachers may recount history, but when they do, they work with different aims and different sets of standards.

A huge trouble with studies of Jesus has already been suggested: scholars talk to one another and form a subculture of their own. Things for which we have little or no evidence, or things proposed by some influential teacher, can get accepted as true by the "scholarly community," or, alternatively, by the "fundamentalist community," just because that's "the way 'everybody' is thinking these days." And such things may change with each passing generation, and in different ways for different people,

---

7. That he was speaking of the Old Testament, and hence of a longer traditioning process, doesn't make his comment irrelevant. Brueggemann, *Introduction to the Old Testament*, 123.

depending on with whom they talk, what books they read, their general outlook, and what has happened in or around the church in their times.

What I already quoted from Nobel laureate De Broglie regarding the "danger which always threatens theorists" of considering current syntheses as definitive and "attributing to them a permanence which they have not got" on the basis of "knowledge which is, and no doubt always will remain, fragmentary," is just as true of biblical studies as of physics.

Despite all these difficulties, the gospels are all we have for understanding the man Jesus. They are a rich treasure to be mined. They will now be treated one by one, much more briefly than they deserve, in the unusual order Mark, Luke, Matthew, and John, since that is the order in which I believe they were written.

One must, however, beware of so concentrating on literary problems in the records we have of Jesus, that we miss the Jesus they are confronting us with.

4

Mark

Mark's gospel . . . a book waiting to be read and enjoyed for
itself, a carefully compiled, flowing account of the story of Jesus
and his disciples, intended to be read and appreciated as a literary whole . . . the story Mark tells is to a large extent the story of
Jesus as seen by his disciples . . . It is about how twelve ordinary
men met Jesus and entered into a new dimension of living.

—W. T. France[1]

MARK, THE SHORTEST OF the gospels, is often passed over by many
ordinary Bible readers. Both Matthew and Luke based their gospels on it, though adding a great deal to their accounts. Mark was written
closer to Jesus' time and is, in some ways, more solid theologically than
either of those authors. However, their works, along with that of John,
have overshadowed it through most of the church's history.

Another scholar wrote recently:

Mark is . . . a fascinating, rewarding piece of literature, and one
of the greatest achievements of modern Biblical scholarship . . . is
its success in rehabilitating what was hitherto the most neglected
Gospel. . . . It seems likely that this evangelist is the first to attempt
to compose a book in which different materials from oral tradition
are gathered together and subordinated to a narrative that reaches
its climax in the death of Christ crucified.[2]

Both Matthew and Luke felt a need to downplay some of Mark's
theological claims in order to advance their own. Thus, they provide
us an important insight into the variety of understandings of Jesus that

1. France, *The Gospel*, 2, 28.
2. Goodacre, *The Case Against Q*, 40.

were active in the first-century church. After grasping the different interpretations the three gospels give, the reader is faced with the choice as to which of the three interpretations he should take as basic. Or must we turn to some other source? I find Mark the most satisfactory gospel, especially if carefully complemented theologically—and occasionally historically—by the others.

The other books now referred to as "gospels" show signs of having been written, or collected, much later (with the possible exception of Q, which we will discuss later). The so-called "gospel of Thomas," for instance, is just a collection of sayings, some of which are traceable back to Jesus. Most of them don't seem to fit Jesus' other sayings at all. And they don't really tell us anything about him that's new or useful, unless we are eager to come up with some drastic alternative to the traditional idea of Jesus. (Thomas is important, however, for the history of Gnosticism—whatever that was.)

One reason Mark intrigues the thinker is his awareness that Jesus spoke in parables that often carry more than one meaning, sometimes ironic, and that he himself was a puzzling figure, not easy to understand and perplexing to describe.

Luke and Matthew, writing later, present more of his parables, but in them Jesus has been reduced, in two different ways, to a more straightforward subject, whether by them or by tradition's trend toward the prosaic.

Mark was written about the year 69, in Rome.[3] He probably used what oral material he had picked up in Christian circles. Some of it may even have originated with Peter (Matthew and Luke, in copying Mark, omit some of his references to Peter). Except perhaps for parts of chapters 5 and 13–15, there seems little to show that Mark used any written sources, though, of course, there may have been such. Some may have been simply oft-repeated ritual material.

He was expounding, making a case for what he himself believed. But, if he hadn't been in close agreement with at least some of those he wrote for, and in harmony with whatever well-established rituals they celebrated, his work would likely never have survived. As it was, it was so overshadowed within a few decades by Luke, and then almost completely

---

3. Marcus argues strongly, but for me unsuccessfully, for a Syrian origin for Mark. However, he admits, "a Syrian provenance is not a mathematical certainty, and most of the exegesis would work just as well if the setting were Rome or some other place where Christians were under pressure." Marcus, "Crucifixion," 33–36.

by Matthew, that we have fewer early papyri to draw on for its text than of the others.

How people read Mark depends a lot on how ready they are to believe what he says, rather than what some other source they believe in says. That causes lots of disagreements that closer looks at the limited evidence may not be enough to resolve. So the crucial questions are: Where did Mark get his information, and how reliable were his sources? How much of its arrangement was his work, and why did he do the arranging he did?

How much or how little came to Mark directly from eyewitnesses we can't say. Possibly none. He may have had to rely entirely on reports retold many times, or some bits may have come to him directly. For example, he identified Simon of Cyrene, who helped carry Jesus' cross, as "the father of Alexander and Rufus," as if his readers would know them.[4] If so, they could constitute an interesting link (both Matthew and Luke, writing for different audiences, skipped that). But most of his material was probably passed down through at least several speakers.

Thus, it's not likely that Mark himself had ever heard or seen Jesus. It is quite possible that he had heard someone like Peter who knew or had seen him, and likely that he got some information no more distantly than third-hand. We can't, of course, be sure of either, but equally can't be as sure as many claim, that he didn't.

Mark shows some knowledge of conditions in Jerusalem. His is the only gospel that mentions the "Herodians"[5] (except for one place Matthew copies him), and his implications concerning the geography of Jerusalem seem quite sound. (Some contrast this to an apparent confusion about the regions around Galilee, but there can be explanations for that). He also gives translations of the Aramaic sayings he records, and his Greek is often unpolished and shows some Aramaic influence.

If he wrote in Rome, as I believe he did, he wrote where there is some reason to believe Jesus' disciple Peter had at least been a prisoner for some time before his execution. Perhaps he even taught or preached there. That

4. The one referred to as "Rufus" in Romans 16:13 is a possible but debatable candidate for Mark's reference. Rufus was quite a common name.

5. The "Herodians" have been identified with "a group of rabinic [sic] teachers whose prominent place in the Temple administration made them a power to be reckoned with in Jerusalem and beyond as chief partisans of the Herodian settlement." France, *Gospel of Mark*, 151n, quoting Chilton.

doesn't mean Mark knew Peter, though he may have. But if there is truth behind the tradition that Peter ended up in Rome, and if Mark wrote there, it's hardly likely he had never heard any reports of Peter's preaching, and may even have heard some of that himself.[6] At any rate, the available tradition gives stronger support to putting his writing in Rome than in the only serious rival, Alexandria. This, of course, doesn't tell us if any of the book of Mark does in fact go back to Peter. It merely helps tempt us to think so.

That later writers give varying accounts of the relation between Peter and Mark shows the unreliability one must always suspect in such reports. But the consistency with which they relate the two shows it to be unwise to distrust tradition completely. I believe that there are quite a few places in Mark one might be justified in tracing indirectly back to Peter's reminiscences, presented of course in Mark's own way. Unfortunately, we have no way to be sure which ones they might be.[7]

Later reports that Mark was, at one time, Peter's translator or secretary deserve widespread rejection. It could be remotely possible, in fact less unlikely than the even more questionable old claim that Peter himself had an active part in the writing of Mark, or approved it after it was written.

Even if Peter was never in Rome and Mark was written somewhere else, Peter still might have been in the background somewhere. But that Mark wrote in Rome, and that his writing had at least some roots in Petrine tradition, suits the evidence we have, and violates none.

---

6. Leon-Dufour argues that at least a score of texts in Mark may well come directly from Peter's reminiscences. He seems to me far too optimistic. The case must be left open. We can neither demonstrate nor disprove Peter's involvement in Mark. We can't even guess just how probable it was. Or how reliable was Peter's memory. Leon-Dufour, *The Gospels*, 138–41.

7. It is interesting that in his *St. Paul vs. St. Peter*, the English scholar Goulder identifies the author of Mark with John Mark—something few scholars do—but treats him as an opponent of Peter, whom Matthew then feels he must defend. Peter and Paul undoubtedly had some disagreements. There were certainly many different interpretations of Jesus in the early church, but our records (such as 1 Cor 1:12) don't justify attributing all the major disagreements with Paul to a Petrine party. It was James, not Peter, who was chosen to lead the Jerusalem church, where opposition to Paul seems to have centered, and Galatians 2:4 suggests that there were opponents of Paul there, but they do not appear to be leaders in the church, such as James. Though Acts 21:20 agrees, it was written too much later to be much support.

After the first chapter, Peter appears in Mark more often than any other disciple—James and John appear only twice outside of the first list of "the Twelve" (9:2, 10:35), and John by himself (9:38). Andrew shows only twice (1:29, 13:3), and they were all Peter's sidekicks. Someone named Levi occurs once. None of the others appear, except for Judas. Peter appears as spokesman and leader (even though John 6:70 can be read as speaking of Judas as "first" among the Twelve). So a case for Peter's reminiscences reaching Mark, whether directly or indirectly, is hardly weak.

Jesus almost never appears in the story without disciples, at least Peter and his two fellow-fishermen James and John. This suggests that little of Mark's information came down from other disciples, except by some general tradition.

In fact, it is striking that Luke and Matthew[8] don't tell us anything about any of the other "twelve apostles" (except for Judas). John brings in Philip, Thomas, and a possible disciple named Nathaniel. Acts also tells us only of Peter, James, and John. So the Peter-James-John tradition may be the only one we draw on.

That Mark undoubtedly used other sources is evident, for instance, in his two distinct versions of the miracle of feeding a multitude (6:34–44 and 8:1–8). Their differences suggest two different paths of oral transmission. Matthew quotes both, but Luke and John include only the first. But, as his awkward use of the saying in 8:15 shows, he used both to further his comforting puzzled readers by showing that their stupidity was just like the disciples'.

As already said, I can't believe that Mark, writing for a particular church community, would have departed very far from the story of Jesus as it was familiar in that church. Nor can I believe that the main outlines of Jesus' story varied much from church to church at the time he wrote (except perhaps in Galilee, where, apparently, some local traditions may have circulated).

Jesus' story was material important to, in fact constitutive of, the community concerned with it, so we can't just dismiss it as idle hearsay. Mark's material may have been carefully preserved, at least some indirect continuity with things Peter had said, but such scattered items could

8. Where Matthew copies Mark 2:14, the calling of "Levi, son of Alphaeus," he calls him "Matthew." No one knows why. But that is probably why the gospel was ascribed to the disciple Matthew. Since none of the other writers were apostles, that gospel took on special, and I think undeserved, authority.

hardly have come down without any change at all. That doesn't mean we can accept the exact sequence of events Mark gives us as accurate historical narrative—neither Matthew nor Luke did, though they honored it in general. Even if Peter reminisced, he didn't lay down a continuous story, and as we've insisted, Mark was not writing history, but gospel.

Mark presents this series of events and teachings as a narrative. It is clear he arranged them not so much out of an interest in their actual historical sequence, but as a desire to make his points more forcefully.

The clever way he presents Jesus shows brilliant organizing skill—first revealing who Jesus is only to Jesus himself, by a vision. He then starts preaching. He calls four disciples. "Evil spirits" recognize who he is, but people don't. He heals the mother-in-law of one disciple—a private healing—then a whole crowd of health-seekers. But he leaves and goes off by himself to pray, deciding he must go preach the coming kingdom of God no matter how much the crowds seek his healing.

Thus, chapter 1 from verse 21 on presents Jesus as feared by unclean spirits as a dangerous enemy, but sought after and celebrated by the people, most of which were attracted by his healing miracles. The evil spirits recognized him as a serious threat. All the while, his basic motivation was something different: to use both teaching and healing to announce the oncoming kingdom.

Then 2:1—3:6 shows official opposition arising. In 3:6 his death is already plotted. This sets up the controversial theme that marks the work right up to and through the continuous narrative of 11 to 15 (with 13 thrust into the middle).

Thus Mark is a mystery-scenario in three acts, with a postlude. Act I (1:2—8:30) presents him as continuing the Baptist's preaching about coming divine action but with a more optimistic emphasis, demonstrated by healings, teachings, and exorcisms as signs of the kingdom's coming.

Act II (8:22—10:52) presents Jesus trying to disabuse his disciples of their mistaken expectations that he would be a conquering "son of David" Messiah, whose triumph they would share. Instead, he emphasizes that their fate would be to be hated and rejected, even killed, and that humility and obedience, leading to be "servant of all" would be their fate, rather than achieving personal or national ends.

In Act III, we have the fulfillment of Jesus' predictions—first the crowd's mistaken acclaim, then the bitter opposition from the establishment, leading to his arrest, trial, crucifixion, death, and burial. There

Mark's story of Jesus ends, having shown his confusing character, but without any revelation of his importance.

However, Mark added a postlude (16:1–8). Women discovered the tomb empty, and were told that Jesus would meet the disciples in Galilee. Mark says they were so afraid they told nobody, though the other gospels say they did. Mark's point is that the meaning of Jesus' life, especially its climax in resurrection, was not something to be *told*. It had to be discovered by going home to Galilee, by obedience (the several "endings" of Mark, added by others later, obscured this dimension of his gospel).

Jesus posed problems for his hearers because they asked what he saw as the wrong questions. Thus, in Mark 3:22–27, when he is accused of "casting out demons by the prince of demons" he responds with two parables, neither of which really meets the charge. One points out that if Jesus frees Satan's captives, he must have rebelled against Satan, his master. Then Satan's realm is falling apart, leaving rule of the world to God.

The other answer is, if Jesus is a still stronger burglar-devil who can rob Satan of his victims, to oppress them himself, then the Pharisees are claiming that healing folk must be evil. Saying that is obviously a horrible sin, amounting to "blaspheming against the Holy Spirit." After all, God is giver of life and freedom.

Scholars have argued strenuously about how his answer meets the accusation. But he is not so much defending himself against the accusation as saying that if one assumes that Jesus healing people is evil, that it enslaves them like Satan rather than frees them, one must accept either one or the other of his alternatives. But to hold that freeing folk oppressed by disease or demon-possession is an evil thing is to blaspheme God's new work of freeing them, which Jesus was proclaiming and demonstrating.

In short, here as elsewhere, Jesus refuses to defend himself, but rather his mission. He seeks to challenge folk to criticize themselves. What was important to him, and should have been so to them, was that a new level of healing was going on, showing God's new way of dealing with human woes.

What, then, was Mark's overall aim? Many theories have been offered, some of them concentrating on him as trying to establish that "Son of God" is a proper title for Jesus. I read him, rather, as showing that "Son of God" is a deep, confusing title, one not to be bandied about easily or reduced to some clear description.⁹ He presents the disciples as stupid, not so much to criticize them as to show that coming to see what "Son of God" means takes a long, difficult, even threatening, course of deep commitment, even suffering.

Consider: the first revealing climax of the gospel, "Do you not yet understand" (8:21)? Then, the stepwise healing of a blind man, which leads up to the question, "Who do you say I am?" This brings about an answer that shows his disciples still had only a dim perception of whom they were following.

The story about the blind man who needed two curative touches from Jesus is often interpreted by identifying Peter's saying, "You're Messiah," with the man's clear sight after the second healing.¹⁰ It's obvious to me that it is the indistinct seeing after the first touch that Peter represents. There is much in the rest of Mark to show that the disciples thought of "Messiah" as "conquering son of David," something Jesus rejected right up to the crucifixion.

In Mark, Jesus was indeed the presence of God's imminent victory over the dark forces of evil. He is tested by the devil, apparently coming off victorious. Then, as soon as he appears as a public figure, evil spirits recognize that he was a threat to their dominance. His popularity as a healer and wonder-worker, with victories over evil influences, are stressed, with his insistence that his main aim was to announce the "coming kingdom," when evil would finally be overcome, though he didn't know how or when. His twelve special followers were also "to cast out evil spirits," at which they found themselves less than competent (9:28).

Mark tells of the popular misunderstanding of what Jesus was doing, wherein people assumed that the victory over evil would be easy and glorious. Officialdom plotted against him, showing that the established religious and political leaders themselves represented the evil forces while

9. The title of Mark (1:1) was probably added later. "Son (of God)" then first appears in 1:11, and Jesus is immediately driven into temptation to wrestle with it. A madman says it 5:7; in 9:7 it baffles three disciples; in 14:61 the high priest says it, but clearly rejects it. In 15:39 a Roman soldier says "a son of God," whatever a pagan might mean by that. Mark took "Son of God" to point to a much deeper, more poetical mystery than did either Luke or Matthew.

10. Matthew changes Peter's ambiguous answer, "the Messiah (the Son of David)," into "the Christ, the Son of the Living God." By his time, the church couldn't have Peter be wrong, or have Jesus not be the Davidic "Anointed One" ("Messiah," or "Christ").

masquerading as institutions of light. Clearly, something more than a son of David was needed.

The second part of Mark tells of Jesus' withdrawal from the crowds that still pursued him. In fact, "five thousand men" gathered in the desert, apparently (according to John) "to make him king." He fed them and then escaped. Herod was suspicious of him, so he traveled outside the territories of Herod, which meant outside of Galilee. Having given up on the crowds, he concentrated on developing and clarifying his disciples' confused views about him and the kingdom they were to proclaim.

Three times he predicts the "Son of man" will be killed in Jerusalem, but will "rise from the dead." Then he deliberately leads the Twelve and a collection of hangers-on to Jerusalem, knowing he, and probably his disciples, too, would be killed there.

Once in Jerusalem (Act 3), Jesus enrages the ruling groups by presenting himself as a non-standard Messianic figure, cleansing the temple, suggesting its downfall, answering all their challenges successfully, and baffling them with a question and a story of his own.

Another of the Twelve now appears, Judas, to "deliver" him to the posse sent by the temple authorities. They have already decided to have the Romans kill him, but hold a hearing to discover a charge that would convince the Roman Procurator, Pilate. Jesus makes two admissions: that he is indeed a messianic figure, and that the "Son of man" will end up judging his accusers. Both are ways of denying the rightfulness of their authority. For Pilate, they translate this into Roman terms, that is, that he is a political subversive, aiming to replace the Roman Caesar as "King of the Jews."

Pilate, despite doubts about the officials' allegations, condemns him. Jesus is beaten, mocked, and crucified, just as he himself predicted. He was buried, which he didn't predict, but assumed. In an abrupt ending to the gospel, his body is missing. (We discuss the resurrection stories in a later chapter.)

One can doubt that things were that neat. As a pious Jew, Jesus probably made a number of trips to Jerusalem, though Mark tells only of one—the last. Jesus' whole career hardly unfolded in the progressive manner Mark relates. And the later writers who copied his work changed the emphasis of quite a few of his stories to suit their own theologies and interests.

Yet since Mark was not inventing a new story, but structuring materials already moderately familiar to those for whom he was writing—Christians who may already have more than once heard a rough chronology of Jesus' life (some may even have heard Peter preach)—his freedom to remold his material was probably more limited than first appears. Here I find myself deeply intrigued by the agreement between his evident interests and Paul's concerns in writing to the church in Rome.[11]

Mark's basic organizing principle is that the crowds, the authorities, and even the disciples misunderstood Jesus as claiming to be "the son of David," but the disciples, by facing up to his crucifixion and resurrection (but not before), finally came to recognize him as "Son of God."[12] This same distinction appears in Paul's letter when he distinguishes between Jesus as "one who, defined according to the flesh, was indeed David's son" but, as "one who, according to the Spirit of Holiness, was more authoritatively defined, by his resurrection from the dead, as Son of God,"[13] a point he makes in no other letter.[14]

Paul wrote Romans to a church where there were problems between Jewish Christians and Gentile ones.[15] If Mark wrote for the same church more than a dozen years later, it would appear that Paul's letter had not been as successful as he had hoped. The problems still involved the tension between "son of David" and "Son of God" as the central meaning of "Christ."

---

11. My understanding of the situation in Rome is based on my own reading of Romans, discussions in Donfried, *The Romans Debate*, and Beker, *Paul The Apostle*, and other writers as well.

12. Though using "Son of God" and "Christ" (= Messiah), Mark never refers to Jesus as "Lord" (Mark 11:3 may appear to, but see 11:5). *Kyrios*, "Lord" appears 9 times in the gospel: 6 times of God, not Jesus: 4 times in Old Testament quotes, once in the "wee Apocalypse" (13:20), once by Jesus (referring to God) to the Gerasene demoniac (5:19), and 3 times of men, as "boss" or "Sir" (2:28, 7:28, 12:9). In Mark, the "dove" and the "voice from heaven" at Jesus' baptism were known only to him. Luke and Matthew miss this. They make them public data.

13. Romans 1:3–4 (translation mine). Philippians 2 credits Jesus' glorification to his *obedience*, referring to the shame of the cross.

14. This same issue may have occurred at other places in the church, but at least we have evidence of it in Rome, where we know there was a sizeable and longstanding Jewish settlement, which had been driven out by Claudius, but later reinstated (without synagogue privileges) by Nero before Paul wrote.

15. The Roman historian Suetonius tells of riots between Christians and, apparently, Jews, before Nero, during Claudius' reign. We can assume some occurred later, also.

When Paul wrote, those inner church problems would have been intensified by the frightening news of the war in Judea between Jews and Romans, and the upset politics in Rome. There, in the year 69, the death of Nero, who had persecuted Christians, was followed by ongoing conflict as three would-be emperors—Galba, Otho, and Vitellius—successively rose to power and then were eliminated, all in the same year, 69. The throne was finally settled by the calling of Vespasian back from leading the siege of Jerusalem. He would be the next emperor.

This upset situation would also account for a characteristic of Mark not yet mentioned: his evident purpose of strengthening Christians in the face of opposition, criticism, and threat. Mark reports antagonism toward Jesus early, and builds his narrative around its growth. Opposition is to be expected, even death.

Many of what appear to be Mark's additions to tradition harmonize with points made by Paul—that all foods are ritually pure, that one must distinguish between Jewish religious culture (for Paul, "circumcision") and the moral law, that true morality is not mere conformity, that obedience to civil authorities requires that civil taxes are to be paid, that following Jesus demands the death of self, and can lead to "tribulation, distress, persecution . . . or peril, or the sword" (Rom 8:35).

These and other parallels may simply represent items widespread in the tradition. In that case, they at least show that both Paul and Mark stood in the same line of tradition, which would increase the likelihood that it was the main line, probably the most authentic line.

Mark certainly put in editorial explanations of his own, without identifying them, though some can be identified with some confidence. He also amplifies sayings made by Jesus, by telling us the disciples misunderstood, so that later, often "in the house," Jesus "explains" what he meant in ways more directly applicable to the church for which Mark was writing. His gospel has to be read in that light, and each of the other gospels similarly. That means we can't just skim through them. They need to be lived with, patiently listened to, soaked up, and set in the situation for which they were written—so far as we can discern.

Since the chronologies of both Matthew and Luke are very largely based on Mark, they show that they either didn't know of any competing account, or else didn't consider such accounts to have any reliability (and we must remember that at that time a written Mark would have had no more authority than spoken tradition). They accepted Mark's account as basic, no matter how much they modified and enlarged it with other traditional influences, as well as possibly some of their own.

That means we have to accept his account in the main, for lack of any significant competition, despite real grounds for questioning Mark's arrangement (but see our later comments on John). Both Matthew and Luke rearranged some things to suit themselves. Even though Mark wasn't trying to write accurate history, and instead organized his account so his order of events served his theological purpose, that purpose was to interpret events reported in the tradition, in accordance with the tradition as he knew it. For this reason, we can't be too quick to claim that he invented his order of events only for private theological purposes.[16]

In any case, it's the only real order we have. As one famous scholar, Manson, put it two generations ago, "It is not a case of preferring Mark's order to that of Matthew or Luke. It is a case of Mark's order or none at all."[17]

Those who are afraid to be wrong opt for "none at all"; those of us who are willing to risk it go along rather gingerly with Mark's order, in the main. He may have omitted much, and he surely has arranged stories and sayings in a theological rather than a purely historical way, but he gives us an overall order of events that was acceptable to believers in his time.

Many scholars today would fall short of even Manson's degree of confidence in Mark's narrative. However, current doubts about the broad lines of Mark's story are apparently based on books that assumed that community tradition didn't set any limits to his freedom to write whatever his theology moved him to invent. He appears to have had no one *written* context, but that does not mean there was no limiting context at all for his writing.

The order of the reported events isn't the only problem. Each of the gospels presents a different picture of Jesus, and we have to decide which of them we most readily accept, and what parts we question. This is hard for the average believer, who reads any gospel in the light of the others, largely because the things that they report we interpret in terms of ideas of Jesus we have already absorbed from many sources.

---

16. The twentieth-century "form critics" claimed that the tradition was just a hodge-podge of discreet items handed down separately, with different items used for different purposes. Their influence has waned.

17. Manson, *The Teaching of Jesus*, 26.

Not only that, but only a very small part of Jesus' (probable) thirty-odd years is covered, and he undoubtedly did and said many things not appearing in any of the gospels. What these were we also tend to fill in on the basis of ideas we already hold about Jesus. Still, the four gospels give us a great deal of material to wrestle with, and it is reasonable to hold that Jesus was a complex enough figure that no one gospel could be adequate.

As already indicated, one has to follow Mark's general order, not only because that's all we have, but because if one looks for some order in the parts of Luke or Matthew that they didn't get from Mark, something roughly like Mark's order still emerges. If Mark's order was wrong, so, apparently, was the Christian community generally. And if we make too much of that, we are simply at sea, with no points of reference at all.

As this is not a "life of Jesus" book, we have not covered Mark's narrative in detail. Later on we will address a few events I find either particularly revealing, or pose problems to be mulled over. Some of them will receive interpretations different from those usually given.

Since you are encouraged to read through Mark for yourself, there is no need to expand upon the short sketch given above. Though a few salient elements of the story may be pointed out.

1. Jesus, though baptized and tempted, does no preaching until the Baptist is imprisoned. Apparently he was to follow up the Baptist's work.
2. Where the Baptist preached, "repent," Jesus added, "and believe the good news." Apparently, he looked beyond judgment to God's promise.
3. His relation to evil spirits and disease was to deliver people from them, as a sign of the still greater blessings of the coming kingdom.
4. He was more interested in announcing the kingdom than in being a popular miracle-worker, indicating he was not to be understood as the latter.
5. He chose and sent out disciples ("the twelve") to spread the "good news," which he later taught must expect to be killed for their witness.
6. He met opposition from recognized religious scholars ("scribes"), meticulous sectarians ("Pharisees"), the political establishment ("Herodians"), and the religious establishment ("priests," "Sadducees").
7. After the Baptist was executed, Jesus stayed out of Herod's kingdom, seeking privacy to teach his disciples, but later returned and headed toward Jerusalem.

8. He taught them not to consider him a messianic deliverer, but a prophet who is to be killed in Jerusalem, as prophets had been, by the religious and political powers.

9. His predictions of what would happen when he got to Jerusalem were fulfilled, though it is difficult to tell to what extent Mark's account of these prophecies was influenced by the fact he was writing after the events that fulfilled them.

Though Mark tells how he was arrested by the priestly authorities and turned over to the Roman Procurator, who crucified him, some have argued that there is no independent evidence of such opposition by the Judeans. That would imply it was the Romans alone who crucified him, not the official leaders of the Jews.

France remarks:

> There is sufficiently clear continuity between this gospel perspective and the enigmatic later rabbinic (Pharisaic) references to Jesus as a *mesith*, a false teacher who was trying "to lead Israel" astray, to suggest a basic historical probability in the gospel's portrayal of Jesus' confrontation with the Pharisees of his day.[18]

However, though Jesus met serious opposition from Pharisees, Mark does not implicate them as the parties that instigated his execution, but rather the high priest and his Sadducee minions. Jesus threatened the dominant Jewish power structure, not ordinary Jews. This is important in understanding later developments.

Mark makes it plain—as do the other gospels—that Jesus' positions on tradition, religious observance, and interpretation of Scripture were affirmative, but were seen as deviant and in violation of what the religious authorities demanded. He could hardly have avoided meeting opposition from all parties with power.

In his home synagogue in Nazareth, he met unbelief and rejection by those who knew his family, and whom he had grown up with.

When he was teaching his disciples apart from the crowds, they still lacked understanding. Peter, speaking for the disciples, calls him "Messiah," but Jesus rejects the title. Their idea is not his idea, and they resist his three clarifying announcements that "the Son of man" must be put to death by the authorities.

18. France, *The Gospel*, 115.

Still, they follow him to Jerusalem. The account of Jesus' arrival in Jerusalem raises a serious problem for Mark's chronology (not the only one). Though he writes as if all the Jerusalem events he narrates occurred within one week, those early in the week fit better the Feast of Tabernacles in the Fall, while those later are set squarely within the Passover week in the Spring. Fifty years ago, Manson made the suggestion that Mark had combined the two feasts.[19]

There seems evidence that Jesus carried on a ministry in Perea, near the Jordan River, between the two festivals. (Luke put that Perean ministry before Jesus' arrival in Jerusalem. John also puts him there just before Passover. Mark puts him at least in Jericho.) Not a few have since gone along with this or some variant of it.

In Jerusalem he teaches publicly, is welcomed by a crowd, disturbs the authorities by driving commercial interests out of the temple, answers critics, and condemns the scribes. Next we find the "little apocalypse," wherein he tells his disciples about the coming end of the age, most of which account is widely held not to go back to Jesus.[20] Then, at a last Passover dinner, he inaugurates the "Last Supper," the bread-and-wine ritual that has marked the church ever since. Finally, he is secretly arrested with the connivance of one of his disciples, "tried" in a kangaroo court by the Jewish authorities, turned over to the Roman governor, crucified, and buried.

His ending, a short account of women finding the tomb empty on the first day of the following week, seems so unsatisfactory that later writers tried to write their own endings to the gospel. Some think Mark's original ending was lost, some that he never finished the book.[21] I find his last verse, Mark 16:8, to be a very effective, even though abrupt, ending. It

19. *Bulletin of the John Rylands Library* referred to in Manson's *The Servant Messiah*, 78.

20. Here we find the "coming" of the "Son of man" in "clouds with great power and glory," apparently from heaven to earth. In the relevant Daniel passage, he "comes with the clouds of heaven" but *not to earth*. Rather it is to be "presented" before "the Ancient of Days." One can wonder whether chapter 13's "coming of the Son of man" represents Mark's understanding or some other's which he has included. Verses 5 through 31 don't sound to me like they belong with what precedes, nor are they consistent with what follows. But Mark did include them.

21. "It is customary to assume another ending which for reasons unknown to us almost immediately disappeared. To me this reasoning is entirely unconvincing . . . Nor does it appear to me that the present ending is unsatisfactory . . . [it] forms a highly dramatic and magnificent conclusion . . . He lets the curtain fall on this brief,

recalls, in Greek, Genesis 18:15, though at times the temptation to speculate on what he would have written had he gone further is hard to resist.
We will return to Mark's last words when discussing the resurrection.

This discussion more or less outlines Mark's story. Scholars have de-
spaired of ever establishing its historical reliability, but also of ever coming
up with a defensible alternative (some earlier ones, like the Frenchman
Renan, tried, but today no one thinks any alternative account can gain
much confirmation).

We have said little about what Mark quotes of Jesus' sayings. Those
who stress that Jesus is a moral teacher, major on "his teachings," so they
gravitate to Matthew or Luke. Mark ascribes many sayings to Jesus, nearly
all of which were copied into those other two gospels, but Mark is more
interested in presenting Jesus himself, a figure in history announcing a
change in history involving him as the crucified Son of man and, covertly,
as "Son of God."

Further, the more I study Mark, the more convinced I am that he
added more than a few expansions of his own to his Jesus-quotations, as
both Luke and Matthew probably also did. Though I confess a probable
bias, Mark's additions seem to me to be, in each case, somewhat more
closely relevant to what Jesus was saying than those of the other two, but it
is more impression than a carefully and critically worked-out conclusion.

Over a century ago, Wrede, writing in German, claimed that Mark
treats Jesus' "Messiahship" and "Son-of-God-ship" as a "secret" the disciples did not understand, which seems to be the case. He then argued
that "the Messianic secret" was evidence that the "primitive church" did
not believe in either assertion about Jesus. Mark, therefore, had to use
the device of "secret" to cover up the fact that he was advancing those
"mythological innovations."[22]

Wrede followed a school that tended to interpret New Testament
language in terms of Hellenistic "god-man" myths, which made "son of
god" language immediately suspect as applied to Jesus. Its popularity at
the time, as "the latest thing" in 1901, added to the influence of his ideas.

This played into the preferences of much of the advanced German
scholarship of the time, and undercut the faith in Mark that English and

---

but triumphant, epilogue with the last word freighted with delightful and portentous
irony." Enslin, *Literature*, 388. So also Hooker, *Gospel*, 391f.; Schweizer, *Good News*, 373;
Williamson, *Mark*, 286. But cf. France, *Gospel*, 684.

22. See appendix, "The Messianic Secret Motif" in Marcus, *Mark 1–8*, 526ff.

American scholarship maintained. Throughout the twentieth century it has led, with some of its sequels, to a widespread custom of downplaying Mark as a historical source. And that has been a powerful motive for shifting attention from Mark to "Q" as the "most reliable" source for knowledge of the Jesus the Galilean.

Most certainly Mark did treat Jesus' idea of Messiahship and his "divine Sonship" as confusing to, even hidden from, the disciples until after The Resurrection. Just what conclusions we may draw from that are unclear, for a number of reasons. One can take, as I do, Mark's account of "Peter's confession" (8:29–30) as indicating Jesus was *not* willing to accept the title "Christ" or "Messiah," at least on his disciples' terms (contrary to Matthew's account); and there is still much room for argument over just what Paul understood "Son of God" to mean, (he usually implies subordination to the Father, and Philippians 2:6 is still debated).

It seems to me that a title such as "Son of God" could certainly have emerged in the primitive church without being a result of Hellenistic influence, especially since we do not know exactly what those who first used it meant by it. That it was taken as understood within the first generation of Christians is shown by Paul's usage, and we have no trace at all that those who opposed Paul took exception to his language about the Christ, though they certainly did to his language about the law.

"Son of God," whatever it meant at the time, seems to have been used to emphasize *already-existing* claims of the primitive Christian community, which was struggling to develop a suitable vocabulary for its "foolish" new gospel. Thus Mark's "tactic" was addressed to a group wherein what Paul called "God's nonsense" involved some dispute about how properly to refer to Jesus.[23]

No one would have invented such terms unless they already believed in Jesus' transcendent uniqueness, and neither term could have arisen overnight, or without some communal reason on one side and some argument on the other. In addition, as already argued, Mark would hardly have written things that many in the community he was writing for did not already hold.

---

23. The complexity of Paul's argument in Romans indicates that the church in Rome was a multiplex community containing many different disagreements. Since Paul's letter could hardly end all those arguments, they undoubtedly remained for Mark to have to deal with.

Jesus could have referred to "the Son" and to God as "the Father" without ever calling himself "the Son of God," leaving his followers the problem of just what exactly he meant by those terms—a problem still being argued about.[24]

It is quite evident that Mark organized and edited his materials to suit his editorial policy. But it is difficult to see how one gets from that to the idea that he was promoting innovations, unless one has decided ahead of time that his reports were false. Mark's gospel itself surely can't be shown to be evidence for that.

Wrede's whole case seems to rest on a prior assumption about Paul's thought. Paul admittedly deviated, at least in degree, from the most conservative party in the Jerusalem church, a party that may have had disagreements within itself with respect to the applicability of the Jewish law to Gentile Christians, but also, perhaps, about "Son of David" as applied to Jesus. That doesn't mean that he also deviated drastically from the church as a whole in his estimate of Jesus himself.

It is evident, however, from the epistle of James and that to the Romans, and from Acts,[25] that there were intense arguments going on in the church over just how to interpret Jesus' relation to the Israelite background of both "Messiah" (that is, "Christ") and "Lord." The four gospels present four stages in the developing split between the two Jewish sects—Judaism and Christianity—that eventually survived.

Luke, writing later than Mark and for the Gentiles, tries to minimize the growing gulf by tying the gospel to the Jewish tradition of world history, tracing Jesus all the way back to the creation of Adam. Matthew, writing still later but for readers much closer to a Jewish background, fights briskly against the growing strength of the revitalized Pharisee tradition. He emphasized that Jesus was the new and true lawgiver and that events in the Jesus story fulfill specific ancient biblical prophecies. Finally, John contrasts believers in Jesus with the confusions among Jewish half-believers, and Jewish opponents. They represent, in part, the variety of viewpoints about Jesus that the church had to sort out as it defined itself. Mark, writing earliest, shows little patience for such a variety of partisanships. He limits Jesus' opposition to "Pharisees," "Herodians," and

---

24. Psalm 2, a coronation psalm, calls the new king of Israel God's son.

25. See Romans 3:2, 31; 6:1–2, 15; 7:12; 9:4–5; James 2:19–26; and Acts 21:20–21.

evil spirits. Then, only at the end, to otherwise unidentified "scribes," the temple priests and the short-lived mob at the crucifixion.

Mark indicates that Jesus' resurrection occurred, and that he will confront the disciples when they return to Galilee, and then says no more about him. The disciples must learn what the resurrection means by obeying his direction to go back to Galilee and there be confronted by the Risen One. This implicit acknowledgment that "Son of God" is a title beyond description—understandable only by meeting, hearing, and obeying—is Mark's closing and impressive *tour de force*.

To sum up, Mark presents his readers with an account of Jesus directed toward showing that:

1. "Son of God" is an appropriate title for Jesus, but one not at all easily understood, even by his closest associates;
2. Jesus' teaching was focused on his task of proclaiming that god was about to judge and alter fundamentally the world's demonic power structures oppressing mankind, and that his miracles are part of God's imminent overthrow of such institutions.
3. Jesus' death and his resurrection are difficult to understand perhaps even for Jesus himself, but necessary for the kingdom.
4. Those who follow him will be persecuted, perhaps killed, but even if they fall away, Jesus will still call them back to continue his work.

Before presenting my construction of Jesus' early years we must look more briefly at the other gospels. Then, after my stories, we take up a selected few of the many questions about Jesus that many have puzzled over.

5

Luke

The gospel of Luke . . . is no hit-or-miss work, but a carefully
and artistically prepared account. . . . [it] may then be described
in words largely of his own choosing as a biographical "treatise
concerning all that Jesus began both to do and to teach."

—Morton S. Enslin[1]

L UKE'S GOSPEL IS NOT just an expanded edition of Mark (as Matthew is),
but a distinctly different work, put together for a different purpose.
His highly formal introduction addresses "Theophilus," someone with
great respect, to help him *know the truth* about what he had been told.
He claims to have drawn upon "many" who compiled "narratives" based
upon "eyewitnesses," that he has followed "accurately" and "for some time
past" and has arranged "in order." Though he may have exaggerated, there
is no reason not to believe him, in general.

It looks as if he used any sources he could find (1:1–4), collecting
many sayings and stories apparently unavailable to Mark. His second
volume, the book of Acts, shows that he picked up things from survivors
or tradition-bearers from earlier churches such as Jerusalem, Damascus,
and Antioch, and possibly some Roman records in Caesarea and Corinth.
He may even have listened to some reports from Galilee.

As a skillful writer, Luke often let his imagination fill out the connections between the separate pieces he had received. In Acts he ascribes
to past figures oratory he could hardly have found in records, and we
can assume he may have done the same in his gospel. We have no way of
knowing. Yet what he says is part of the records we must use. That they
were largely based upon persons' memories or traditions simply means

1. Enslin, *Literature*, 403.

that historians in that day didn't have the sorts of files and records we have now.

Luke's gospel shows that he wrote later than 70, after the temple in Jerusalem was destroyed, but probably no later than 85. (His second volume, Acts, may have been considerably later.) Copying, but often rewriting, about two-thirds of Mark, he skips from Mark 6:44 to 8:27 entirely as well as a number of shorter bits. Though he claims to have used many believable sources, we cannot assume they were all equally reliable. He may even have added to them. That he took some liberties with history has been suggested.[2]

Contrary to much church opinion, Luke was probably written before Matthew, so that is the order in which we will discuss them.[3]

It appears Luke was concerned with laying out his ideas of how history led from Adam to Jesus. Luke's second book, Acts, seems to aim at convincing "Theophilus" that Jesus was the true continuation of Jewish history. The Jewish church, he held, was the true continuation of Judaism and the Gentile church—the world church—a true continuation of the Jewish church.

Fujita's *Introducing the Bible* puts it, "It is Luke's fundamental conviction that God's salvation of the world develops through history,"[4] but he goes on to stress how Luke also emphasized Jesus' concern for the poor and for women: "Luke underscores the fact that Jesus was and is a neighbor in the real and true sense of the word . . . he is not only *with* the people but also and genuinely *for* the people."[5] Later, in Acts, Luke stresses the mission to Gentiles. And he represents Rome as not being responsible for Jesus' death.

2. Luke's "second volume," Acts, was no doubt written considerably after Luke, perhaps even ten years later. It has been dated as late as 120, but for tendentious reasons. Hengel remarks, "The work on the gospels and acts may possibly have been extended over a number of years. In other words, in the sphere of dividing Luke's sources, which are of the utmost significance for the Jesus tradition, apart from Mark we can no longer gain any real clarity, but only express conjectures with more or less of a basis." *The Four Gospels*, 141. Study has forced me to lose some confidence in him or his sources, and hence, in the literal reliability of his copying the "Q" material from whatever source or sources he used. Believing that Matthew copied his "Q" material from Luke suggests even less precision for Matthew's version.

3. Some of the reasons for believing Luke wrote first will be given when we discuss Matthew.

4. Fujita, *Introducing the Bible*, 138.

5. Fujita, 139.

Sayings of Jesus found in both Luke and Matthew, but not in Mark, have convinced many scholars that both of them drew on another document called "Q," collected by a supposed "Q community" having an interpretation of Jesus different from the tradition behind Mark and especially Paul.

This view, that Q was a written source for both Luke and Matthew, independently of each other, is embraced very widely today, and all agreements between the two gospels not traceable to Mark are assigned to it.[6] After years of accepting that theory, I have lately come to doubt it. If Matthew used Luke, one can still assume Luke had some such source or sources, and must admit that material used by Luke and borrowed by Matthew may have come to Luke from more than one place, or even was invented. Therefore, holding that Q was a single document, enabling us to characterize a separate Q community seems an over simplification, and is at least speculative.[7]

John S. Kloppenborg-Verbin, one of the most active proponents of Q, acknowledges that the theory is questionable:

> Modern scholarship on the sayings gospel Q is founded on a hypothesis. . . . Because it offers the most economical and plausible account of the form and content of the synoptic gospels, it continues to be by far the most widely accepted solution to the synoptic problem. . . . But it remains a hypothesis. Other early Christian sayings collections have been found, but no papyrus copy of Q has yet been discovered.[8]

As for other views, two scholars, Horsley and Draper, say "the standard view of Q as a collection of sayings is a modern misunderstanding rooted in the accidents of the historical development of Synoptic Gospel studies."[9] Their detailed study argues that rather than being a written

---

6. For a history of how ideas of Q grew up see the introduction to Robinson, *The Sayings Gospel.*

7. Some even carefully distinguish different "levels" or "editions" of Q. Why not several Q's? Those most enthusiastic about Q, sometimes sound as if eager to undercut Paul's testimony to Jesus as the Christ. I don't see how a "source" we ourselves construct can provide a more solid base for our historical understanding than documents whose antiquity is unquestionable. How can two steps involving our fallible (and constantly modified) interpretive theories be more reliable than only one step?

8. Kloppenborg-Verbin, *Excavating Q,* 11.

9. Horsley and Draper, *Whoever,* 166. See also Goodacre, *The Case Against Q,* that, however, assumes that Luke copied Matthew. I conclude the reverse.

document, it was several bodies of quotes or stories that poor, but literate, Jewish followers of Jesus recited orally to celebrate him as the hero of the oppressed.

It seems quite adequate to treat the "Q" material as representing widespread traditions unavailable to Mark. Then Matthew used Luke when he expanded Mark, leaving out those parts of Luke that didn't fit his purposes and adding his own new material.[10]

This approach avoids the temptation to treat Q material as if it all came from a single manuscript, granting it an imagined unity and a single source.

As a convenience, we will use the label "Q" (with quotes) for texts shared by Luke and Matthew but not with Mark, without so assigning them to any one source but Luke. Where Luke got them we can't know.

We cannot identify the other sources Luke used. It's easiest simply to lump them together as "tradition," though some could have been written. Since Luke was a skillful storyteller, he may have expanded on tradition or even created new stories. We don't know. Nor do we know what sources he had for his second volume, Acts, nor how accurate any of them were.[11] It would be very helpful if he had left us footnotes and a bibliography of sources, but he didn't. That wasn't much done in those days.

His additional material that Matthew didn't use (and it is often evident why) includes many familiar events—the Annunciation to Mary, the Christmas shepherds, the repentant crucified "thief," and others. He also gives us powerful parables—Dives and Lazarus, the Good Samaritan, the Prodigal Son, the lost coin, and more—that Matthew doesn't offer.[12] They make Luke's account memorable, and most can certainly be taken as quite typical of Jesus, suggesting that the parables he used come from a rather reliable tradition—or else that our picture of Jesus is deeply influenced by

10. The differences in the "Q" texts in Luke and Matthew beg the question: Who changed what, and why? Whether Luke copied Matthew or Matthew copied Luke hinges on how we interpret those differences. They indicate to me that it was Matthew who did the changing, though this requires interesting views on Matthew's editorial policies. This holds whether "Q" existed separately or not.

11. Whether the "we" sections in Acts 16:10–17 and 21:1–18 represent a written source is believable, but is still argued against.

12. Matthew's omitting these is said to show that he and Luke wrote quite independently of each other. Since several motives for his omissions can be suggested, and he may have had still others, I don't find that argument convincing. They were quite different people, with different viewpoints, writing for different folk, and for different reasons.

Luke's parables. (Luke was such a skilled writer that those who believe he created some of his stories, perhaps even some of the "Q" materials, argue a point worth considering.)[13]

It is clear that Luke aims to assure his apparently highly-placed correspondent that Jesus was not in any sense guilty of subversion, but that his crucifixion was the shameful martyrdom of a beautiful, prayerful, forgiving, and in no way subversive, man.

Christianity, he suggests, is not a new religion, and hence should be legal under Roman law. It cannot be considered to be socially dangerous, but is the true continuation and fulfillment of God's overall plan for history as revealed in the Jewish Bible, all the way back to the creation of Adam. He thus is presenting a matured theological account of history that goes far beyond Mark's, though, since based on the Old Testament, it is largely consistent with the other gospels.

Luke's moral concern and wonderful storytelling have contributed to the impression that Jesus' primary interest was in teaching kindly general moral rules. Rather, Luke shows that he concentrated on announcing the "kingdom," God's imminent invasion of the world's history. If Jesus had been just a moralist, would the common people have "heard him gladly"? Would the Pharisees have objected to his moral teachings? They rejected him not as a moral teacher, but as a false prophet making clear the coming overthrow of the powerful and the comfortable.

As we shall point out, Matthew wrote against the aggressively reorganizing Pharisees by emphasizing that Jesus was an independent and authoritative lawgiver. Luke instead presents Jesus the compassionate man of prayer (a priest?), rather than Matthew's Jesus the Law-giving King. Jesus prays in all the gospels, but Luke has him praying much more often than Mark and Matthew. Luke also speaks much more often than the others of the Holy Spirit as a supernatural power, often driving Jesus' actions.

Luke also seems to be trying to convince Theophilus, and through him, probably, all Christians who needed it, to share what they owned with members less fortunate. His emphasis on generosity and sharing comes through in many places—the story of the rich man who ignored the starving man at his door, for instance, or Zaccheus, who after meeting Jesus, gave half of all he owned to the poor. This was undoubtedly one of

13. This should particularly be noted in the end of the gospel and the early parts of Acts.

Jesus' emphases, but as preparation for God's overthrow of the world they knew, and has certainly been one of his impacts on history. It is Luke who makes the most of it.

Zaccheus' story shows still another side of Luke: that forgiveness was an important part of Jesus' activities and his message. A number of the other parables found only in Luke recommend forgiveness, such as the Good Samaritan, the lost coin, and the Prodigal Son.

There is tenderness in Luke, gentleness quite beyond that of the other gospels. Thus he omits Jesus' cry "My God, why hast thou forsaken me!" from the crucifixion story. He then adds three "words from the cross" appearing nowhere else: "Father, forgive them, for they know not what they do" (Luke 21:34), "Truly I say to you, today you will be with me in Paradise" to the repentant "thief" (21:43), and "Father, into thy hands I commend my spirit" (21:46). Two of these are words of forgiveness, and the third quite different from the outcry Mark reports.

Besides his emphasis on forgiveness, there are four more things that are distinctive of Luke.[14]

1. His Greek is the best in the gospels and sounds deeply influenced by the LXX Greek translation of the Hebrew Scriptures.
2. His stories are told with wonderful skill.
3. He is the most cheerful of the evangelists.
4. He emphasizes Jesus' deep concern for the sufferings of the common folk, the poor, and women.

Luke presents this as evident in both actions and teachings (much of this appears in the "Q-material," but some is distinctively Luke's). Where Matthew accuses the Pharisees of hypocrisy and Mark accuses them of legal nitpicking, Luke treats them as unfeeling and stuck-up.

Luke seems to expand Mark's order of events, but except for his omissions and a few things he moved around, that effect comes primarily from the fact that he had a lot of material with no clear place to put it, so he dumped a huge amount into Jesus' final trip to Jerusalem. It takes Mark only 52 verses to get Jesus there from Galilee. It takes Luke nearly ten chapters! (As a result, Luke is the longest book in the New

---

14. "The note of Joy that is sounded over and over in the gospel of Luke," is spoken of by Beare, *Matthew*, 43.

Testament.) Much of this may reflect Jesus' ministry in the Jordan valley, which Matthew notes in 19:1.

On the other hand, Luke works too hard at making excuses for Pilate and the Romans for executing Jesus, and his account of the crucifixion lacks any of the somberness and tension—and much of the power—written in Mark's account. It's much *nicer*. In Mark, Jesus' death is ugly. In Luke's version, he dies sweetly. At least one scholar concludes, "The death of Christ in its redemptive sense plays no role for Luke, whereas it is central for Paul."[15]

Doubts also may arise when Luke goes beyond Mark in quoting words of Jesus, especially in the early chapters of Acts, where more serious doubts regarding events arise. That the stories, though effective, may contain narrative inventions is something not to be welcomed or celebrated, but it must be faced.

There are, no doubt, many items in Luke that are worth crediting. But, which ones? What we have is the gospel of Luke, his testimony to the Christ.

15. Beker, *Paul The Apostle*, 330.

6

Matthew and John

The gospel of Matthew has been described as a "manual of the life of Christ and of Biblical theology" . . . It implies an organized church life and a moral code. . . . He has used sources . . . but he clearly felt free to interpret, to rearrange, to rewrite drastically, and to suppress.

—Morton S. Enslin[1]

THOUGH MANY SCHOLARS WOULD disagree, I believe Matthew was written later than Luke, no earlier than 85, perhaps as late as 100.[2] The author used both Mark and Luke,[3] but drew more heavily on Mark, plus some additions of his own.[4]

He responds to the changes in Jewish culture and attitudes that emerged about 85,[5] lumping "the scribes" with "the Pharisees" where Mark separates

1. Enslin, *Literature*, 389.

2. Clement's (c. 97) quotation of Matt 5:7 is hardly enough to date Matthew, since it may have been a widespread tradition independent of the two gospel writers. His quotes from Luke do confirm a date for Luke earlier than 97.

3. As already noted, I'm convinced Matthew got his "Q" material from Luke.

4. Eusebius, *History*, (early fourth century) quotes from Papias (early second century) that Jesus' disciple Matthew wrote a collection of Jesus' sayings in Aramaic. If so, it was neither our "Matthew" nor was it "Q."

5. After the temple in Jerusalem (that had cooperated with the Romans) was destroyed (in 70), the leadership of Jewish culture was turned over to the Pharisee Rabbis, relocated on the coast at Jabneh. They constructed a temple-less Judaism, focused on Torah, and presided over by a head rabbinic office, the "House of Law" (Bet Din), set up about 85 under the Pharisee Rabbi Gamaliel II. Rabbi Gutstein wrote of him, [he was] "from c. 80 to c. 110 the leader of the Jewish community at Jabneh . . . Gamaliel's principal aim was to establish unity within it and to achieve unquestioned authority in matters of Jewish Law for the school at Jabneh." (Gustein, "Gamaliel," *Collier's Encyclopedia*, 558–59). He made it official that Christian Jews were no longer Jews and they were to be expelled from synagogues and beaten as heretics (Paul and others had been beaten by local

them, and emphasizing the continuity of Jesus with the Israelite law. So, even though he wrote considerably later than Mark, he stands closer than the others to the conservative faction of the Jewish church in Jerusalem. The church's first head was Jesus' brother Jacob ("James"), who was called by his fellow Jews "James the Just," that is "one who keeps the Law."

That Matthew's theology seems *more primitive* than Luke's need not require an earlier date. The theology of William Jennings Bryan, candidate for President and later Secretary of State, was more *primitive* than the theologies of Calvin or St. Thomas.

We know very little about the church in Jerusalem. Paul gives us some information in Galatians, but at that time was defending himself rather emotionally, so may not have presented the balanced picture we need. Luke's account of the beginnings of the church in Acts is so obviously colored by Luke's special interests that it is hard to draw a historically reliable idea of many things we need to know about the church in Jerusalem.

We do know, however, that Jesus' brother James, who headed the Jerusalem church, was assassinated in 62, and during the war with the Romans (65–70), Christians were driven out of Jerusalem. Matthew's family may even have been among those driven out. Matthew, however, certainly did not write in Jerusalem.[6]

Matthew was writing for a church whose members had much more Jewish background than those that Luke or even Mark wrote for, and shows that he himself had had some rabbinical training and a rabbinical mindset. He was also obviously reacting against some overblown reports of Paul's teaching regarding Jewish law.

In fact, though every gospel recognizes that Jesus was a Jew, Matthew's Jesus is closer to what became traditional Judaism than the Jesus of any other part of the New Testament:

> As the fulfiller of the Scriptures, Jesus is, according to Matthew, the authoritative interpreter of the law . . . modern scholars sometimes call it [Matthew] a "Jewish Christian gospel" . . . [that] emphatically states that Jesus came primarily for Israel's salvation.[7]

---

synagogues much earlier). His efforts, continued by others, led to the eventual triumph of Pharisee Judaism.

6. "It must have originated in an area where church and synagogue were in continual contact and conflict, and where Jewish influence was sufficiently strong to bring serious trouble to the communities of Christian believers." Beare, *The Epistle*, 8.

7. Fujita, *Introducing*, 132–33.

Jesus, he suggests, was a kind of second Moses. However, he had to distinguish Jesus' teaching as "Law" from the way "the Law of Moses," or Torah, was interpreted by the rabbis of the Pharisee party,[8] who had gained much greater influence by Matthew's time than they had had in the time of Jesus.

Some have read Matthew as directed toward the conversion of Jews. It appears more likely he was trying to encourage Jewish Christians to stop cursing the synagogue and accept their exclusion from it as the resurgent Pharisees had made official around the year 85. Thus, Matthew is most intense in his criticisms of the Pharisees, yet it is only he who quotes Jesus as saying, "The scribes and the Pharisees sit in Moses' seat, so practice and observe whatever they tell you, but not what they do."[9] This is a puzzler. It is difficult to believe Jesus would say that and yet disagree so strongly elsewhere. But when put with Matthew's, "Think not I am come to destroy the law and the prophets, but to fulfill them. For truly . . . not an iota, not a dot, will pass away from the law until all is fulfilled (Matt 5:17)" one sees he was treating Jesus as the Christian's rabbi, one doing what he thought Jewish rabbis ought to have been doing, but weren't.

Notice Matthew says, "The scribes *and* the Pharisees." He knew there were scribes who weren't Pharisees, but the non-Pharisee scribes were becoming fewer and fewer, as the Pharisee viewpoint was becoming dominant. When Jesus was alive, Pharisees were just a small minority,[10] less than one percent of the population, but one with some rich and important members who were ambitious to take over Judaism, which they eventually did. The destruction of the temple in 70 gave them the opportunity to dominate and define Judaism, but it took over one hundred

---

8. "Jesus radicalizes but not abolish the law, according to Matthew; he is like a new Moses who on a new mountain radicalizes and reissues the Torah." Beker, *Paul*, 249.

9. Matthew 23:2–3. This might be read negatively as, "Do the scribes, etc., sit in Moses' seat? Then do what they say!" but what follows discourages such a course, and I can find no translation that adopts such a reading.

10. ". . . this period, prior to the destruction of the Second Temple in 70, was characterized by a culture of exceptionally pluralistic halakhic discourse in which virtually all positions were considered worthy of respectful consideration and no pressure was exerted toward imposing uniformity . . . There was a gradual erosion of the early pluralism. . . . The major watershed(s) in the process [was] Rabban Gamaliel's attempt at the academy of Jabneh to sift earlier traditions and testimonies." Segal, in review of Heger, "The Pluralistic Halakhah," 520.

years. When Matthew wrote, they were still struggling aggressively to expand their influence.

That's important, because most Jews and many Christians think of all Jews in Jesus' time in terms of the post-Pharisaic Judaism that has come down to today. They think of the later Jerusalem church, including Jesus' brother James, as largely Pharisee in orientation. (In fact, the Pharisee "oral traditions" were not fully organized and standardized until the editorial work of "Judah the Patriarch"[11] a hundred and sixty or so years after Jesus' death.)

We don't really know how much Jesus' Galilean background included Pharisee emphases, or how much Jesus' synagogues resembled Pharisee synagogues. Mark may have been right when he spoke of "Pharisees from Jerusalem" among those opposing Jesus, and equally right when picturing the majority of Galileans as favoring him while Pharisees, especially Judean ones, opposed him.

One striking example of Matthew's strong pro-Jewish (though anti-Pharisee) outlook is his expansion of the story of Jesus and the Canaanite woman. In Mark 7:28 the woman just "begged him to cast the demon out of her daughter." In Matthew 15:22, she cries, "Have mercy on me, O Lord, son of David," seriously compromising her non-Jewish character. Before presenting the answer Jesus gave in Mark, Matthew quotes him as saying, "I was sent only to the lost sheep of the house of Israel," but nevertheless, later, "O woman, great is your faith!" In Mark he simply says, "For this saying you may go your way; the demon has left your daughter." The contrast between the versions in the two gospels is striking.

Other examples of Matthew's effort to emphasize Jesus' concern with Jews, while rejecting the authority over Judaism the Pharisees claimed, included starting Jesus' genealogy with Abraham (Luke starts with Adam as "Son of God"). Matthew also placed emphasis on Jesus not only as "King of the Jews" (2:2), but also as "Son of David." The title for the expected Messiah occurs very rarely elsewhere.[12]

11. How quickly Judaism became Pharisaized is debated. "It is implausible that the successors of the Pharisees will have won immediate authority. It is entirely possible that the rabbis lacked any say in the Greek-speaking diaspora until well into the third century A.D. or even later." Goodman in Dunn, *Jews and Christians*, 29.

12. "Son of David" as a title occurs in Matthew 1:1, 12:23, 15:22, 21:9,15, and twice in Mark, 3 times in Luke (two simply copy Mark), and never in John (though as "seed of David" once). It appears in Revelation, but only three times in all 22 epistles.

His is also the only gospel that quotes Jesus as commanding his disciples to "Go nowhere among the Gentiles, and enter no town of the Samaritans, but go rather to the lost sheep of the house of Israel," (10:5–6). This pro-Jewish bias doesn't indicate an early date so much as a quite different situation for Matthew.

It is possible, I suppose, to argue stubbornly that Matthew's versions give us the original tradition, which Mark abridged to suit his purposes and his audience. Favoring Mark leads me in the opposite direction. But in either case, difference in attitude between Matthew and both Mark and Luke is evident.

Still, Matthew ends up urging the preaching of the gospel to all peoples. He clearly accepted those parts of Jewish culture Jesus didn't criticize. He simply leaves one wondering how much of it he expected converted Gentiles to adopt.

On the other hand, despite his positive attitude toward Jewish religious tradition in general, Matthew's very negative view of the Pharisees themselves extends to the former Jewish population of Jerusalem. Thus, in rewriting Mark's account of Jesus' trial, he whitewashes Pilate but has the crowd declare, "His blood be on us, and on our children" (Matt 27:25). This not only absolves Rome from guilt but also obviously interprets the destruction of Jerusalem in 70 as punishment, a generation later, for Jesus' crucifixion.[13] (Whether Matthew can be called anti-Semitic depends on a number of questions of definition, history, and interpretation.)[14]

Matthew had to disagree with the Pharisee rabbis without denigrating the Torah itself, which he and his church members alike highly regarded, being like himself good Jewish Christians, though undoubtedly Greek-speaking. He almost treats Christianity as another school of interpretation of Jewish law, with Jesus as the Lawgiver and Primal Teacher. In this, he was "correcting" Mark's emphasis (and perhaps coun-

13. To blame Matthew for later Christian anti-Semitic use of this passage seems unfair to him—though that doesn't excuse Christian anti-Semitism. Matthew was not predicting some future calamity; he was commenting on the past fact that Jews of Jesus' time and their children both suffered terribly when Jerusalem was taken and the temple destroyed. Apparently some Gentile Christians even gloated over this as God's punishment on Jerusalem for crucifying Jesus. But Jewish Christians like Matthew looked on it as the terrible and sad thing it was—if God punishes, it should call forth both terror and sympathy, not gloating.

14. The discussions in Dunn, *Jews and Christians*, 177–87 and 203–11 are helpful on this problem.

teracting Paul's), even while copying most of Mark and adding to it.[15] As for his relation to Paul's writings, it's not at all clear just how much he disagreed with them. Did he favor the folk who had made so much trouble for Paul, or was that controversy settled before he wrote? We have no adequate clue.

Matthew's rearranging of things is seen in the five long speeches he gives to Jesus—the Sermon on the Mount being the best known. Sayings that appear scattered through the two earlier gospels, particularly Luke, he collects into four other lengthy "addresses." Since there are five of them, just as there were five "Books of Moses," he seems to suggest that Jesus either replaced or reinterpreted Moses. His emphasis on Jesus' presumed Davidic ancestry, already mentioned, distinguishes him not only from the other gospels but also from any other New Testament book.[16]

Where in Mark, Jesus emphasized vaguely a coming judgment; Matthew emphasizes, more than any other gospel writer, an eventual fiery Gehenna for sinners. (He appears even to be delighted in such a hell, "where there shall be weeping and gnashing of teeth.")[17] An example of this is his rewriting of Mark's parable of the seed growing secretly (Mark 4:26–29; Matt 13:24–30). Matthew adds that Satan also sows seeds, producing plants that at the final "harvest" are to be gathered up and burned.

This leaves the question: did Matthew understand Jesus better than Mark did? Was Jesus' view of the law closer to Matthew's than to Paul's?[18] Except possibly for the book of James, the rest of the New Testament

15. Mark had been in circulation for twenty or thirty years by the time Matthew wrote, without any real competition, even from Luke. Matthew alters Mark's narrative, but Jesus' sayings in Mark he usually quotes carefully. Mark had more authority for him than did Luke, but Jesus' was of course still greater.

16. Except for Romans 1:3, where Paul was writing carefully to Jewish Christians as well as Greek, David is rarely mentioned in the New Testament. References in Psalms are quoted, 2 Timothy 2:8 says Jesus was "descended from David," Hebrews 11:32 mentions David in a list of ancient worthies, and Revelation 22:16 has the ascended Christ call himself the "offspring of David." Except for Matthew, it's evident that Greek-speaking Christians showed little interest in "son of David" Messianism.

17. If Matthew 13:24–30 is his rewriting of Mark 4:26–29, his emphasis on final judgment shows up clearly. Beare, *Matthew*, 43, remarks "The emphasis on Judgment is so pronounced as to cast a somber pall over the picture of Jesus . . . The terrors of the Day of Judgment hang perpetually over the heads of Matthew's readers. . . . It must be said that there is little trace of a gospel of 'grace abounding for the chief of sinners.'"

18. It is interesting that books about Jesus by Jewish authors, like Vermes *The Religion of Jesus the Jew*, treat Matthew as their favorite source of information.

hardly bears that out. Yet the church has markedly favored Matthew over Mark. I have to admit that my immersion in Mark and Paul, plus my late dating of Matthew, have led me to think the ascendancy of Matthew in the church was unfortunate, at least in the rather legalistic view of Christian morality that it encouraged.

In reading Matthew, one notes a sort of "superstition" not found in Mark and rare elsewhere in the New Testament. Things are revealed in dreams—to Joseph and to Pilate's wife, for instance—and stories occur, like that of the death of Judas (27:3–10), whose only function seems to be to apply an Old Testament passage to events involving Jesus. He probably received most of these from the ongoing growth of the tradition during the years between Mark and Matthew.

Matthew shows more interest in the church and how it should operate than do the others. In fact, his is the only gospel that mentions "the church" at all. But then, it is hard to resist the conclusion that besides writing later he was a conscientious pastor (whatever being a pastor meant at the time).

As already noted, in Matthew, many have found evidence of either rabbinic training or dependence on rabbinic methods, and even some knowledge of Hebrew.[19] He also includes tales, like that of Jesus' birth or of the soldiers at the tomb that raise real doubts. Much more than the others, he wrests Old Testament verses out of their proper context to apply them in questionable ways to events he narrates. The other gospels also interpret Jesus in terms of the Hebrew Bible (often in its Greek translation), but less often and less arbitrarily than does Matthew.

I find myself tempted to be very careful about ascribing to Jesus any of those parts of Matthew that do not appear either in Mark or Luke (and even some of those that do). Abandoning them altogether would rob us of some real—though sometimes puzzling—treasures, like Matthew 25:31–46 and 28:18–20, and much of the Beatitudes. No preacher would want to lose those, and they rather sound like Jesus—or else they have influenced our idea of Jesus. But they at least demand careful handling.

---

19. "He shows the influence of professional training as a Jewish 'scribe' . . . He provides a *gemara* [a commentary] to the sayings of Jesus, in something comparable to the way in which later rabbis built up the Talmud." Beare, *The Gospel*, 9. He also changed Mark's Aramaic "Eloi" (*Alahi*) in Jesus' cry from the cross to the Hebrew "Eli," though he left the Aramaic "sabachtani" unchanged.

One more point about Matthew: although it was some time before the order Matthew, Mark, Luke, and John became the standard order, Matthew quickly became viewed by the church as the most important gospel.

This has often been taken as evidence that it was written before 80 and in a city that was an important Christian center. To me it seems to indicate that it was welcomed as the most suited for the task of teaching Christian morals to Gentile converts, that it was found more impressive than Mark, and that it fitted the situation of the groups of Jewish Christianity in the church and Jewish antagonism outside. In addition it played well into the developing church administrative structure that seemed necessary to cope with pagan opposition and internal dissension. It also provided a counterbalance to the way some of Paul's ideas were being interpreted. Besides, it may have had particularly committed copiers, or a wealthier sponsor of copying and distributing it.

It certainly became the most influential gospel throughout the church's history while it encouraged tendencies toward moralism, just as Luke encouraged kindly emotion and social concern. Matthew in particular has always been the mainstay of those who would reduce Jesus to nothing more than a moral teacher. Despite his more or less evangelical theology, he ends his gospel with Jesus charging the disciples to "go . . . make disciples of all nations . . . *teaching* them *to observe* all I have commanded you." That has invited moralists to limit Jesus' "command" to ethical instruction. Paul saw that as necessary, but not as prime or central.

Not one of these considerations supports the idea that either Matthew or Luke is the best testimony to what Jesus said, did, or was. However, without them we would not have the "Q" material or other items found in one or the other and these are quite important. Despite the value he adds, it is unfortunate that Matthew was granted such primacy. Mark and John are both more profound, and Luke certainly more beautiful.

To sum up, Luke and Matthew accepted the authority of Mark as, in general, the standard account of Jesus' ministry and death, but expanded and *corrected* him for the sake of their readerships and their own theologies. Luke chose to speak better to Greek folk and to use material Mark didn't have or didn't use. Matthew chose to address those Jewish Christians who were being influenced by the growing pressure from the Pharisee revival and to former Greek synagogue adherents who were puzzled (as Paul's Galatians had been) as to how much Jewish tradition Christians should follow.

Both tied the faith more closely to the Old Testament, Luke by emphasizing the gospel's continuity with biblical history and Matthew by emphasizing the Mosaic Law in a Jesus-modified form. Matthew also quoted many earlier passages as predicting Jesus in some detail.

Their two overall views could be characterized thus: For Matthew, it was Moses who launched God's great Ark, the Torah, for the saving of humans. Moses gave directions to get Israel and its converts to the harbor where they would be safe from the coming storms of God's wrath. However, the Jews perverted Torah, so God sent Jesus to correct their reading of it, setting Moses' Ark back on course.

For Luke, God had the Ark for all of mankind in mind when he created Adam, and Judaism was just one of the seas the obedient sailed until, finally, by passing through the Gibraltar of crucifixion and resurrection, they reached the open ocean of the gospel of love available to the entire world, should they respond by repenting.

That both Luke and Matthew were written significantly later than Mark shows in their evident rejection of Judaism in its actual state. We read that:

> Matthew is much more Jewish and sympathetic toward the Torah than Paul, yet much more hostile in his treatment of Jews as a people . . . Thus the people of Israel as a whole are responsible for Jesus' death. . . . in Luke, the gospel story is marked by the increasing hostility between Jesus and the company of Pharisees and Sadducees which foreshadows the hour of their final condemnation. . . . For Luke [especially in Acts] . . . the Jew fails because he is ignorant and morally corrupt. For John, Matthew and Luke, the church is the successor to Israel; it is the "New Israel."[20]

I would not say that the church for Matthew is "the New Israel"; Christ's church is rather "the true Israel reformed."

So we turn to John, and find a different kind of puzzle. What he says is at least ninety percent different from the other three, though his story of Jesus' trial and crucifixion parallels their accounts significantly. In John, Jesus speaks in long theological addresses, claims he obeys "The

20. Beker, *Paul*, 329–30 [bracketed comment mine]. This last does not apply to Paul. Research has shown that he, writing earlier, considered Israel still to be God's chosen people, alongside the church.

Father" implicitly, and will return from where he came down. John clearly embodies a very different tradition about Jesus and very different thinking about that tradition. The problem of how much of his traditional material is historical, and how much figurative, though a basic problem with all the gospels, is at its worst in John.

Much of his material is undoubtedly traditional, but of a quite separate tradition, undoubtedly one developing in geographical or social isolation from the others.

Since there is so much difficulty in drawing on John for historical data (he presents the theologian with much material and many problems), we will refer to him rarely until a later chapter on his prologue.

Both Matthew and Luke felt a need to downplay some of Mark's theological claims in order to advance their own. So after grasping the different interpretations the three gospels give, the reader is faced with the choice as to which of the three interpretations should be taken as basic. Or, must we turn to some other source? Where is it to be found?

It has been clear that I find Mark the most satisfactory gospel,[21] especially if carefully complemented by sayings in Luke and Matthew, and theologically, but hardly historically, by John.[22] But like the others, we cannot take even Mark's account as completely true historically, nor as one fully acceptable to some of the other scattered early Christian groups.

Despite their limitations, what we can reasonably believe about Jesus depends on all those four gospels. We are then left with five questions:

1. How do we find reliable answers about him? How do we confirm them?
2. What did he do? Under what circumstances? How do we know?
3. What did he say? Under what circumstances? How do we know?

21. The Jewish literary scholar Harold Bloom reports, "I am fascinated by the mysterious gospel of Mark. Matthew does not find me, and Luke and Acts arouse only my skepticism, while John hates me and I respond in kind." Bloom, *Jesus and Yahweh*, 174.

22. Some object to relying too closely on the gospels, arguing that, on the basis of contemporary sociological thinking, it grants them a "privileged position" over against other ancient literature. As a matter of academic probity this is quite proper. There is, however, much difficulty in establishing that other works are *as old* as the inescapable dates for Mark, and especially for Paul, whose works are certainly the oldest sources we have regarding early Christianity. Granting some appropriate degree of privilege to those two for one's understanding seems quite sensible. And even if one is a convinced non-Christian (not just playing at being non-Christian for academic reasons), privilege is to be granted to Christian history.

4. What happened to him? Who did it? Why?

5. What did his followers think of him? Did they agree with one another? Did their understanding change? When? How or why?

My present answers not already indicated, nor many of my arguments for them, will not be laid out in full detail. That would require another book. But they are implicit in everything I say about Jesus, and I hope that what I give of those answers will become part of your wrestling with the questions.

Of the questions numbered above, the last two are crucial. If Jesus died and was resurrected, or even was vindicated in some other way, that must have changed how his followers understood him, spoke about him, and acted. If he died but was not resurrected or otherwise vindicated, his followers would undoubtedly have understood his career in a different way. But then their influence, and his, would hardly have lasted as it has.

Authors discussing Jesus can in fact be separated into two groups: those who assume, explicitly or tacitly, that there was no resurrection, no vindication, and therefore, interpret Jesus and his followers on that basis, and those who interpret him as vindicated by his resurrection. Again, we see the resurrection, or something equivalent, as *the basic issue* in studying Jesus and his followers. (Some, however, ignore The Resurrection as something not properly available to critical historical or sociological methods.[23] With such, it is hard to tell what is denial and what is methodological discipline).

To put it another way: the fundamental question is whether "the Resurrection" was a creation of his followers or a unique act of God. Historians look for human causes for everything, because we don't know how to cope intellectually with a unique act of God. We have no suitable heading in our mental indexes under which to file it. So the basic question for our self-understanding is: does honest, responsible thinking require that our human methods be able to cope with everything?

23. Such as Burton Mack. I have tried to be as sympathetic as possible in studying the latter's *Who Wrote the New Testament?* Writing with obvious scholarship, in the important historical tradition of Reimarus, Strauss, and Wrede (perhaps Kautsky? Goodenough?), he bases his whole case on certain sociological commitments and seems to me to pass over a number of sorts of evidence I find quite deserving, and then grants to Q and Thomas more than they deserve. When he says of Mark (154) "we have to regard it as a major achievement in early Christian mythmaking . . . we have an obvious fiction, masterfully composed," I can only consider him cavalier.

Further, a sixth item must be added to the five questions above. Historians have pointed out that there is a necessity, in historical thinking, for intuition as well as reason. Answers to the five questions need to be synthesized—integrated into one coherent picture—by creative intuition.

It should be obvious that intuition that takes resurrection seriously will offer a quite different unity in its answer from one rejecting it. And it should be quite obvious that despite the many problems connected with doing so, I take The Resurrection, whatever it was, with utmost seriousness, even though that raises very difficult, probably insoluble, philosophic problems. (Such problems are not uncommon in philosophy; problems raised by ancient philosophers in Greece, China, and India are still challenging today for those philosophers who haven't settled for the "answers" so far proposed for them.)[24]

The gospels give us four different "portraits" of Jesus. I share a belief once widely held, but now less widely approved, that in learning about Jesus, Mark, and Paul give us the place to start. However, my reasons are not just the old reasons; they come from studying and questioning the newer developments as best I can.

Mark, as already stated, was proclaiming gospel, "good news," while not seeking to meet our expectations, whatever they might be. Both Matthew and Luke accepted him as their main source, and we should do the same. Paul, of course, is our earliest source, offering interpretation of the risen Christ but little about the historical Jesus. So while Mark may be considered as closest to Paul, Luke and Matthew should be seen as two later and quite different responses to Paul. And that means using all three of them carefully.

Here this chapter must end, so we can go on to my stories of Jesus' early life, and to discussion of several problems raised by both my students and colleagues. Some of them are crucial to interpreting Jesus, and one, Jesus' birth, is more an area of unquestioned popular celebration, though in academic circles still debated.

---

24. My book on the ancient Chinese philosopher Xunzi received diametrically opposed reviews. To many ancient problems contrary answers are still offered.

7

A Preface to the Stories

It is in the face of fear and doubt that we find faith. . . . Jesus
developed, and his development involved conflict. He also developed in the context of a particular time and place. . . . Jesus
. . . perfectly manifested humanity in his own particular human
context.

—William C. Placher [1]

"THINKING ABOUT JESUS" MAY require an overview of his life, or at
least of his public ministry, his teaching, his preaching. We have the
"gospels" that do that, four of them. They represent the thinking about
Jesus' final months shortly after his time. Each writer drew on materials
passed down, either by word of mouth or in writing, from those who had
known, seen, or heard him, or their hearers. Based on their accounts,
there are also numerous much-later accounts called, "lives of Jesus," to
which readers might refer.

Many of these ignore the fact that the rest of the New Testament
says very little about his teachings or preaching, but concentrate on what
he was shown to be by his actions or passion.[2] They form the key to his
importance. But they must be interpreted in terms of what he had already
become.

To deal with him as a human person, but a unique one, we have to
use a longer narrative than the gospels give us, since talking about a person requires narrative, as each of us is our own story. And stories imply
antecedents, so biographies start early. A lack of facts about Jesus' early

1. Placher, *Jesus the Savior*, 36.

2. "Jesus research, especially by Protestant scholars, should make a fundamental
break with its focus on Jesus' authentic words and make its main theme the work of Jesus
as a whole." Theissen and Winter, *The Quest*, 199.

life means that every such story reflects the author's theology. Thus, many of the traditional stories overwhelm his humanity with pious ornaments that destroy it, or at least obscure it.

The stories presented here as an introduction to Mark's account of Jesus reflect my own ideas as to how his distinctive character was molded during his early years. They give a helpful background for some of the unusual positions I later advocate. It would make no sense to claim that these stories tell "what actually happened" or that they are a historian's attempt to reconstruct "what must have happened (I guess, on the basis of the available evidence understood in light of my presuppositions)." They grew from a need to crystallize on paper how my imagination understands what preceded the story the gospels tell us. The only importance such fiction might have comes from our seriously trying to understand that strange figure, Jesus of Nazareth, who, the gospel proclaims, was resurrected from the dead as the Lord Christ and who by his life, teachings, death, and resurrection has influenced uncountable lives, and continues to do so.

Since I have often been turned-off by those who try to impersonate an ancient character, I write in the first person with considerable unease, for fear I might sound as if I think I'm Jesus or something even approaching that. Nevertheless, how Jesus reacted to his milieu and how he felt about himself as a person growing up (at some point he *had* to be a teenager!) can hardly be presented without imagination.

The stories have no intrinsic authority. As already pointed out, I am not an eyewitness, nor a professional historian, or a Greek or New Testament specialist. But neither were the writers of the gospels upon whom we are so dependent. These stories do occasionally depart somewhat from accounts in the gospels, but in ways that I believe are reasonable and not untrue to their testimony. The items that are relevant to our later discussions are the important ones. The rest only supply context.

These writings parallel the gospel stories, but with some unusual interpretations. They explore Jesus being baptized, going through a strange experience of "receiving the Spirit," and struggling with the confusion of what it meant. The stories continue with him finally understanding his career as choosing and establishing the "True Israel," being the "Son of man" as prophesied by Daniel, and in modifying the Baptist's preaching of the soon-to-arrive end of the age. My account of choosing his first disciples follows Mark closely.

There my imagined narrative ends.

8

Jesus' Early Years

Is not this the carpenter, the son of Mary and brother of James and Joses and Judas and Simon, and are not his sisters here with us?

—Mark 6:3

MY NAME IS JOSHUA, son of Joseph—or, in our local Aramaic language, Yeshua bar-Yoseph. Though I am in my early thirties, I still live, when I'm home, here in Nazareth with my mother Miriam and my four brothers Jacob, Joseph,[1] Judah, and Simeon, whom we call "Jake," "Joe," "Jud," and "Sim." All of the names are very ordinary, and in fact, Joshua is one of the most common names given sons in Galilee, where we live. My two sisters, Leah, Joe's twin, and Ruth, who is older than Jud, are now married and living in town with their husbands and babies. Our father died some time ago; I will tell about that later.

My mother is a beautiful, loving, patient, hard-working person who has kept demanding of us the same moral and religious standards as our father. She has dark hair and eyes, but rather light skin. Most of the time she smiles a smile as cheerful as a summer day, but when we get out of line, or one of the neighbors is officious, she is ready with a brisk anger that gets things done but hurts no one. I must admit, however, I never saw her more than just a little put out at our father.

As for my brothers, Jake, less than two years younger than me, is the smartest. He's taller than I am, skinny but wiry, has a long, angular face, a large, sharp nose, wavy brown hair, and piercing eyes that try to penetrate

---

1. In Mark 6:3 he is called "Josetos," which seems to be the same as "Joses." Matthew 13:55 corrects this to "Joseph," according to the best manuscripts, though many have "Joses" there, a typical Greek respelling, too. "Joseph" is probably correct. Other manuscripts have "Jose," and a few "John."

behind every surface appearance. He's my favorite conversation partner, since he usually understands what I'm saying, and tells me when he doesn't or when he disagrees. He never pretends anything that isn't true.

As I said, Joe is Leah's twin. He's a bit on the chubby side with a roundish face and black eyes set like raisins in a cookie. He has a friendly disposition, loves music, and would go about humming all the time if we didn't shut him up. He's not as smart as Jake, but doesn't care about that. He'd rather just be comfortable and enjoy life.

Jud was always a very quiet boy, though he has started to open up a bit lately. His brown hair shows a hint of red, and like many a younger brother, has an explosive temper to go with it. It still isn't clear what he wants to do, or make of himself. We don't push him. He can be stubborn enough without that. Even though he's so quiet, one can sense his inner strength. No one pushes him around.

Sim has always been the baby. He's not very strong, and has been sick more frequently than any other of us, but Mother is very kind and gentle with him, as if she doesn't want to lose him. His disposition is sweet as a beautiful sunrise, and gentle as a ewe with her lamb. Unlike the rest of us boys, he never gets rowdy, but he hardly ever makes a joke, either.

Jake hopes to be married to a very likable girl, but her family hasn't agreed yet just what her dowry will be, and he hasn't worked out new living arrangements—he doesn't fancy living with her folks. Her mother is a somewhat careless housekeeper, not like Mother, and he's very particular about where things are and what shape they're in. His wife is going to have to learn neatness from him, or he is going to have to be very forgiving. I suspect quite a bit of both.

Besides, with my being gone so much of the time now, if Jake marries, then Joe, Jud, and Sim will have to take over the support of our mother, and neither Jake nor I have been the teacher of carpentry that our father was. Our reputation, especially Jake's, might get them started, but the younger boys are going to have to teach themselves a lot to make a go of it. I'm afraid none of the three have the self-discipline, at least not yet, to turn themselves into even average craftsmen. Though Joe is the most likely to make good, if he sticks at it. They don't have our father, as Jake and I had, to demand fine workmanship while encouraging us at the same time.

Next to Jake, I was close to Leah. She grew up rather tall and thin, but when young, was compact, always cheerful, and very lively. She played noisy, even rough, games with Jake and me—until Father would remind her that she was to grow up to be a quiet and reserved woman. She tried. She is brighter than our other sister, Ruth, the quiet one. Ruth loved to sew, and became very good at it. They both, according to custom, married young.

I wish Leah had wed someone else. Her husband has beaten her occasionally in his fits of anger. But I must admit that even he, being an Israelite, is kinder to her than some of the husbands I saw beating their wives in the city of Sepphoris, six miles away and largely Greek. I can't put up with women being mistreated. I never could.

Father never struck Mother or the girls, of course, but if he had, I don't know what I would have done. Women, even though they so often talk about nothing more than their families and the neighborhood gossip, are just as much human beings, images of God, as men. In fact, our mother is a better image of God than most men I know. I guess that's why I don't understand why so many men look down on women. Our sisters did take part in our family discussions about life and things religious, and their comments made as much sense as did us boys'. But, come to think of it, they never did speak up like that in public. Few women try to, and they are rather unkindly criticized for doing so.

Perhaps it's ironic, perhaps just luck, but Ruth's husband is about the kindest, quietest fellow you'd ever meet. The only thing bad about him—which we pity her for—is that he is a tanner, so constantly smells of hides and rotting tanbark. In fact, our law holds that if a bride finds that her husband is a tanner, and she wasn't told, she can have the marriage annulled. Ruth knew that, and knew how he smelled, but she also knew he was a kind man. She loves her husband very much, smell or no smell. But it does raise a problem when he joins her in visiting us. We welcome him, despite the smell.

Carrying on his trade requires a great deal of water. That's why they live near the well. And why he is, perhaps, the only husband in town who helps his wife carry water from the well, which is really a cistern fed by a spring on the other side of town.

Our parents were a wonderful, open, loving couple. At a very early age, watching my playmates' parents, I came to realize how wonderful ours were, even when Jake and I, and sometimes our sisters, fretted under their rather strict discipline. They were not only wonderful to us, but also to each other. As I grew older and heard neighboring men talk about their wives, I realized how much more respect our parents had for each other than seemed true of the parents of many of our friends. I also thought how much warmer our own home felt than some of our neighbors'.

In fact, one of our neighbors, a rather short-tempered chap, suddenly divorced his wife one day, even though she was left with only a very small dowry. They had no children and her family members had either died, lived far away, or didn't take much interest in her. She ended up having to labor at the only trade a lone, untrained woman could ply in our small town.

Most of the neighbor women turned against her, but Mother didn't. She tried to help, though we didn't have much to help with at the time. Mother invited her to dinner several times, and there were neighbors who criticized all of us for "eating with a sinner." Mother simply said, "She's our neighbor and she's hungry. It's her husband who is the sinner." The poor woman finally went to Sepphoris, which seemed to promise more of her unfortunate business than she found here. Everyone lost track of her after that. She just seemed to disappear. She either died or sold herself as a slave.

This saddened the whole family for she had been a very warm, friendly neighbor whose husband had degraded her by divorcing her. Surely God didn't intend the laws he gave Moses to allow men to treat women so hard-heartedly or wickedly. Maybe God only allowed that law because he knew we men could be such beasts; I'm sure he didn't create anyone to be treated that way.

Until we were older, Jake and I just took our parents' love for granted, as children do, but later we wondered about the connection between their love for each other and their love for us. Each year seemed to bring new insight into what it meant. We rang all the changes on the problem, and finally decided—I don't know where we got the insight—that they were so very loving because they had such deep respect for themselves and for each other. Still later I realized that their love of God lay behind that respect. I came to see that love of God, love for one's self, and love of others are all tied up together.

Our father was a carpenter, like his father and grandfather before him, but an even more skilled craftsman than they had been. Up in the large Greek city of Sepphoris, many of the folk he did work for called him a "*tekton*," as if he were just another ordinary laborer the well-to-do despised. Though, because of the quality of his work, they did pay him a bit more than most. (Not much more, and that more didn't support us quite as well as you might think, since his skills demanded the best tools he could afford.) He kept his tools finely honed, and also preferred to work with the most carefully selected wood available, some of which either had to come from the Jordan Valley, or all the way from Lebanon, which made it expensive.

Several times he was urged to move us to Sepphoris for the sake of business, but he just said, "I'm an Israelite, and won't have my children brought up in an impure Gentile city where customs don't follow Torah. I won't have my sons going naked in a gymnasium, with boys living impure lives."

Despite the demand for his work, there had been more than a few times when crops were poor and we found our meal, oil, or wine running very low. We knew that more would not soon be available, or if it were, only at frightening prices. And there were other times, as soldiers foraged nearby, when we didn't know whether we could keep what we had. But no matter how grim the future looked, our parents would remind us, "God gave us Israelites manna and quails in the wilderness; he will not fail us now," and he never did. There was always something to eat.

We were no worse off than our neighbors, none of whom could be called prosperous. In fact, many had a harder time than we did. Practically everyone in town was quite thankful that God gave us whatever we received. Just a few weren't quite sure.

Folk here in Nazareth, however, didn't call Father a "*tekton*," which was a Greek word applied to anyone who worked with his hands, wasn't a farmer, and didn't carve statues. It implied a low standing. Our villagers respected Father as a "*naggarah*," a carpenter, since plying a trade was not looked down upon among Israelites—in fact, important scribes also knew a trade, and had their sons taught trades.

In referring to Father, folk often attached to *naggarah* some word like "master" or "fine," in tribute to his exceptional skill and care. His work showed a love of well-made things and a remarkable discipline—love that blessed our whole family and discipline that shaped all six of us kids.

Known for his skill in joinery and cabinetry, he tried to transmit those skills to his sons, especially to Jake and me. Unfortunately, we never got beyond being just good journeyman carpenters, though we did inherit some of his fine tools. So after he died, we got only a few jobs in Sepphoris and had to take over support of the family mainly on the basis of a reputation among our Nazareth neighbors. We were regarded as more ordinary, but reliable, workmen and so quite acceptable. Some dismissed me as "the carpenter's son," but others, showing some respect, called me "the carpenter." I don't know why Jake, who was a better workman than me, was always treated, as long as I was around, as my assistant. Probably it was just that I was older.

Part of the problem was that neither of us had Father's love for the craft. When he took a fine piece of wood, worked it, and finished it, one could see him light up with delight at the finished product. Jake and I were more likely just to feel relieved that we had gotten through the job successfully and in a way that we could respect.

On the other hand, where Father loved the Scriptures, so far as he knew them, we both were completely fascinated by them, first hearing them in synagogue and later studying them. Father could read and even write a little bit, which was unusual in Nazareth, and very useful for a skilled craftsman, though he hadn't had much opportunity to study. Instead, he had a good memory for what he heard. We listened carefully in synagogue and tried to memorize what we could, but we also loved to think and to argue, to extend the Scripture message by telling stories, and even to compose poetry—perhaps not very good poetry, but at least imaginative. Father's parental authority and his need for our help, of course, made us his companions in his work, but even then our hearts were still in our questionings, our rethinkings, and our arguments.

This little town of Nazareth lay in the more-or-less fertile part of Galilee—what was called "lower Galilee." In the eyes of those in Jerusalem, who believed they defined what a good Israelite should be, Galilee was suspect. They called it "Galilee of the Gentiles," and I guess they thought they had good reason for doing so. Eight hundred years ago or so, the Assyrians took away as captives most of the Israelites in what is now Galilee, and replaced them with other sorts of folk. More than one hundred years later, the Babylonians took away those in what we now call Judea. About seventy years after that, the Persians, who had conquered the Babylonians, allowed them—at least some of them—to return to Judea (so the Greeks call them, and us, too, "Jews"). Now, over five hundred years later, the Judeans still aren't sure we Galileans quite qualify as "Jews." (We tend to call ourselves Israelites, rather than Jews, anyway.)

They and we both had a bad relationship with the folk—Samaritans—who lived between Galilee and Judea. Though we in Galilee went to the Jerusalem temple for the holy festivals, the Samaritans had their own "temple" (until it was destroyed by the Romans). Many in Judea felt we also were religiously inferior, at least somewhat. After all, many of us had ancestors who were not Israelites. Also, there was more Greek spoken in Galilee than in Judea, except along the Judean coast, where the Romans kept most of their armies and did most of their business, and in Jerusalem, where most of the educated and well-to-do lived (but also a great lot of poor).

We had our own faithful pieties. We knew that so long as we kept the commandments, we remained within the covenant, and had a right to consider ourselves quite as much Israelites as the Jews in Judea. We were careful about cleanliness and purity, we prayed and recited the Shema,[2] we observed at least the basic dietary laws in Torah, though without all the Pharisee elaborations. Some of the houses in town even had cisterns for religious bathing. We knew our sins were forgiven, quite as much as were the sins of Judeans', if we repented for the sake of "the fathers" Abraham, Isaac, Jacob, and Moses, and by the sacrifices and prayers of the priests in Jerusalem.

We went to synagogue and kept the Sabbath (Father lost many jobs in Sepphoris because he wouldn't work, or even show up, on the Sabbath). We were more careful regarding the Sabbath than the law required, not out of fear of breaking a law, but just out of thankfulness for the opportunity for rest the Sabbath gave.

For instance, the Sabbath law doesn't forbid cooking. But, when the weather suited it, Mother would spend Friday afternoon heating up the stone oven thoroughly (which took quite a bit of extra straw and twigs, since wood that wasn't just scraps was too scarce to use as fuel). Then, before sundown brought in the Sabbath, she'd put in a pot of lentils or fava beans, the only kinds we had, add garlic and any available herbs, and let them cook overnight as the oven cooled. When nights were chilly, the heat given off by the cooling oven helped us sleep more soundly. Feeling good when we got up was especially appropriate for the Sabbath.

If we had been like most of the folk in Nazareth, we would have had neighbors who were relatives, some closely related. Most small towns in Galilee were largely made up of a few clans; sometimes interrelated ones. Our relatives in Nazareth were few and not very close, third cousins or

2. The Shema', Deut 6:4: "Hear, O Israel: The LORD our God is one LORD; and thou shalt love the LORD thy God with all thy heart, and with all thy soul, and with all thy might."

something. Father explained what had happened: our great-grandfather had inherited the family farmland, farther south near Nain, which had been in the family for generations. When he died, his sons couldn't pay all the debts he had incurred, and lost the farm. The boys, having picked up different sorts of skills on the farm, settled in different towns and improved their skills; they had been raised with more ambition and more discipline than most of the farm boys who were similarly cast out on their own by exploitative moneylenders.

Our grandfather had worked for a time in Gennesaret, then in Capernaum (where Father was born), but finally moved, with his wife and son, to Nazareth. But on visits to our grandmother's family in Capernaum (after grandfather died), Father met Mother and convinced her family, through a marriage broker, that he was a good prospect. They married and he brought her back to Nazareth. That is why we had no close Nazareth relatives, and were rather marked people, considered as not really clan members by those whose families had lived in Nazareth for generations and who felt they owned the town.

We had relatives, some sort of cousins, in Jerusalem, whom we saw (but didn't stay with) when we went up there for some of the great festivals—not all the festivals, for it was always a question whether we could spare the time. The time for the feasts, of course, belonged to God, but it was hard to spend the days it took to walk the ninety miles or so there and then walk back. (It was only about sixty-five miles in a straight line, but the groups we traveled with never wanted to go through Samaria, so our route, down the Jordan valley, was quite a bit longer.)

Often we spent the lesser feasts at home in Nazareth. But neither Father nor Mother felt right about missing Passover in Jerusalem, and, for us boys, it was always thrilling to see the impressive temple, and to listen to the great scholars teaching their pupils or arguing with one another on the temple steps.

Our relatives in Jerusalem liked to tease me about the time when I was twelve. I guess I became so absorbed in the scribes' discussions, even chipping in with questions and ideas of my own, that I stayed there while the family set out to return home, thinking I was traveling with our Capernaum cousins. The way they told it, (though I was really only voicing some of my youthful doubts), I was "correcting" the great scribes' interpretation of Scripture! They took that to be hilarious, their small-town country cousin "correcting" the established authorities of the big city, the world center of biblical learning! I'm sure they told their neighbors that story, so I had a bit of undeserved reputation in Jerusalem even when a young boy! If the learned authorities heard it, I'm sure they wouldn't resent such a report. They'd just laugh.

The reason we didn't stay with our Jerusalem relatives during the festivals was that they were just too busy. Shobai, the father, was a Levite serving in the temple, and during a festival he had so much to do it didn't seem right to take up much of his or the family's time. Besides, their young son, David, was enthusiastic about growing up to be a Levite, and spent a good deal of time just hanging around the temple. He even ran errands for the high priest, when that official couldn't locate one of his usual messengers.

He was a disappointment to Jake and me, because though he knew a great deal about the temple rituals and the calendar rules in Torah, he wasn't much interested in the rest of the Scriptures, and steered away from questions about the Bible. He claimed he intended to study eventually and would have plenty of time when he was older. If we started a discussion with him, instead of dealing directly with the problem, he would come up with imaginary stories that he believed had something to do with what we were talking about, but whose relevance wasn't clear to us. The stories we told, to explain what we thought, always had a definite point. At least, we saw them that way.

Instead of staying there, our family stayed with our other, even more distant, relatives in Bethphage, just east of Jerusalem. They, Matthai and his wife Hannah, had three children, Lazarus, Martha, and Miriam. Lazarus was fourteen years older than me, a rather tall fellow with an impish sense of humor. He loved to play tricks on his sisters, who always seemed to enjoy them. Martha was four years younger than he, and Miriam six, so they were all our seniors, but they took us under their wings and we all got along very well. It was always a joy to visit there.

More recently, things were not so pleasant. Lazarus married, but his wife became very sickly and they had no children. Martha married, but lost her husband and both children in an epidemic. Mary's husband was caught in a riot in Jerusalem and killed by Roman soldiers. After a number of years, Esther, Lazarus' wife, died, so the two sisters lived with and took care of him.

As if that were not enough tragedy, Lazarus came down with a very virulent leprosy and had to move to the leper colony called Bethany, or "house of the poor," just east of Bethphage. The two sisters moved with him, and we feared they would catch leprosy also, and eventually they did. Our whole family was disturbed by what happened, but Mother insisted that family ties overrule fears, and that lepers were still the same persons as they had been when well, so on our festival visits we began staying in Bethany instead of Bethphage.

I'm getting ahead of my story. Besides our relatives in Capernaum, Mother's sisters and their families, we have some distant ones, second cousins, in Bethsaida. Bethsaida and Capernaum are both quite different from Nazareth. There's more Greek spoken in Capernaum, because it's on two main trade routes, but even Greek is spoken in the smaller village, Bethsaida.[3] I suppose that's natural, since Bethsaida is on the other side of the lake, the east side, in the realm of Herod's half-brother Philip, who encourages things Greek. Both rulers pretend to be Jews, but are really Idumeans.

In fact, when we visited Bethsaida, I was quite impressed by the knowledge of Greek exhibited by two neighboring boys, Simon and Andrew. Their names showed their parents' acceptance of Greek, as "Andrew" is a purely Greek name, and "Simon" is the Greek form of Simeon, my brother's name. However, their background was thoroughly Israelite, and Aramaic was their mother tongue. They attended synagogue regularly—the Aramaic-speaking synagogue, where the Torah was read in Hebrew, not another one they told me about, where it was read in Greek. Jake and I argued with them that Torah read in Greek couldn't still be Torah, but they just called us narrow-minded.

I was shocked because the Greek I heard while helping my father in Sepphoris, and after a while began to make a little sense of, didn't seem to be a language in which anything genuinely sacred could be said. Father did say, though, that it was full of words that were the names of their "gods." But when I thought about it, I realized that the Aramaic part of our home synagogue service never seemed to be quite as impressively holy as the Hebrew Scripture reading.

3. Rami Aray, in "Hellenism in the Towns," 42, says, "Hellenism was introduced by Herod the Great . . . His dynasty carried on this mission"; however, he also says that "little traces of Hellenism were found [by archaeologists] . . . in Bethsaida," yet remarks "in 30 A.D., Philip the son of Herod, elevated the city to a status of a Greek City." I conclude that there must have been considerable informal Hellenization before Philip's action.

Later I learned there were Greek-speaking synagogues in Sepphoris, and also in Tiberias, a city on our side of the same lake in which Simon and Andrew and their father Jochanan[4] fished. Still, it took both Jake and me quite a while to recognize that God could speak in Greek quite as well as in Hebrew, and what God might say in Greek would still be God's word.

And that brings us to the other difference. Though there were a number of fishermen in Capernaum, its north-south trade route and the very fertile country around it supported a number of other businesses as well as drying, salting, and shipping fish. As a result, it was a tax-collecting post, and had a unit of soldiers stationed there to safeguard and enforce the collection. Although Bethsaida was close to one of the same trade routes—the one to Damascus—its folk were mostly fishermen. The lakeshore was lined with boats, and with men washing or mending their fishing gear. Only a few soldiers or tax collectors are stationed there.

Simon and Andrew showed me their father's boat. He had made quite a success of fishing, selling much of their catch to the salt-fish trade that shipped it as far north as Caesarea Philippi, northeast to Damascus, and even south to Jerusalem.

Some years later I heard that both their parents had died. The two sons inherited the boat and the business, and stayed for a while in Bethsaida. Then they moved across to Capernaum and did very well, eventually having a number of hired hands to help with the fishing.

Andrew was the gentler, kinder one of the two, quieter, and more likeable. He worked hard, but wouldn't have made a successful boss. Simon was a born leader; when I was with him, he always had a suggestion as to what we should be doing, and usually started doing it right away. He was exciting to be with. On a later visit, he and Andrew invited me to go fishing with them, and I was delighted at the prospect, but when Simon saw a storm coming up, he canceled the trip. I've never yet got that boat ride, despite having been there since. I'm sure I'll get back there again before long, and will collect on that promise. We also had rather distant relatives in Cana, about ten miles to the north of Nazareth, beyond Sepphoris, but we hardly ever got over to see them. In fact, it always took some special family event for them to invite us.

4. John calls Peter "Simon, son of John" (John 1:42, 21:15–17); Matthew calls him "Simon bar-Jona" (Matt 16:17). I take John's tradition to be the more reliable, for rather weak reasons it would take some time to present, and still more to argue for.

Before going on with my story, there's something else I must tell you. The Scriptures say that a first-born son, the "son that opens the womb," belongs to God,[5] and must be bought back from God by the family with the proper sacrifices. My mother told me about that when I was quite small. She also told me that circumstances had prevented them from completing that responsibility, so God still had a special claim on me. She said I must find out just what he wanted of me. That claim hung on in the back of my mind. I could never get rid of it. So always, through my childhood, my youth, and my manhood to date, I have had the feeling I must determine where my special "belonging to God" will lead me.

One possibility suggested itself when our cousins in Jerusalem proudly claimed that, on their mother's side—which was how we were related to them—they were descended from King David. That was exciting to us boys, since it was their mother who was related to our father, and that suggested we were, too. For me it evaporated quickly when I asked Father if we were really David's descendants. He said, "Who knows? David lived long ago, and had many wives and lots of children. Maybe we number among the thousands of his descendants, or maybe we don't. What's important is whether we are faithful members of the covenant, not who our ancient ancestors were." That was the end of that, so far as I was concerned. At least, what I was destined for wasn't defined by our relatives' claims about our ancestry.

But something about it did bother me. David was a warrior, a conqueror, and people expected the coming Messiah to be "the Conquering Lion of Judah" like David. It seemed to me that God didn't work much by conquering. He called Abraham *out of* the idolatry of Ur and Haran; He didn't conquer them. He didn't conquer the Egyptians either; he *rescued* us Israelites out of Egypt. Solomon followed in David's steps; he had great conquering armies, but his taxes and son's arrogance lost most of his kingdom.

The Babylonians conquered us; we didn't conquer them. And God saved a remnant of us, and brought us back to our land. Did we conquer anyone at all? No. We won independence, finally, only to forfeit it by our unfaithful behavior, by not loving God with all that we are. And so we ended up under Roman rule. If God works in history, he doesn't do it by

---

5. Exodus 13:2.

conquering, though maybe Satan tries to. God's ways are more mysterious, more like a caring Creator than a Conqueror.

Jake, however, clung to the idea we were descended from David, the great conqueror, taking it to be too important to ignore. Every now and then he'd remind me of it.

But whether a descendent of the great king or not, what was my calling to be? That question stewed in the back of my mind all through my youth. The fact I was named Joshua added to it, since it meant "God is salvation" or "God is victory," and father liked to remind me that it was Joshua, not Moses, who led Israel into the Promised Land. Did that mean I was to lead in some way? I couldn't be sure.

As I said at the beginning, Nazareth is in the more fertile part of Galilee, which means that despite some almost bare stretches hardly fit even for grazing sheep, we do have beautiful green fields around us in the spring and fields glowing gold and white, ready for harvest, in summer. I had lots of thinking to do, and spent what time I could wandering in the fields, admiring the wild flowers that sprang up here and there, and watching the birds—tiny song birds, large threatening hawks, and an occasional vulture—ride the air. I felt a real kinship with them, as God's human among God's wild creatures, enjoying God's provision for all.

Recollection of God's provision was undoubtedly due to the Kiddush we recited before every meal, thanking God for bringing grain and grapes from the earth for our food. But I couldn't ignore that there were hawks and vultures among us humans, including landlords, moneylenders, tax collectors, thieves, Roman soldiers, and others.

The pity I felt for the hawks' prey merged with the pity I felt for our acquaintances that had, like our ancestors, lost their land. Many family inheritances had been lost to moneylenders, taxmen and other wealthy chaps with both the power to take folks' wealth and the "legal" immunity provided by soldiers to keep from having to give it back.

God had also taken my peace of mind. I was destined for some special divine purpose, but what was it? Possibility after possibility came to mind, but none settled there long. As I got older, time to get started seemed to be growing shorter and shorter. Was I to spend my whole life wondering rather than doing? The Psalm says to "wait on the Lord."[6] I found that a very hard lesson to learn. Even hard-headed, practical Jake couldn't quite

6. Psalm 27:14.

understand my problem, or why it so occupied me. For him, as always, everything practical should be done and finished; even questions about ideas should be threshed out and settled.

As I grew older, both these matters—treatment of the poor and my own calling—dampened my pleasure in going to Jerusalem for the great feasts. There I saw great wealth, alongside deep poverty and oppression. The temple itself seemed on the side of the wealthy, the exploiters. The temple was full of moneychangers, and there was much gossip about the many ways the temple organization fleeced the people and sided with the Roman oppressors.

On the other hand, if I was destined in some way to fulfill a call from God, what business did I have criticizing God's chosen priesthood, those who offered sacrifices for the sins of the whole people? How could I be thankful for my situation?

On free time, when we were in Jerusalem, I haunted the steps of the temple, where as a boy I so enjoyed hearing the scribes discuss Scripture. I was disappointed. Their discussions no longer seemed to catch the spirit of Scripture. Some spoke as if temple rituals and priestly holiness were all that the texts were about. Others spoke as if the poverty and suffering all around simply didn't exist. Neither way was how I heard the prophets, or Torah, or the Writings.[7] In them, God was on the side of the poor and dis-possessed, a God of justice, but of kindness and encouragement as well.

Jake was no help. He maintained that the temple and the priesthood were established in Torah, and represented God Himself. One could not love God with all one is without loving and respecting them. Without the temple sacrifices our failures to keep the law perfectly would never be forgiven! They embodied the Covenant!

I couldn't see how that could any longer be true. After all, the high priesthood hardly represented God's choice. It was not conferred by holy lot, not even by an Israelite ruler, but by the powerful overlords, first Herod's father, then his son Archelaus, then the Roman procurator, and none of those had the authority of Torah behind them. The priests' family's wealth and their subservience to the Romans were more important than their piety. And how they ran the temple was shameful!

I was sure more study would help. The answer to everything really important must be in the Scriptures. I had to know them better. I had

---

7. The Torah, prophets, and Writings make up the Hebrew Bible. Christians call them the Old Testament.

to become a learned scribe! So we must go on to that. I've already mentioned our family's piety, and the love Jake and I had for the Scriptures. In the synagogue, the Scriptures were read aloud in Hebrew, and then applied in Aramaic by whoever was speaking that Sabbath. At home we discussed what had been read and said—in Aramaic of course,[8] but that wasn't because we couldn't, with some effort, follow the general sense of the Hebrew.

After all, the languages were related. It soon became automatic to notice where words were almost the same, except for accent, or where Hebrew used a long vowel where Aramaic had a short one, or sounded a *sh* for a *th* or a *z* for a *d*. Things like that. One often had to rearrange the words, but in a way that still made sense. It took longer to get the hang of the verbs; in some forms they were quite like Aramaic, in others different. And sometimes the same word meant something different in the two languages. Hebrew took some getting used to, but to us it began to make sense.

Father had made sure we learned to read Aramaic, and since Hebrew was written with the same letters, Jake and I received permission, during the week as well as Sabbath afternoons, to try to read some of the scrolls at the synagogue.

When we discovered that some of the books had parts in Aramaic we avidly turned to those. Ezra was a bit of a bore, but Daniel was more interesting. I was particularly excited by a number of the stories: the lion's den, the fiery furnace, and especially the part where the true Israel, "the saints of the Most High," represented by "a Son of man," suffered oppression and defeat under a beast but eventually "inherited the kingdom."[9] Why that particular passage caught me up into it, I don't know, but it rang in my memory again and again.

Aware, however, that practically all the rest of the Scriptures were written in Hebrew, Jake called me back to working on the Hebrew text.

---

8. "What evidence there is does not seem to demonstrate that the Jews of the first century A.D. needed an Aramaic translation at all. The use of Hebrew as a literary language at Qumran is well noted, and there is some indication of it as a colloquial tongue. Fitzmyer . . . points out that 'pockets of Palestinian Jews also used Hebrew, even though its use was not widespread'. . . whatever the functions of the Targum may have been . . . providing a biblical text for the unlearned masses was not one of them." Golomb, *A Grammar of Targum Neofiti*, 5. And Fitzmyer, *A Wandering Aramean*, 45: "Little can actually be said about Jesus' use of Hebrew. That Hebrew was being used in first-century Palestine is beyond doubt."

9. Daniel 7:13–22.

I told our parents I would like to study to be a scribe, an expert in the Scriptures. So they sent me, often accompanied by Jake, to an elderly man who wasn't officially a scribe but who sometimes spoke very learnedly in synagogue. He liked to be addressed by his Hebrew name, Jozadak ben Hanani Hakkohen. He wasn't an active priest, so the Hakkohen was perhaps a little improper, but he was proud of being descended from the priests, the Cohens of Anathoth whom King Solomon had excluded from the Jerusalem priesthood for political reasons.[10]

Since the prophet Jeremiah was one of the "Cohens of Anathoth," Jozadak felt closely akin to Jeremiah, even though he admitted that what genealogy his family had didn't show he was a direct descendant of the prophet. He had proper reverence for Torah, but showed a still greater interest in the prophets and the Psalms, and spent more time with us on them than on Torah. His devoutness impressed us quite as much as his learning. But his emphasis on prophets and writings made our curriculum different from that for an "expert on the Law." And the more I studied, the less sure I became that I was to end up a scribe—at least not an ordinary one.

One day Jozadak remarked, "The 'new covenant' Jeremiah spoke of[11] need not be identified with Torah as now understood. Many folk make Torah the whole thing, the Pharisees even drown the prophets in Torah, or, rather, in their traditions' interpretation of Torah. But God gave the prophets to counterbalance the Torah, to focus it, to advance our thinking about it, not just to apply it. God is as truly God of the prophets and psalmists as He is of Torah. The great prophets don't just echo Moses!"

Another time he burst out, "If Jeremiah, Amos, Hosea, Micah, or Isaiah were here now they would say many of the same things to the landowners, moneylenders and the government, and the Jerusalem priests as they did in their day.[12] The Scriptures show God to be a God of the poor, the oppressed, of widows and orphans, of prisoners and captives, and His

---

10. See 2 Kings 2:26–27 and Jeremiah 1:1.

11. See Jeremiah 31:31–33.

12. Jeremiah 1:10, 18–19, 2:7–8: "See, I appoint you this day Over nations and kingdoms . . . against the whole land—Against kings and officers, and against its priests and citizens. They will attack you, But they shall not overcome you. . . . Hear the word of the LORD, O house of Jacob . . . you came and defiled my land, you made my possession abhorrent, the priests never asked themselves, Where is the Lord?' The guardians of the Teaching ignored Me, The rulers rebelled against Me" etc. (trans. JPS *Tanakh*, 1999).

'righteousness' means his faithfulness in doing acts of freeing oppressed folk. To call God 'our God' is to take the part of the poor and oppressed! The Pharisees aim at being good, at obeying Torah, but they go along with the rich, the powerful. They speak of God's restoring of Israel, but don't really share the suffering of the people!"

His vehemence at such times scared us, as we remembered how many rebellions, some local and some large, there had been in Galilee. Rebellions against just those same landowners, moneylenders and the powerful office-holders whom they supported, rebellions that had sometimes brought in Roman soldiers and ended in mass crucifixions or enslavements.[13]

Father had told me, "When you were little, a leader named Athronges stirred up rebellion and fought against the Romans. Many Galileans followed him. His followers in Sepphoris were put down by Roman soldiers under Varus, who burnt the city and made slaves of its inhabitants."[14] He told me this when, working in Sepphoris, we saw laboring men being treated harshly by the armed "peace keepers."

Despite our fears, the more we studied Scripture, the more we saw that Jozadak was right. The prophets would never have approved the way the common people were badly treated by the well to do, both in the city and in the villages. God's will, as revealed to the prophets, or in Torah for that matter, was certainly not embodied in society.

This bothered Jake more than it did me; he could never have been a rebel. He seemed to love order, to be always on the right side. And, despite Jozadak's arguments, he wasn't sure that the Torah shouldn't be followed more strictly by most ordinary Galileans, as well as by the powerful. He found great comfort in clear rules, while I was always wondering whether any rules could really be as final as he claimed.

The story of Jonah impressed me especially: all God required of the people of Nineveh was repentance! They were saved without sacrifices, temple or Torah. Not even a covenant. God was so gracious that even His prophet Jonah was offended. Jake told me I made too much of Jonah, but I couldn't stop thinking about him.[15]

---

13. See Horsley and Hanson, *Bandits*, 48: "brigands were an important factor in Jewish society. They figured prominently in Herod's rise to power. In the mid-first century, they provided leadership for Jewish peasants seeking justice. . . ."

14. Josephus, *Antiquities*, 17.10. 9.

15. Compare Brueggemann's understanding of Jonah: "Jonah concerns a recurring and endlessly powerful resistance to reduce YHWH's character, so large in mercy and

I was still troubled as to what my future was to be. On Sabbath afternoons I often walked out into the "desert," the land that couldn't be cultivated, to find solitude for thinking and praying. Sometimes I went into the pasturelands, among the sheep and the shepherds, who became quite used to me. They more or less left me alone—it was helpful that shepherds are not very talkative folk.

Jozadak pointed out to us that Jeremiah said that God would keep Israel "as a shepherd keeps his flock," and a Psalm calls God "Shepherd of Israel,"[16] so the way the shepherds tended their sheep gained deep meaning for me. The sheep could largely do what they chose, so long as they stayed together and kept out of danger, but the shepherd was constantly aware of what they were doing. If needful, the animals would be herded, even forcefully the few times it was necessary. The rest of the time the sheep just grazed and rested, while the lambs played.

The lambs played, and I watched them with delight. Especially their "king of the hill" game, where one would mount a hummock and another would butt him off and take over his place, only to be bumped off in his turn. It made me think of the course of history and how one conqueror after another, each with his short moment of glory, is doomed to be replaced.

How like the lives of lesser men, too: competing, vying, devoting their lives to replacing some predecessor in some local high place, no matter how small or unimpressive. But lambs were not like humans. The weaker ones who never attained the summit even for a brief moment still had all they could eat and the security provided by the older sheep and the shepherds. Though the smaller and more timid ones never attained eminence, they weren't ever oppressed or demeaned, either.

There were, of course, wolves. I never saw any, but the shepherds talked of them, and were always on the lookout for them.

The lambs were like little children, devoid of guile, full of celebration, as God intended all His created ones to be, even us humans.

The sheep of any age weren't conscious of the shepherds' care for them, yet those men had a name for each one of them and treated them as individuals. As I told Jake, one learned a lot about God's care and humans' need to care and to be cared for by watching shepherds and their sheep.

---

comprehensive in compassion, to the local convenience of the inside community of Israel. . . . an Israel who . . . resists the awareness that the same generosity extends to "the other" who is "unlike" . . . *Introduction*, 232.

16. Jeremiah 31:10 and Psalm 80:1.

At the same time, it was evident the sheep, unlike myself, had no problems as to who they were. A vague sense that I was to shepherd Israel came over me, but what did that mean? Rather than clear matters up, it made things worse. How was I to prepare for a future whose nature I couldn't even guess?

Hoping for some help, I went to talk with our local resident priest, Eliezer, who lived on the other side of town for the eleven months of the year in which he wasn't on duty in the temple in Jerusalem.[17] When he recognized my deep interest in the Scriptures, he accepted me as one he could trust, but instead of giving me the spiritual advice I sought, he poured out his own anger.

"Ordinary priests suffer oppression! I'm a consecrated and active priest, yet I'm hardly able to live. With poor harvests and the demands of their creditors, the tithes folk give are often so small, and yet the higher priests in Jerusalem demand I give them so much more than the law demands! I willingly give them what God expects, a tithe of what is given me, but they demand more, and more, and more. And the rulers back them up, so the village judges are afraid to do anything! I'm glad I act as an unofficial scribe to the town, competing with the official area scribe. Otherwise I couldn't support my family. And when crops fail, folk can't pay me to write their letters, or even their leases, bills of sale, or receipts."

The service of God was clearly a victim to the service of the powerful, whether political or ecclesiastical. The prophets' criticism of the people's "shepherds" certainly applied to our times. Any real shepherd to Israel would have to be at great odds with the established institutions.

When I told Jozadak about my visit to Eliezer he thundered, "Prophet after prophet criticized the priests for their hard-heartedness toward the poor and their conniving with the rich. And now the priests in Jerusalem grind the faces of their own poor priests around the country! The woes of the prophets will yet fall on the entire priesthood! God may even withdraw from the Temple!"

His fury reminded me that his pride in being a Cohen didn't extend to the central hierarchy, even though he wasn't dependent, as Eliezer was, on a priest's livelihood. The banishment of the Cohens of Anathoth nearly a thousand years before seemed to him to be reflected in the temple politics of the present, a sore still festering after all those intervening

17. We don't know where all the priests lived when off duty. Having one living in Nazareth is unlikely, but was it impossible? That liberty is at least good for the story.

generations. The holiness of the hierarchy was still made unholy by its political rulers!

I went back to work, but my studies and meditations affected my efficiency. Father and Jake were quite patient, but each had limits. I know I shouldn't have let my indistinct future interfere with my quite distinct present responsibilities, but, as Father clearly recognized, I was not superhuman. I could only wrestle with so much at a time, and was having trouble directing my efforts successfully. Surely, I thought, this can't go on forever. If God has a special task for me, He will let me know—when He chooses. But when in the dark, it is not easy to go on waiting for light—and waiting, and waiting . . . and waiting.

∾

When I was twenty-two, and Jake and I were working with Father in Sepphoris, we undertook a large job that required more help then just the two of us could supply. Since Father still considered the other boys too young to work in the big city, he hired Critias, a much-traveled worker originally from Crete, to help us. He was tall, muscular, and good-looking, with a square face, and yellow hair like the poet's "golden-haired dawn" he told us about. More important, though a relative newcomer to Sepphoris, he already had a good reputation among both craftsmen and laborers; something I gathered was rare for Cretans.

He was talkative as a rooster at sunrise, and, being relatively new to town, was curious about us Jews. During the breaks in work, while Father was occupied with some finer details, he, Jake, and I fell into serious discussions. It was the first time either of us had had personal discussions of any but mere practical consequence with an out-and-out Gentile. It was a struggle, because he had even more difficulty with our smattering of Greek[18] than we did with the slivers of Aramaic he had picked up in Mesopotamia and Egypt. And we had as much trouble coming to see his point of view as he had with ours.

Our discussion was rough and broken up. I'll try to report it more smoothly and clearer than it actually was, but as true to its meanings as I can.

18. "The general evidence . . . would suggest the likelihood that Jesus did speak Greek." Fitzmyer, *A Wandering Aramean*, 37. But how well?

"Why do you Jews say that God spoke to humans only in your history, no one else's? And through a book! Our gods speak to us directly, through sybils and augurs, and through our great poets who don't need to be written down, because in every town we have men who can recite them. Is your God an untrustworthy trader, whose word is no good unless some scribe writes it down like a contract? And why would God give a book that is written in a barbaric tongue like yours, or any like it, when Greek, the language of true human culture, was available? Is your God ignorant, or just uncultured?"

Jake broke in, "Stop! That's too many questions at once! God didn't speak to us just through a book. He spoke through his saving actions. He brought our whole people out of slavery in Egypt, with many signs of his power. He made a covenant with us to be his people. And he spoke to us through a long series of prophets. It's because we have the books that we don't need sybils and augurs. Those are more likely to be the untrustworthy business men you're talking about."

"How can he be a god if he binds himself with a covenant? A god is completely free; he can do whatever he wants! No one can force him to keep a contract! Nature established governments and law courts to force people to be trustworthy, to keep their promises. That guarantees peace; it guarantees civilization. But the gods themselves don't have to be forced to be trustworthy. They just follow their own reason!"

I responded. "God is completely trustworthy. That's how He is. That is why we Jews trust Him even if we are killed for it. How can any of your gods be worth worshiping, when even your swear words reflect stories about them doing all sorts of evil things? And you say they often disagree! How can they disagree and still be divine? There can only be one God, who created everything else."

Critias had a reply. "Of course there's only one god, in the sense of Nature. Nature is Reason, and because the one ultimate is Reason or Nature, it is reasonable for there to be many gods to deal with all the many facets of things, and so they exist as part of Nature. If it's Nature, it must be Reason! Nature rules over everything. How could your one God be the god of more than one nation, or the God of more than one independent city? When two cities fight each other, which one does your God support? Does he support both of them? In that case, he's stupid. Does he support only one? Then he's unfair."

Jake was furious by this time. "God created us humans to do his will. But we didn't. So he chose just one nation, us, not because we deserved it, but so there would be at least one people in the world committed to obeying him in all the details of life, to be an example to the rest. How could He expect us to be that unless He gave us the Torah, a book written in a language we could understand, to guide us and tell us his will? You must admit, Jews live much more moral lives than do you Greeks."

"Not the best of us. Our sages are the highest embodiment of what humans can be. They follow Nature. They live by Reason. They don't let their passions rule their behavior. Our philosophers and our poets, too, have taught us things much deeper than your books, no matter how ancient you claim them to be."

Jake had the last word, just as Father beckoned us to get back to work. "Then why do you have so much more drunkenness, adultery, fornication, theft, murder, and impiety than do we Jews?"

At that, we all went back to work. As the job progressed, Critias asked us several times about what the Scriptures said, or the significance of some of our customs, like Sabbath or not eating pork. The subject of gods never came up again.

However, on the last day of his working with us, Critias took a new tack. "I was talking with a friend," said he, "a friend who has some knowledge of philosophy, much more than I do. He said something that puts well what we Greeks believe, and I think I can quote him rather accurately. He explained that 'One of our greatest sages, Zeno the Stoic, said we must bring our will into line with everything that actually happens, so that nothing occurs that is contrary to our will and we do not wish for anything that does not happen. Then we are following Nature, obeying the shape of what is real.

"When we do that, we order our lives so that we get what we will, and avoid everything we want to avoid. If you will only what actually happens, and will everything what actually does happen, and give up being troubled by what is not in your power, you can live your life free from pain, fear, and distraction." That's how he put it. So I say the best of us Greeks follow Nature and Reason, ignore physical pain, sidestep all mental pain, and become full citizens of the universe.

"I wish I too were like that. I'm not, but I know that's what a human life ought to be. That's being like one of the gods. It's not trembling at their power, or trying to cajole them with sacrifices. It's being true to

Nature. But I understand that in the Jerusalem temple you Jews sacrifice animals every day. Your books make you so afraid of not obeying all kinds of unreasonable rules that you can't just look at Nature and see how it is all reasonable and to be followed. You don't have any science, only superstition."

That made me burst out like one of the prophets. "That's not doing anything for the folk God is interested in! That does nothing for the widows and orphans, the poor, the sick, the imprisoned. That doesn't bring righteousness! That's just selfishness. If that's what you think the gods expect of us, how can you think they're worth worshiping?"

At that point, our conversation was interrupted, so Jake and I never had much chance to respond further, though we were bursting with a desire to keep going. But Critias had raised a number of questions in my mind, not questions about the Scriptures, but about what the best and highest type of human life is. He almost made a philosopher out of me, for at least a moment, but certainly not a Greek one.

Jake and I had a number of discussions after that, discussions that showed how seriously we took Torah, and God's Covenant, and the fact that God is not "Nature," but a being far greater, its Creator and Ruler. In fact, the prophets predict God's ultimate triumph over all the evils that infest and infect the world, but in His own time and in His own way. Many of us wish that time is coming soon, in our lifetime, in fact!

Jake suggested that Critias' idea of a lot of lesser gods in charge of different earthly functions, under the umbrella of one high god, Nature, wasn't too much different from our idea of angels being part of the created world. But it was clear to us that God had to be God, not just nature. Otherwise there would be no real reason for righteousness, for living disciplined and devoted lives, for ending the oppression and exploitation we saw all around, and for hoping God would turn history and the world to a more righteous course. It seemed no wonder to us that Gentiles, despite Critias' claim of high thoughts, really had little interest in embodying God's kind of righteousness in their lives, their society, or in their treatment of other peoples.

But both of us agreed that we Israelites could do much better than we have been doing. That brought me back to wondering what God might do next to right the terrible wrongs seen all around us, in Jerusalem, Sepphoris, or, for that matter, in Nazareth. There was certainly much for us Jews to repent of!

Our discussions went further. We recalled what the Psalm says: "He made known His ways to Moses, His acts to the Children of Israel."[19] The "ways" he showed to Moses were the laws of Torah, but the people were much more impressed with his "acts," like releasing them from Egypt, keeping them alive in the desert, giving them the Promised Land. We succeeding Israelites adopted other gods, and when we did think of God, we were interested in His power, His favor, and His guarantee of our nationhood. We were less interested in His directions for life, and eventually His "act" was to take us captive to Babylon, to remind us that following His "ways" was as important as trusting in His "acts."

We came to two conclusions in our discussions: one was that the Gentiles ascribed all "acts" to "Nature," which lies behind all history, so they had no special revealing act of a "giving of the Law" to demand righteous "ways" of living from them. They had no act of binding by a covenant to define who they were beyond just being products of "nature." We came to realize that our pride in being Israelites was something different from their pride in being Greeks, or Romans, or Syrians. They are proud of their status in their own eyes. We are proud of the status God has graciously given us, a "peculiar people," despite how we behave.

Our second conclusion was a question. If our Israelite world was as full of evils as we saw it to be, and simply having the Torah was not amending it, isn't it time for God to renew His "mighty acts" and *do* something for the world that Torah and covenant were not at present enabling us to do? Oughtn't we to look for God's intervention in our history soon?

I took this to heart more seriously than did Jake. He still had greater faith than I did in Torah as the answer to everything. Besides, he took more lightly than I the idea that kept gnawing in the back of my mind: that I had been set aside for a special calling, one that I still couldn't define. I felt God would have to act in some way before I could know. What would that be? I had no way to find out, nothing to do but wait.

---

19. Psalm 103:7.

9

Jesus' Early Manhood

Therefore he had to be made like his brethren in every respect
. . . For because he himself has suffered and been tempted, he is
able to help those who are tempted.

Hebrews 2:17–18

A T TWENTY-SEVEN, I HAD been expected to marry for some time,
though that had hardly been a major item in my plans. Yet, at a time
when business was better than usual, our family was healthy, and spring
was well advanced toward summer, marriage looked very attractive, and
so did Rachel, daughter of Elisha ben Ucal. When I approached her family,
they were willing, so we soon held the happy celebration, and she moved
into our house as my wife. Mother was glad to have her help, now that
both Leah and Ruth were married and living with their husbands, and
Mother was feeling the wear and tear of long years of hard work.

Marriage[1] did bring problems and stresses, but it was also a high
point in discovering that thanking God did involve all one's heart, all one's
life impulses, and all one's strength. And, I felt, all of one's being. (I don't
like that word "soul"; apparently the Greeks talk a great deal about "soul,"
but it misses so very much of our word *nephesh*, used in the Shema', where,
as Jozadak taught us, it includes everything about one that has anything
to do with being alive and breathing.)

Soon Rachel delighted my parents and me with the announcement
that they could expect a grandchild. Our rejoicing became somewhat tem-
pered when her morning sickness tended to last most of the day. She ate,
but often lost her dinner. She lost weight, instead of gaining it. Neighbor
women offered all sorts of advice, and though the local man honored for

---

1. Most have thought Jesus never married. See my reasons offered in Appendix A.

his medical lore prescribed treatments, his success was only temporary and disappointing. Soon he warned us to be prepared for miscarriage, but for a month or two nothing of the sort happened.

Rachel had from the first been a great help to Mother in the housework, but now she had to be restrained from any great effort. "I'm not being a good daughter-in-law," she complained. "Mother Mary works so hard, she's such a careful housekeeper, and I have to watch her slave away. I'm not a good daughter-in-law at all!"

I was at a loss to answer her. What comforting words could I offer? All I could do was encourage her not to fret, and try to help with things myself, when home, and encourage my brothers to do the same. Mother, however, had trouble entrusting what she felt was woman's work to us men, and, I fear, we were not as troubled as we should have been to let her do so.

We lost the baby. We also lost much more than that, for Rachel's bleeding wouldn't stop, and she developed a raging fever. The doctor couldn't do anything about it, and we had to watch her die. My life collapsed with her. How could God, who so graciously put her into my life, take her away from me? What sense did it make for Him to create one so beautiful, so sweet, so full of life, so loving, only to take her away?

The funeral and burial was an abyss in history, a shadowy deadness that faded into daylight only slowly.

I hadn't talked with Jozadak for a long time, due to an unusual load of work. Now I felt the need for his wisdom. His wife opened their door to me, asked me in, but told me he wasn't well, and had been sleeping. He heard my voice, however, and called to me.

When I told him of my grief, he replied, "Read Job. Read Psalms. Pray. I know no other answer, but to tell you to take everything as God's lessons. He is giving you a chance to learn something deep, something important, something you have to find out by seeing through this darkness to whatever light he has for you on the other side of it. Ask for God's answer, not some human's." That seemed at the time to be no answer at all. It took time—a long time—to show me he was right. And, at a time like that, what else is there?

Then we suffered an even greater loss for the family. Father had gone to Sepphoris alone, because only a few finishing touches were still necessary on a difficult job for a wealthy family. When he didn't return that night, Jake and I went to find him, with no success. The next day we went back, and made inquiries. Finally we found someone who had been there, but only as a spectator.

This was his report: "When the job was finished, your father expected to be paid, but the chief steward would not pay him what had been agreed upon. When your father objected, the steward got nasty, called him a 'stupid villager' and asked what he was going to do about it. Your father simply repeated that he expected his employer's promised word to be kept. The steward became angry and shoved him violently. He tripped and fell backward, with his head striking the corner of a large stone. He never moved after that. The steward ordered his body carted away and disposed of. I don't know where they took it, but by now it's probably buried under garbage.

"It's a shame, but there's nothing you can do. The steward will lie, his employer will back him up, and his wealth gives him such status with the judges that you won't have a chance for anything to be done about it."

What we did, Jake and I, was to go to the wealthy man's house. The steward answered the door. When we asked for Father's pay for his work, the steward refused, but the wealthy man himself overheard and broke in, "Oh, give them half of it, that'll shut them up." Or something like that. He said it in Greek, and we knew from his tone of voice there was no point in arguing.

We took the money from the grudging steward, who had probably pocketed some himself, with the tacit collusion of his employer. We had heard more than once that that sort of thing was not uncommon. In Nazareth, we could have appealed to the local judge or even to the town elders. In the big city of Sepphoris, one from a village didn't have much of a chance.

I was also deprived of my conversations with Jozadak. The next time I went to his house, two weeks later, his wife Gomer met me at the door to say, "Jozadak died during the night. I'm busy preparing his body for burial. Please come see me later." So Jake and I lost our mentor.

All these events, piled one on top of another, put me into deep depression. For some weeks I wasn't much good to anybody, and began to spend whole nights out in the open, praying. Jozadak's advice, I knew, was right, but "the other side of the darkness" he had spoken of failed to appear. I was finally able at least to go through the motions of living, "waiting on the Lord," dully, like a dead tree waiting to be chopped down.

I waited on the Lord, all right, but on a Lord who seemed to be very slow in showing mercy on my grief.

I believed, of course—like nearly everyone except the Sadducees—that on the distant but coming "last day" all the dead would be resurrected, to face final judgment. But the far-off future didn't do much for the present.

One thing did seem to help—a little. On the other side of town there was an olive grove. They are open to the public, since no one can eat olives right off the tree. I found solitude there. The trees soothed me with a strange kindness, their crooked branches and gnarled limbs echoing the twistings of my soul, their silence calming me, the whispering of their leaves offering the prayers I couldn't put into words. They silently joined my stolid waiting on the Lord, and sustained me. Olive trees became my haven, my assurance that some day, somehow, my life would find its definition.

But the trees were a crowd, a community, and their silent compassion toward me helped me see that the ills I was going through are the common lot of humankind, to be shared in and suffered together. As yet, that burden of ills could only be suffered in the silence of their company.

As you know, olives are too bitter to eat until they are soaked in brine or lye. I felt my life to be an olive, hoping that the brine and lye of my losses would eventually lead to something more palatable, something more nourishing to those about me. But life is sometimes so slow that a mere mortal can hardly get through it.

A need for the comfort of olive groves became part of my life. They have become for me a special place to pray. I found I needed the wilderness places when it was crowds of other people who weighed me down. When my problem was myself, olive trees were my comfort, their roots my prayer-bench.

I knew my dead loved ones would never come back. I knew I must go on. I also knew that death is the natural fate of all of us. Anything beyond that is entirely up to God.

After those terrible months of loss, the routines of life took over, dully. I felt more like a spectator at a meaningless drama than an actor in a significant one.

I was now Nazareth's carpenter. Even though there were days when I felt so troubled I didn't work, and Jake and Joe took over the jobs alone, I was still called "the carpenter," and Jake "the carpenter's brother." Joe, Jud, and Sim were simply known by their names (Sim rarely helped with the work, but stayed home and helped Mother quite cheerfully). There were profitable months and unprofitable ones, interesting jobs and routine ones, difficult tasks and work that we sailed through quite blithely. But none of them lit up my darkness.

Looking back, I can see what a poor head of the family I made. Carpentry was not my life work, I knew, but what it was to be I did not know, and that bore down on me heavily. When there was no available work, I spent more and more time in the open spaces thinking, or among the olive trees praying. I found myself feeling quite guilty at leaving so much of the family work to my brothers, and of spending so much time alone. Even the family began to consider me somewhat odd, and before long, so did my neighbors. Unlike my brothers, especially Jake, those neighbors had no idea of what I was going through. They simply noticed I was not behaving as they thought I should, and I knew they were appropriately disapproving.

The deaths of Rachel and Father seemed to me dark shadows cast by the massive, looming evil not merely infecting the world, but plowed deep into its subsoil—evil that struck down the good, evil that was contrary to love, freedom, and everything that should make human existence a shining forth of God's image.

Though I hungered for Jozadak's counsel and felt his absence as a loss, his death did not seem part of that evil. He was old, had lived a good and holy life, and, as the Psalm puts it, he had "seen his children's children" and completed his human allotment of time. He had "passed his days as a tale that is told." His death seemed a normal end, even as it was a gentle one.

The others' deaths could only be signs of radical evil infecting the world. And so must the trials of all those in Galilee who suffered from hunger, cruelty, exploitation, or imprisonment, all reflections of the same evil influences. Also the sorrows of Eliezer the priest, who, trying to serve God, was victimized by the higher-up priests who should have been as concerned with God's will as he was. Even God's holy temple in Jerusalem seemed defiled by a political priesthood. I was tempted to think God would abandon his polluted temple, leaving it to be destroyed by the ungodly, as Jozadak told us He had done in Jeremiah's day.

To face my sorrow, that old scholar had told me to read Job and the Psalms. Almost avidly, I did. They made things worse. They presented the world as full of irrational evils permitted by God. They promised that God's permission would not last forever, but how long must the world wait for God to rescue it? Or to rescue us common folk from the evil powers that dominate the world? The more I thought on the mystery of evil, the more a sense of call grew in me. That call was yet to be focused or crystallized. I began to feel I was on the road to something that most certainly was to be, but what twists and bends there would be in its course, and where it would end up, were still hidden in the fog of the future.

I went back to my youthful enthusiasms, Jonah and Daniel. I felt I had been already thrown into the sea and gobbled up by a big fish, thrown into a lion's den and cast into a fiery furnace. I knew I would somehow have to show up in some Nineveh, some place where the world's wickedness flourished, to preach, knew I would somehow have to stand up to the ruling powers, and somehow have to be involved when the Beast "made war" against "one like a Son of man." Humbly, almost gingerly, I felt that eventually I would in some way be involved when "the saints of the Most High" were vindicated and "inherited the kingdom," though why I felt that way I still don't know.

Word came to our village of a strange figure whose preaching, down south along the Jordan River, was drawing crowds. His name was Jochanan,[2] or John, known as "the Baptist," because he used the water of the river in his ritual of cleansing for those who repented of Israel's sins. I certainly felt a need to repent of my confusions, of my failing my family, and of my submergence in a people of Israel who were so snared in sinful acts and institutions. I felt I needed to be freed from my own involvement in the whole world-system.

Jake apparently had some of the same feelings and suggested we go to hear John, though he added, half seriously, "What do we need to repent of? We've been very loyal to the covenant." I replied, more seriously, "Perhaps that feeling is just why we ought to go."[3] When we were about ready to leave, however, a demanding job came up that Jake wasn't willing to leave to Joe and Jud, so he told me to go alone, and he would join me there later.

I took along some money and supplies—mostly raisins, dried figs and almonds, which would keep one alive—and set out by myself, but

2. Originally *Jehochanan*, then *Jochanan*. In Greek, *Ioannes*, in English, John.

3. Following a suggestion in the apocryphal "gospel of the Hebrews." See R. Miller, *The Complete Gospels*, 430F.

soon chanced upon a group that was also heading to hear the Baptist. We chatted about a lot of things, but it struck me how large a part of their interest in his preaching was tied to the reports that he was predicting the Day of the Lord. On this Day, the prophesied cataclysm was to end the power of Gentile evil in the world and establish us Israelites as the righteous rulers, under God, of the entire kingdom God would set up.

I suggested that the book of Jonah told us that repentance saved Nineveh's Gentiles from disaster, and it did, so why should it be just Israel who should repent? Besides, Daniel predicted that "the kingdom" would be given to "the saints of the Most High," obviously a faithful remnant, not just any temporarily repentant Jews. They maintained, however, that the preaching predicted immediate disaster for everyone, except that any Israelite could escape the coming wrath by repenting so that destruction would fall on the Gentiles. That was something they enjoyed looking forward to: we not only would inherit the earth, but would enjoy watching all the other nations being destroyed!

This bothered me since I was so oppressed by the way the world's evil infected both Jews and Gentiles. Surely God wanted all humans to repent! As I understood the Scriptures, any "kingdom of God" should embrace the salvation of everyone who turned to God. He certainly didn't like Jonah's hoping that the repentant Ninevites would be destroyed![4] That's what I had learned from my interest in Jonah. So I had some feelings of doubt about John before ever seeing or hearing him.

We headed south down the hot, dry Jordan Valley, paralleling the river, but not walking right along its edge. That was impossible, because "the jungle of the Jordan," an infrequently broken hedge of dense Tamarisk and feathery but long-thorned Acacia, encroached. There were also Pistache trees, but not the Persian kind that are grown in the farmlands and bear edible nuts. Besides, the river wound around, and had often cut itself down into the ground far enough to be almost in a gorge.

Now and then, through a break in the trees, we could see the water flowing, sometimes dashing madly through some narrow rapids, sometimes flowing slowly and gracefully through a placid area. We drank the water whenever we could get to it, for the heat was oppressive.

---

4. "Jonah . . . is a presentation of the way in which the gracious God who rescues Israel (and Jonah in 2:9) is the God who intends to save Nineveh as well." Brueggemann, *Introduction*, 232.

Occasionally we met a caravan to Tiberias or Capernaum or on farther north. Many of them carried salt from the great salt sea the Jordan flowed into—salt for the salting of fish as well as other uses. Once we caught up with a slow caravan moving in our own direction, laden, among other things, with the salt's ultimate product, fish from the lake to the north, salted and dried.

We bought some from it, for a change of diet. While eating, it occurred to me the fish might have been caught by Andrew and Simon, my Bethsaida friends. I'd not seen them for quite a while. I'd not even thought of them, but the resolve to look them up soon shaped itself in my mind.

Our two-and-a-half-day journey suddenly was over. We came upon the Baptist preaching. He was standing where a stream dying from the hot season grudgingly added what water it could to the already amply filled Jordan. The small delta the stream had flooded during the year's early rains left a wide break in the trees, leading to a sand spit that jutted out into the river, protected on its upriver side by some impressive rocks. Behind the preacher, the river, here quite wide, slouched by sullenly, as if ashamed to be flowing so slowly.

Quite obviously it was he, John the Baptist. He was bearded and dirty, clothed in a disreputable camel's-hair tunic with a soiled, worn leather belt around it. Even so, he immediately impressed me as a noble figure. He looked exactly as I had always imagined Elijah to look! In fact, it was hard to resist the impression that he *was* Elijah returned to earth, to prophesy to our age, just as Malachi had predicted. The sound of his resonant voice struck us some time before we could make out what he was saying. A small crowd, some sitting, some standing, occupied the ground before him, listening intently.

Quickly we moved within earshot. "The Lord will come and not be slow," he declaimed. "As an avenger He will come to destroy the wicked and to save those who repent and keep His covenant, and He will come soon. I am His herald. His winnowing-fork is in His hand and with His fan he is ready to blow away the chaff—all the nations of the world with their evil ways. He will clear this earth like a threshing-floor, and burn the chaff with unquenchable fire. No evil will stand before Him. But the righteous, those who repent of their sins and confess them, those who testify to their repentance by the washing of baptism, will be His harvest, His good wheat, which He will gather into His own granary. They shall be a righteous nation, and shall inherit the earth."

Something about him gripped everyone there. Whatever appre-hensions I may have had about his preaching were overwhelmed by his presence. I felt there was no man in the world like him, nor had there been such before, except perhaps for Moses and Elijah. He dominated just by the magic of his intensity, the fire in his eyes, the authority of his declarations.

He continued to preach for another half hour, saying essentially the same things in a torrent of ever-changing metaphors and striking dic-tion, giving few details one could remember, but forcing one to join in his thinking by overriding one's own mental processes with the sheer momentum of his oratory. This was a prophet indeed! No one hearing him could doubt, while he was speaking, that the Spirit of the Lord was upon him.

It was after he had finished, about sundown, which doubts began to set in. Something about his predictions disturbed me. I needed Jake to talk to, but he hadn't arrived. I wondered if further work was going to keep him from ever getting here. Without him to talk to, my need to leave, to be by myself, to think things through, became pressing. John was surely a prophet, and hence one who must be listened to. His call for repentance was irresistible. I ought not leave until I had joined those baptized with the waters of repentance.

The next morning, when he called for penitents, I was surely one of them, though hesitant. Was I ready? I waited as long as I could, but finally joined the line reaching down to the water's edge. The Baptist stood waist-deep in the river, and as each one came to him, the prophet listened to his confession and then gestured to him to immerse himself in the stream. He did not touch them except to steady some who teetered as they waded out or to help a few straighten up afterwards.

I couldn't hear him make any ceremonial mutterings during the pro-cess; the symbolism of washing oneself completely clean of the accumu-lated defilements of one's past was too directly impressive. Words would have added nothing to it; in our Israelite tradition, one baptizes oneself.

He did, however, require two or three to repeat their dunking, as they hadn't completely immersed themselves.

When each baptizee came back to shore, one could see his relief, his elevation of spirit, and his joy in facing forward to a holier life. The natural question, "How effectively or how long will that elation hold up?" crossed my mind but was immediately quashed. I willed to maintain my confidence in the rite, which was new to me, though I knew it wasn't new to Israel's religion.

My turn arrived. I confessed to the Lord my impatience with him, my indecision, my inadequacy as a family head, my involvement in Israel's departures from the covenant, and my anger at the authorities. Then I waded out to John, repeated my confession, and submerged myself with my eyes open, unwilling to miss anything of the experience. The blotting out of the world, the clean feeling of the water and its reinvigorating temperature, may all have added something to the submersion, but, when I straightened up, I felt much more than those items could explain. I, too, was carried away, rapt. The whole surrounding scene disappeared, and I saw the heavens split forcibly, and a man come down to me.

How I knew him before he spoke, I do not know, but I did. He placed his hand on my head, saying, "I am Jonah, God's prophet, sent to place His Spirit upon you as it came upon me."[5] The vision then disappeared; the river, the trees, the people all reappeared, and I found myself just reaching shore. I must have looked dazed, since the next man in line asked me anxiously, "What happened? Without thinking, I blurted out, "God's Spirit came down from heaven as Jonah and touched me," but I immediately thought better of it and said nothing more. He went ahead into the river to take his turn.

That night my internal turmoil returned. "Trust God," I told myself. "You have been called to witness to this generation's Nineveh. Wait on the Lord." It wasn't easy, but I slept. Listening to other baptizees talk about returning to their old lives now that their security had been established, I realized the crowds surrounding John were not all "the saints of the Most High." Those would have to be a more deeply committed group.

The next morning I awoke knowing that I had to leave the camp and go off by myself to untangle my thoughts. As I was about to leave, a fellow came up to me and said, with a condescending smirk, "They are saying this morning that yesterday, when you were baptized, you saw the Spirit of God come flying down from heaven on you." "*Flying* down?" I gasped.

---

5. Mark 1:10 says, "the Spirit as a dove came down *into* (*eis*) him." Luke and Matthew both change this to "upon" (*ep'* for *epi*). *Eis* can indeed be read as "upon," but then, why did they change it? The Aramaic "*b-*" could be taken either way. "Upon" emphasizes the physical visibility of the "dove" and—indeed, Luke says it came down "bodily" (*somatiko*)—while "into" emphasizes the personal significance of its bestowal.

Irritated, as if what he said was obvious, he snapped as he turned away, "Yes. Doves fly, you know." Then, with an air of superiority, he strode off.

I was dumbfounded for the moment. A bird? A dove? Flying? But the explanation came quickly enough. The name "Jonah" *means* "dove." When I said to that earlier man, "God's Spirit came down from heaven as Jonah and touched my head," what he understood was "God's Spirit came down as a dove," and so on. And he had told others, starting a rumor that had apparently run all through the crowd.

A dove? All through the Scriptures doves stand for stupidity, fear, or mourning—well, once for a girl's beautiful eyes. Doves had nothing to do with God's Spirit! It was Jonah I saw, a prophet, whom the Scriptures confirmed as a bearer of God's Spirit. A dove indeed!

And nothing could be done about it. Rumors take on a life of their own. Who can stop them? And what did it matter? I could expect the story to be forgotten eventually. Why would anyone perpetuate it? The vision was my own; it was private. It was directed to my own problems, not to anything of public import. What mattered to me was the vision itself; what some rumor said about it was of no consequence. It would surely die out, of its own incongruity.

The vision itself most certainly did matter. It certified my call just as its occurrence in my baptism implied John's true standing as a prophet. God had favored me, much more highly than I deserved! I was to follow the Spirit's instructions, whatever they might turn out to be. For the first time, I had confidence that my future was unfolding. I was on the edge of my life work. I was to be a herald of God's Kingdom, just as the Baptist was. Except, and this was the problem, I couldn't honestly proclaim exactly what he was proclaiming. His attitude did not square with Jonah, who had laid the Spirit on me. God showed Jonah that He willed to spare Nineveh, not destroy it.

What was my message to be? The need to go off by myself became greater than ever.

Jake hadn't yet arrived. I suspected he wouldn't make it. He was too conscientious about work. But I had to get away. Taking what little was left of my supplies, I decamped as fast as I could, forded the river where it was wide and shallow, and headed into the desert beyond—a desert of wild beasts, evil beings, and hardships, but a desert apart from society and its demands, its snares, and its misunderstandings, a desert that was nature as God had created it, unaltered by human concerns. The threats of nature I deemed less destructive to the spirit than the threats of society.

The desert was a place of thinking, of purging oneself of nonessentials. This was a place where one met no idols or socially approved fictions. One was just confronted with the hard facts of nature, with wild animals, with oneself, and who knows with what evil forces? And, as always, confronted with God.

Why was it Jonah who was sent to me? That bothered me. Was it that I was being a Jonah, finding reasons not to go where I was sent? Was it that I, like Jonah, was angry with God for not letting life turn out as I wished? Had Jonah been given yet another message, one to me as a new Nineveh who needed still more repentance? These interpretations of the question I worked through, but none of them seemed convincing. Why, then, was Jonah sent? I could see the evil all around me; the world looked like a Nineveh. But simply calling to repentance was not enough; John the Baptist had already done that. What was I called to do?

Then a worse thought hit me. Was I to be left to determine what my calling was to be? But might I make a wrong choice, and end up trying to use God's gift for the devil's purposes? After all, he tempts. How would I know what choice was right? Hadn't there been false prophets, like Hananiah in Jeremiah? Of all the things I saw needed to be done, which one was I called to do? Jonah hadn't been any help!

But finally, though my musings led me nowhere, I relaxed. Time might bring the answer. I knew the temptation would leave me only "for a season," as the saying goes. But that horrible trial receded.

I decided to leave the desert and head home, nearly starved. The Jordan I crossed at the same ford as before. As I passed the crowds still pressing about John and his preaching, I saw that my old Bethsaida friend Andrew was among them. He said Simon was there somewhere, but not nearby, and pressed me to stay, at least until he located his brother and brought him to me. I told him, rather sadly, that I had to go. I had already been baptized, and really had to get back to the family. I had already been gone too long.

He did give me some news. Their father had died and they had inherited the boat, and had, for business reasons, moved across the lake to Capernaum. He explained that it was easier to sell their fish in Capernaum, since the main trade route from the south divided just north of there. One branch continued northeast past Bethsaida, skirting the hills known as the Golan and going on to Damascus, while the other went straight north to Caesarea Philippi. They got a better price for their fish in Capernaum, too.

It was good talking with him, and I hated to miss Simon, but knew I must go. So I headed back home to Nazareth and the family.

All of them were glad to see me back, of course, and were very relieved that I seemed a little less disorganized. Jake wanted a full account of what I had heard, seen, and done. When I gave him a rather long but still incomplete report, he said I should not let my doubts and confusions rule my life. "The *Shema'* is enough, and the Torah sets out all that is necessary for fulfilling it, and the prophets explain its application. Why have all these problems?" I had no answer, except to say, "But I am I," and leave it at that.

The house routines went on as before, and I fitted into them with as much comfort as before. Waiting on the Lord did not require doing nothing. Now that I was home, Jake left the work over to me so he could go hear the Baptist himself. I threw myself into carpentry to drown out the noise in the back of my mind.

The family said I needed calm and quiet; I needed to stay home until my mind settled down. They had learned to get along without me quite well, but they still loved me, and didn't want me to make a fool of myself, or to embarrass them—although they wouldn't admit that. It was bad enough that the neighbors already thought I was a bit odd; I shouldn't make it even more obvious. It wasn't that they were critical; they were just sympathetic and protective. They still respected me and believed I was someone special, though wrestling with something real, something profound.

Of course, we still went as a family to synagogue every Sabbath. There was no resident scribe of the sort some call a "rabbi." It was a normal synagogue, a community meeting-place where the town gathered to assemble as God's people, to hear and discuss Torah and the prophets, and to sing and pray. We were there to sense our unity as the people of God and enjoy each other as a particular community.

After the readings, there was opportunity for someone, usually one of the older men, to comment on or apply the Scripture. Jozadak's death had robbed us of the commentator Jake and I thought most interesting and worthwhile. With him gone, much of the comment was often rather trite or of little relevance.

One Sabbath, the Torah reading was the passage in Deuteronomy[6] telling the Israelites that when they entered the land of Canaan they were to wipe out the previous inhabitants, the "Hittites, the Girgashites, the Amorites," and so forth. "You must utterly destroy them; you will make no covenant with them, and show no mercy to them." Reuben bar Ehud, one of the ones who first brought us news of the Baptist, spoke up, applying the reading to our situation. Though a relative newcomer in town, he was already well known for his short temper and radical leanings, "The Romans, the Syrians, the Greeks have made themselves not merely the inhabitants of this land, but its rulers. It's our land, given to us by God Himself. In Torah, as we have heard this morning, even though they are 'nations greater and mightier,' we are commanded to wipe them out, and show no mercy. God will send us a hero to lead us to victory against all the evil nations. He is about to establish his kingdom. We shall fight, and we shall win!"

He went on at length, clearly fired up by John's preaching and, undoubtedly, the talk of those who heard John—and also by his own inability to pay the unbearable interest on his loans. Defaulting had caused him to lose his inherited farm and forced him to move to Nazareth, out of reach of his tormentors, to find work and escape debtors' prison. Everyone felt deep sympathy for his situation, and more than a few obviously relished what he said. However, it was clear neither he nor anyone else would, in fact, rise up in rebellion until some inspiring leader filled them with some illusory hope of success.

I was quite sure they would be slow to follow any such leader, since his declared program would inevitably put them under threat of attack by the army. Their emotional backing of Reuben's position was more an expression of their own insecurities than any leaning toward action. Still, many found some comfort in just hearing his outburst.

It was probably unwise, but my own struggles forced me to respond. "If God was merciful to Nineveh as a result of Jonah's preaching, can't he show mercy even to Romans, Syrians, and Greeks? He can do all things. Must he meet fire with fire? How can evil and hatred destroy evil and hatred? Can't he bring in His kingdom otherwise than through rebellion, anger and cruelty? Must he use Satan's ways to overcome Satan?"

---

6. Deut 7:1–11.

There was immediate uproar. "You're no true Israelite!" "Who can believe that?" "Our fathers died fighting for God and His Torah!" "Are you a coward?" "Treason to our nation!" Silenced by groans, hisses, and many other sayings, I sat down. I thought I had said something reasonable, and was not at all prepared for such anger, or for so huge an exhibition of mistrust in me, something that had never been shown to me as "the carpenter."

The next day, a kindly old gentleman named Isaac bar Baruch accosted me. "Son, I knew your father. He was a good man. I've watched you grow up. You have a good, righteous family. I think rising in rebellion is just as foolish as you do, but surely, being an Israelite, you must share the hope of our fathers, that God will restore the kingdom to us, in glory and power."

That raised a new question in me. How should "the saints of the Most High" respond when the Beast "made war upon them"? Surely just telling the Beast to repent would be silly. What kind of courage does God demand of his saints? What is the place of fighting back?

A few days later Jake returned, having listened to John, confessed his sins (which we all knew must be few), and been baptized. He was greatly impressed by John's preaching, and quite convinced that there must be some Messiah to appear soon, in fulfillment of John's prophecies. He was not as negative as I about the way John's preaching was interpreted by some hearers as pointing toward rebellion. His expectations of God's Kingdom were more nationalistic than mine. Perhaps "more nationalistic" isn't the right way to put it, as he wasn't really very politically minded. Better would be "more focused on the uniqueness of our way of life, and more distrustful of Gentile ways." We both had recognized that some time ago.

Andrew and Simon he didn't see—they had already left—but he met two friends of theirs, Jacob and Jochanan,[7] sons of Zabdai (who, however, was usually called by the Greek form of his name, Zebedaios or Zebedee). They confirmed the news that Simon and Andrew had moved to Capernaum, but added that Simon had married the only remaining daughter of a rather well to do widow, and the four of them lived in the widow's house.

He had other comments to make about his trip. "A group of Pharisees were there, not like the Pharisees here in Galilee, who are so very devout,

7. "James" and "John."

and fine characters, even if they add strange items to the law and don't criticize the political authorities, except for their bitter opposition to the Sadducees in the Jerusalem temple. These Pharisees must have been from Jerusalem, and they weren't there to listen, but to heckle John. 'Show us a sign from heaven,' they sneered, 'and then we'll believe you.'"

"His answer was to the point: 'My message is my sign. If you don't believe it without some other sign, you wouldn't believe if you were given a sign. You are a brood of vipers, and need to repent.'"

"That answer ruffled their pride. They went away, saying, 'If he were a true prophet, he would demand that everyone obey the complete law, as given to the fathers.'" Jake went on, "I suppose they meant those 'fathers' of their own tradition, as Jozadak told us. I guess John's mistake, in their eyes, is that he stuck to what Torah actually says, not to what their group says it says."

That wasn't quite fair to the Pharisees, as I reminded him. "They care for what Torah says. They just so concentrate on being sure they haven't transgressed even a detail of the written law that they forget what Torah demands at the level of ordinary people's lives. They forget that 'Torah' means *instruction*, instruction of the heart and of social life. All of life, not just strict rules as to how to deal with details."

"Well, that bunch of Jerusalem Pharisees seemed to me farther from the spirit of Torah than a number of ordinary people with Pharisee leanings we have here in Nazareth. But I'm afraid even they might be offended if someone came right out and treated their tradition as questionable interpretation of Scripture. Jozadak had told us Pharisees once ruled the country, under a queen named Alexandra, but lost their power. They probably would like to regain it. They certainly tend to side with the wealthy and powerful rather than the poor."

Then Jake came back to his impression that John the Baptist must be right: a Messiah-figure is about to appear. In fact, he wondered to me, half teasing, half serious, but quite openly, whether I might not be the one.

I snorted at the idea. Me, the Messiah? Certainly I would not be one to fulfill the dreams of Reuben bar Ehud, or the crowds surrounding the Baptist. Conquer and destroy the Romans? That would mean adding further pain and calamity to our already distressed people, and when, since the days of Joshua, had warfare brought about greater obedience to God?

Jake's only comment was a quiet, "Joshua, the kind of Messiah that is needed is a real 'Joshua,' a 'God saves,' a shepherd of Israel." I knew he meant well, but I was sure I would never claim the title "Messiah." I wasn't cut out for it. Yet I loved him for his respect and faith toward me.

Still, his suggestion was troubling. It upset me so much that I turned our current job over to him and the younger brothers and headed for the olive grove, in as great an inner turmoil as ever. My unsure self, or perhaps the devil, had returned.

After a long session of prayer there, I felt I must go back into the open spaces to sort out my thoughts further. I found a lonely spot on a small rocky hillock, asked for guidance, and let my thoughts rove.

I thought of Moses, called to lead his people. He, I had read, brought down manna, "bread of heaven," to feed his hungry people. Many of my people didn't have enough to eat; was I to be another Moses, a supplier of bread to them? But there would have been bread enough for all, if the world stopped taking it away from those in need to give it to those who needed nothing. God's will that everyone be fed would not be fulfilled simply by multiplying bread, as long as there were those who would snatch it out of hungry mouths.

Besides, Moses dealt with a people wandering in the desert, who had not yet entered the promised "land flowing with milk and honey." My people had occupied their land, but rapacious institutions of debt and force had taken their ancestral holdings away. Simply providing more bread would be no answer.

Were what John's followers so eagerly looked forward to what was needed: a divine leader who would conquer the forces that ruled the evil world and deprived folk of their daily bread? That would be a mighty work, a miraculous work, an earthshaking exhibition of power! Was I to become a miracle worker, an instrument of divine power?

But was there anyone who really needed nothing at all? Those who boasted they needed nothing still had great need: to live according to God's will. "Man shall not live by bread alone" is as true of the rich as of the poor. Through Israel, Moses gave the world all the law that was required. What was needed, as Jeremiah saw, were hearts with the law written on them, rather than engraved on stone tablets. And that was something one could not do simply by preaching or teaching. Surely I was not to follow Moses in either function, as bread-giver or as law-giver.

I thought of Elijah and Elisha. They were men of power. Both worked wonderful signs, both stood up to kings and armies. Elijah called down fire from heaven to defeat the priests of Baal. Elisha parted waters, made undrinkable water sweet, filled a dry spring-bed with water, multiplied vessels of oil, and healed the Syrian hero Naaman. What wonderful deeds! Signs of God's favor! Yet did even they turn the people of Israel to righteousness, let alone the rest of the world? After them, prophet after prophet was sent to the people, and they still did not change their ways. Surely I was not called to be a prophet of signs, like Elijah or Elisha.

The ushering in of God's Kingdom would not be accomplished by miracles, no matter how powerful. Miracles might be signs of God's working, but no one has ever been made internally obedient by some external miracle. Would any miracles turn Israel to righteousness, let alone the rest of the world? After Elijah and Elisha, prophet after prophet was sent to the people, and they still did not change their ways. Surely I was not called to be a prophet of signs.

My thoughts returned to Daniel, and how "one like a son of man"[8] was to be in some way the epitome of "the saints of the Most High God," and "to him was given dominion and glory and kingdom, that all peoples, nations, and tongues should serve him." I could not shake my strange identification with that figure. I felt both that it was I, and that it wasn't. It couldn't be I, since he was "the saints of the Most High," and was I even one "saint"? Jake may not have been a *Qaddish*, a "saint," but he was close to being the *Tsaddiq*, the "righteous man," in the family. He probably should be called "Jacob the just." He'd make a better "Son of man" than I.

But the world's problem was, it seemed, quite obvious: that dominion over all peoples, nations, and tongues, even Israel, had been given to Satan, or his representative, "the Beast," the holder of power. Was the "Son of man" called to conquer the world? That was surely a temptation, an enticing prospect, and one that so many Jews looked forward to as God's deliverance. What would be more glorious than to succeed where all the other self-styled "messiahs" had failed?

That, too, had to be set aside. The power that kept the world's rulers in office was itself evil; it led to pride, arrogance, alliance with the servile, and with deceivers. It set its own will to security, gain, or pleasure above God's will for the world. God's Kingdom could not be attained by the

8. Dan 7:14. cf. Pierre Grelot: "Dan 7:13f. speaks of the Son of man, a symbolic personage who is contrasted with the beasts which are the symbols of human empires. Whatever the origin of this image, it does not refer directly to the Messiah but to the kingdom of God which will take the place of the earthly kingdoms, and to the 'people of the saints of the Most High,' in whom the kingdom will be vested." *Sacramentum Mundi*, IV, 16a.

ways of the world. To think so is to yield to the temptings of the Evil One who rules the world as it is.

In Daniel's prophecy, the "beast" was first to "make war with the saints, and prevail over them." The world's evil powers were destined to have their way with the "saints of the Most High." Not "one like a Son of man," but "the Ancient of days" Himself was to bring about the victory, on behalf of the beleaguered saints. The "saints of the most high" were not to conquer; they were to be overwhelmed. Their destiny of "receiving the kingdom" was not to come about by their own military or political victories; it was to be a postlude to their suffering and defeat. Only God Himself would bring the victory, in his own way—and how that would come about hadn't been revealed.

It then struck me forcefully that this was what the *Shema'* demanded: loving God with "all your strength" meant always allowing God to lead, rather than dashing ahead into a fray, inflated with one's own glory. It meant allowing God to lead even if it seemed heading for defeat. "The ways of the Almighty are past finding out" can be a bitter pill. Serving Him can mean the death of one's ambitions; or, simply, one's death.

Suddenly things came clear. I knew the answer to my doubts. I was called to be *completely obedient*, no matter what it cost. I was to establish "the Saints of the Most High," the "Son of man," and to be faithful, even if it meant to death. I now understood that the coming "Realm of God" had to come in the form of complete obedience, obedience more complete than that of the Pharisees, obedience that accepted everyone, even the lowest, as God's chosen beloved. It had to be the obedience that trusted God—the compassionate God of the book of Jonah—for everything, as a little child trusted his father, obedience that would lead to being over- whelmed by the world's evil, so the "Ancient of Days" would, in His own way, achieve a victory that would be His, rather than ours.

Didn't God tell Moses to say to Pharaoh, "Israel is my first-born son"? Through Jeremiah, didn't He say, "Is Ephraim my dear son?" and "Therefore my heart yearns for him, I will surely have mercy on him"? Didn't He say, through Hosea, "Out of Egypt have I called my son"? Didn't He say in the Psalm, "Like as a father shows steadfast love toward his children, so is the Lord steadfast and loving to those who obey Him"?[9]

---

9. Exod 4:22; Jer 31:20; Hos 11:1; Ps 103:13.

I must call Israel to *accept being a son* to *God*, an obedient, trusting, loving son, to the One who called Himself their Father. Those who wouldn't accept such a role couldn't be the true Israel, the "saints of the Most High."

If we, the "saints," were to represent the true Israel, if we were to be sons, we must pray to God as "Father." I prayed so, addressing Him as I had addressed my human father, as "Abba," and it felt perfectly right. I spent the rest of the day, pouring out myself before Him with no reservations, no defenses. It was as if He had really replaced my father, so I was no more "bar-Yoseph," but "bar-Alaha," "son of God." And "the saints of the Most High" must become the same, praying in full confidence to "Abba."

Yet I recognized that, along with proclaiming the coming of God's Kingdom, my task must include calling together "the saints of the Most High" to whom God would also be "Father." I was to bring them together as Moses called the Israelite rabble together in the wilderness. It was to "the saints," the "*Qaddishin*," the true Israel, that the kingdom was to be given. Whatever the successful warfare of the Beast against us was to be, and however the Father would faithfully vindicate us, had to be left to the future. It was not my task to prophesy, but to proclaim and lead, to obey and trust, whatever more the future might teach or demand.

The next Sabbath we went to synagogue. No longer was I unsettled. A deep, serene confidence filled me. I *knew*. I did not know what would happen, but I knew myself to be completely in the hands of God. I no longer needed to know what would happen to me, but I knew what I must do. I had a new confidence and, at last, deep serenity.

Since it was only a few weeks since Reuben's outburst, the synagogue reading the next Sabbath was still from Deuteronomy. It was the passage that says,

> And because you hearken to these ordinances, and keep and do them, the Lord your God will keep with you the covenant and steadfast love which he swore to your fathers to keep; he will love you, bless you, and multiply you; he will also bless the fruit of your body and the fruit of your ground, your grain and your wine and your oil . . . you will be blessed above all peoples . . . and the LORD will take away from you all sickness.[10]

10. Deut 7:12–15.

When comment on the reading was invited, I stood up and spoke. "Here God promised good things, very good things, to his people, if they kept his covenant perfectly. But we did not, we have not, we are not doing so now. Simply telling us to obey earnestly and lovingly hasn't worked; we are a stiff-necked and error-ridden people. His patience will not last forever. The time is here when he will act to bring in His Kingdom. It is upon us, at the door, demanding that we repent our sins and begin to act as citizens of His Kingdom. We must do this by giving up pride and thoughts of vengeance, loving our neighbors and our enemies, forgiving those who do us harm, sharing what we own with others, and obeying in all our thinking, all our natural impulses, and all our leverage on life.

At that point Reuben leapt to his feet and roared, lightening flashing in his face and thunder in his voice, completely carried away by rage. "Do you think you are God? I know what you are. You are evil! You are one of those who would have us all killed! Love the Romans? Love the tax collectors? Love the moneylenders? God told us to kill the gentiles! The Psalm that was sung this morning said, 'He will subdue peoples under us, and nations under our feet.'[11] You don't speak for God. You have an evil spirit!"

I was amazed at how calm and confident I felt. I confronted him face to face, and, despite his anger, he flinched.

"No, Reuben, it's your spirit that is evil. You are dominated by anger and hatred. Cast those out from yourself. God calls you to live as His image. He is God of peace, patience, and kindness, not of war and hatred. Until we see how God is bringing in His kingdom, we must repent, change our ways to be like God's ways, God who loves evildoers as well as doers of good. He sends his rain on the unjust as well as the just."

Except for my family, who were obviously anxious for me, nearly everyone there seemed to agree with him. They turned into an angry, shouting mob. "Nonsense!" "Where did you get those new ideas?" "Don't you trust God to save us?" "Go do your carpentry, don't try to teach us!" I don't remember all the many other things that were screamed at me. The

11. Psalm 47:3. Reuben's knowledge of Aramaic would give him some sense for the meaning of the Hebrew, and he would take the *pi'el* Hebrew verb here, *yadebber*, as imperfect, and hence as future, as KJV does. It is ambiguous. It can also be taken as past, as does *An American Translation* and, apparently, LXX. Most translators now take it as a continuative present (ASV, RSV, NEB, JPST). The unusual meaning for the root *dabar* as "subdue"(see BDB, 182, giving possible Aramaic and Arabic parallels) is testified to by the LXX *upetaxe* (aorist, but what sort of aorist?).

family urged me to leave, and the mob evidently agreed, since they pushed us out the door. I guess all of us were lucky not to have been hurt.

The walk home with the family was somber. Our whole relationship to our hometown had been shattered. Things would never be the same again.

Shortly thereafter, however, word came that John the Baptist had been arrested by King Herod—or rather Tetrarch Herod, since the Roman Emperor had refused to allow him his father's title "king." John's arrest moved me deeply, on two grounds. It seemed to me an indisputable certification than John was indeed a true prophet, since the word of the Lord had always led to prophets' arrest, imprisonment, mistreatment, or death. That his proclamation of the coming divine action was a genuine message from God was beyond doubt. The realm of God was indeed threatening to arrive.

That established something further: with him removed from the scene, who would continue to spread the news that the kingdom of God is approaching, is very near? Surely this was my signal to step up and preach!

Jake and the others didn't think so, but it was clear that someone new must take over its proclamation. And that person, I knew, had to be myself.

Thus ended my long period of wondering, learning, and preparation. I still didn't feel completely prepared, but I had to act. And I realized that my hometown was no place to start proclaiming or organizing anything. How can you lead those who remember you as a youngster, who find you familiar to them in quite different roles, who remember you playing children's games or whistling while you work, who have already rebelled against your message, who don't trust you to be anything but what they already imagine you ought to be?

After talking with the family, I set out alone for Capernaum and Bethsaida, to start my mission there. I would come to be known as "Joshua *of* Nazareth," but now it would mean "Joshua *from* Nazareth." Nazareth had ceased to be the hometown it had always been previously, despite my family's continuing support. I faced having no home but prayer and obedience.

I walked the twenty miles or so to Capernaum, and went to the home of our Aunt Thamar, her husband Shemaiah and their youngest son Tobiah (their two other children were grown and gone). They were pleased to see me, but when I told them what I was about, that I must be John's successor in announcing that God's Kingdom is near at hand, their discomfort was obvious. They had just attained some stature in the public's eyes—Shemaiah had been elected a ruler of the synagogue—and didn't want to be embarrassed or to upset people.

I stayed with them that night, but knew I must leave the next morning.

So, after eating breakfast and thanking them for their hospitality, I walked down to the waterfront, where I sought out Simon and Andrew. They were with their hired hands in their boat, moored close to shore, drying their nets after a night's fishing. They'd obviously had a good catch and had already sold it to the buyer.

I called to them. Andrew dropped his net and ran to me. When I explained why I was there, he ran and got his brother Simon. After they both joined me, they called instructions to their retainers to take care of everything. I explained that I was organizing a "true Israel" to go about with me teaching and preaching about God's coming rule, and eventually to go out preaching on their own, and they were enthusiastic. Listening to John had fired their imaginations, and Simon in particular set me wondering if he would quite understand how my outlook differed from John's.

It was evident it would take a lot of teaching to get them to realize that our course would be like that of the old prophets: we would meet resistance, antagonism, hardship, danger, even death. They received that reminder as if it made the undertaking even more adventuresome.

When I pointed out that we three would not be enough, that we needed more members, they suggested their fishing acquaintances Jacob and Jochanan, sons of Zabdai or Zebedee. They and their father had also moved to Capernaum. When I approached them, they left their father and his hired hands with his boat and joined us.

Frankly, I was somewhat appalled. Jake had been my associate for so many years, and had been a thoughtful and devoted foil for my deepest thoughts. These new colleagues were boisterous—at least three of them were. Andrew was more reserved. But all four were serious in their convictions, even if not in their manner.

The two Zebediah sons were loud and full of fun, but also full of illusions of leadership and great things. Simon, though ownership of the boat had matured him a great deal since last I'd seen him, was still a spontaneous and natural leader; he would be problem enough. I was sure he would be faithful, at least up to a point. But those two! "Sons of Tumult" I called them. Compared to them, Simon was a comfort, but I could sense leadership struggles in the offing.

I knew I would have to find others. Though the experience of the Nazareth synagogue suggested that no matter how large a following I might get on the basis of a popular reputation, only a minority would seriously respond to my teaching. Of that minority I would have to pick twelve to represent the New Israel, to be its committed center. And how truly those will represent the "saints of the Most High," the "Son of man," how many will stay true through the opposition and what the disaster we will surely meet will be, no one could tell. The detailed ways of God are beyond prediction.

10

A Note on Method

> It is a mischief that critical observations which any intelligent
> man can make for himself, should be ascribed to atheism or
> unbelief . . . when interpreted like any other book, by the same
> rules of evidence and the same canons of criticism, the Bible
> will remain unlike any other book; . . . it will create a new in-
> terest and make for itself a new kind of authority by the life
> that is in it.
>
> —Benjamin Jowett[1]

I T IS EASY TO read the Bible and jump to conclusions. It is hard work,
often yielding less than firm results, to study it diligently and critically,
with what tools and background knowledge one can command, while
keeping an open mind. Only after being painfully aware of the many ways
in which we not only make mistakes but also often fool ourselves, in both
methods and conclusions, can we offer our findings to others, and even
then, it must be done with appropriate caution.

In what follows, unless my view is quite unusual, I won't argue for
things I see as at least as well grounded in facts as alternative positions.
None of these will be *proved*, because in these areas, where we have so little
to go on, nothing can be. I invite the reader to disagree wherever he sees
cause. Where confirmation seems too slim, I simply admit that my guesses
are just guesses, but at least guesses informed by such data as we have.

Of course, every opinion one advances should have "appropriate
confirmation." But what is that? It may depend on who one's colleagues
or brothers-in-thinking are. Where colleagues are very careful and very

---

1. From "On the interpretation of Scripture," in *Essays and Reviews* (1860), extracted
in Reardon, *Religious Thought*, 312.

critical, they often function as an intellectual conscience, even in ways they shouldn't. But they can help define what we take to be "reasonable."

I shall work within this definition: what is "appropriately confirmed" is whatever I believe based on evidence that *the total evidence available to me* does not make me ashamed for holding. That turns aside rejection on the basis of both current fashionable theories and pedantic claims of "respectable formal standards," which are hardly appropriate to the sort of material we have to work with.

One point clearly brought out in the philosophy of science must always be kept in mind: conclusions can never be more precise than the data on which they are based. Any treatment of the life of Jesus is burdened with the fact that all our data is very imprecise. Because translations of that data add still more imprecision, references to the original languages must be used. And our dictionaries, word-studies, and grammars in those languages may still need correction.

Gospel writers were concerned with the *meaning* of Jesus' career, its meaning for them, not its precise details. They were more concerned with the edification of their hearers than the satisfaction of anonymous critical "referees." Accepting much of their interpretations of Jesus doesn't require us to be unquestioning as to their reported facts, especially when they disagree. So reading them for details must be subordinated to reading them for meaning, and our critical evaluations must deal with that meaning, so far as we are able.

The language of human meanings is poetry, song, metaphor, ritual, and narrative. Meaning comes out of freedom, not timeless concepts or the mechanical explanations that result from replacing facts with formal concepts.[2] And the background against which those authors expressed meaning was their own century and the literary and folklore remains of the centuries preceding—especially what was in the Hebrew Bible, whether they read it in Hebrew or, more likely, in Greek translation.

When a philosopher hears "poetry," he is likely to think something rather negative: "nothing but mere poetry!" as if that negates any truth beyond what is literal. But poetry involves being serious about meanings that go beyond literal language. One sensitive writer has characterized a poem quite aptly as "an imaginary garden with real hedgehogs in it." That indicates where poetic truth lies: whether the literal meanings be imagi-

---

2. Rather than distinguish types, I include under the term "poetry" all kinds of non-literal speech.

nary or literally true, the real communication hides and must be looked for with open sensitivity, patience, and a recognition that discovery may be a long process. In fact, the reader may never reach it.[3]

Such is the language not only of poetry, but also of genuine literary writing, of history, and even biography. A case history presents dead facts, while a biography presents a live person. The Bible has always been most fruitfully read as an extended poem, a largely "historical" poem, but a poem in which there hides the Great Hedgehog, God, for whom no prose is adequate and even poetry is but stumbling gestures. He reveals Himself as He chooses, hiding between the lines. The meaning of the gospels does not lie in their words taken flatly, but it is nevertheless there for those who patiently wait to hear it.

Since part of the gospel writers' own century was contact with Jesus' followers or their hearers, it is difficult to know how many of their "meanings," as well as their facts, were derived first- or second-hand and how many were gleaned from even more indirect sources. Conservative thinkers may claim too much for the former, others may be tempted to make too much of the latter. What Donne's poem called "mean ways," avoiding both extremes, seems justified, if not required.

However, between their time and ours, printing was developed and books became the prime intellectual currency. Before that, knowledge and truth were primarily communicated in words by someone *who knew*, uttered face-to-face with a trusting listener. Books made the relation between writer and reader impersonal, so much so that the modern world often treats *truth* as something necessarily impersonal, something that can reside in books. In fact, if something is spoken by a person rather than printed in a book, its truth is taken as probably corrupted. (Every professor who disagrees with a textbook faces this in his classroom.) The "Enlightenment" resulted from books.[4] Once printing was widespread, truth had to be expressible "objectively," that is, impersonally, and hence in literal, conceptual speech, preferably common-sense talk. If too abstruse for that, then delivered in "scientific" language. In any case, truth

3. Luther spoke of the Christ as the "divine incognito."

4. "In the communicational history of human culture, the advent of printing constitutes a revolution . . . For printing . . . involves reliance on . . . the assurance of being able to reproduce by mechanical means "the same" alphabetic forms . . . Printing meant being able to discount for all practical purposes the variation due to the individual scribe . . . [or] oral communication." Harris, *The Language Machine*, 52.

was considered to be independent of people. Even the Bible, formerly read as personal communication, whether from God or its authors, was, for many, no longer primarily *listened to* for its deep echoes of things prose cannot communicate. Now it had to be taken "literally," prosaically, printed word for printed word. When both God and the ancients had been reduced to words printed on paper, literalism, and then its child, fundamentalism, were born.

Radio made some difference. At least, we got the news audibly from trusted and honored reporters. But radio didn't give the face-to-face evidence of truthfulness that personal contact would have. Movies tended to make even pretended "truth" something we *see*, though the technology of cartoons made us see quite impossible and hence, unbelievable, things. Television advanced this, complicating it by the fantastic ability of electronic technology to present the most unbelievable images quite as vividly as genuine applications. "I saw it with my own eyes" no longer means something is believable. It may be only entertaining rather than convincing. Seen miracles that once might have represented the presence of God or the devil now represent only technology.

Along with such developments, advertising majored on making speech, illustration, and written text, all three, into means of persuading to action—perhaps even concealing truth rather than communicating it. Politicizing of publication, removing it farther from the moral restraints of journalistic conscience, also contributed. Everyone who speaks or writes is now suspected of having ulterior motives, axes to grind, something to sell, or ideological dishonesties.[5]

How can a modern thinker with this background trust ancient documents that report miraculous events, when television shows us daily unbelievable but entertaining prodigies, and advertisers and politicians care little about truth? Images, appearances, profits, and partisanships drown reality. Language is to be "spun," believing is to be cozened.

Indeed, the last generation has seen some scholars go overboard in reading the gospels not as attempts to communicate truth, but as propaganda instruments in political contests within the church. To do that is

5. Philosophers such as Foucault have even made such claims respectable. The gospels, like the rest of the Bible, were certainly written in response to particular problems, some of them disagreements. But interpreting all those as power struggles makes "power" so broad a term that it oversimplifies, losing its usefulness by swallowing up many valuable distinctions.

to forget that the authors were primarily concerned to present the *gospel*, good news, whatever their theological slants.

Despite Luther's warning that the Bible functions as "the Word of God" in *oral* and *aural* ways, that is, when it is discussed communally by believing persons, the Bible has been, these past centuries, reduced first to impersonal printed words and now, apparently, to a mass of partisan polemics. The claim that the Bible is an unquestioned authority is in tatters, first crippled by the straitjacket of "literal language" and then drowned in the deluge of new resources for language distortion.

For two-and-a-quarter centuries, ever since the time of Reimarus (1778), learned discussions of Jesus' life have been tied up with arguments about and criticism of the reliability of our sources of information about him. A decent respect for the present generation of New Testament scholars requires that any book, even one admittedly not a contribution to historical research or criticism, should give some acknowledgment of both why it reflects some skepticism and why it does not at the same time embrace some of the "latest" positions.[6]

In these discussions, something of each is present. I've already summarized my fiction dealing with a part of Jesus' life about which we have very little information. They present in narrative, and hence in somewhat poetic language, results of seriously trying to understand the strange figure of Jesus of Nazareth.

So far as it has been possible for me to keep up with a rapidly increasing mass of discoveries, what is written here responds to two hundred years of careful criticism of the gospels and our increased, though still incomplete, knowledge of their first-century conditions. Study of what has been learned about the existing gospel records and their ancient contexts forces one to try to reconcile discrepancies, unifying their testimony, and discerning details of their message.

As for the discussions that follow, they are, I hope, demonstrations of the fact that one may have deep respect for both the gospel story and the traditions of the church, and still have responsible skepticism about many things. I hope everything that appears in this book shows that

---

6. "Scholarship on Christian origins often suffers a misplaced positivism that assumes that certain things are known as "facts," either because they are espoused by a large number of scholars or because alternative scenarios have not (yet) been advanced. . . . No volume of support for a *hypothesis* will ever turn it into a fact." Kloppenborg-Verbin, *Excavating Q,* 3.

doing your homework with an open mind does not necessarily destroy faith—though it may influence how the faith is expressed.

Being a philosopher is a far thing from dealing with life's questions from the aloof comfort of some out-of-this-world viewpoint. Being a believer is a far thing from being an unthinking and naive embodiment of tradition. Both, in fact, can drive one to be a deeply immersed and thoughtful student of all the facts that may call tradition, the philosophical tradition as well as the religious, into question.

In following discussions what is fundamental is, I believe, treated as indispensable for the thinking Christian. However, a number of things in the tradition that are not basic have been questioned, and at times modified or even rejected—but rejected in favor of what in faith, I believe, are not perversions, but real alternative understandings.

11

Jesus' Birth

> In dealing with the birth narratives it is particularly difficult
> to locate the original author. Today, everyone admits that to
> some degree these narratives are a distillation of a community's
> experience. . . . Even if we could name a particular editor, the
> matter of intention may elude us. Seldom does the writer of
> such stories have a single, definable purpose.
>
> —Paul S. Minear[1]

SHOULDN'T JESUS' MORAL TEACHINGS now be summarized, since that
is how so many have understood him to be important? No. Jesus was
not a moralist, though thinkers as diverse as Jefferson and Gandhi took
him to be one. Instead, he was announcing that God was about to liberate
humans from their self-serving but self-destructive ways. By what means,
Jesus was not able to describe, but had complete confidence in. God
would somehow create a core of "true Israelites" who would be attacked
and martyred, but who would, in God's own time, be vindicated in a new
order of human affairs.

Those who want to grant him importance without taking seriously
what he saw himself as doing are left to celebrate only his moral instructions and example. So they line up with one side of Matthew. But Jesus
was not just an Israelite Confucius. He was a prophet, a "forth-teller" of
coming acts of God in history.

People of the "New Israel" would need instruction as to how they
were to behave *as co-heralds with him* of the coming evils: persecution, perhaps death, followed by judgment on the persecutors and final
vindication. True, to embody the truth of their proclamation, their

1. Minear, *The Bible and the Historian*, 90.

120

behavior was to be as fitting of the kingdom as their pre-kingdom situation would allow, but Jesus never claimed he was laying down "the Constitution of the Kingdom." That would be up to the Father.

Since those teachings can be read in the gospels by anyone, each can easily construct his own summary. Instead, some of the problems raised for many thinking about Jesus will be dealt with.

These problems are raised by the contents of the gospels themselves. They are problems for naive believers as well as the learned, and problems that have exercised critics as well as seekers. It seems more fruitful to deal at some length with a few prominent or celebrated ones than to attempt to touch on a large selection. Though no answers can be final, no arguments conclusive, one must do what he can.

That Jesus was born is no problem. *How* he was born became a much-discussed one, so some remarks about it are in order.

What are the simple facts about Jesus' origins? Paul speaks of Jesus as "born of a woman," which seems undeniable. C. J. Cadoux, in his *The Life of Jesus*, first published in 1948, said bluntly, "The date of his birth was about 7–5 B.C., and the place in all probability Nazareth itself."[2] Most biblical scholars would agree,[3] since neither the story of Jesus' birth in Matthew nor the one in Luke stand up under scrutiny as history.[4]

Jesus was known as "Jesus of Nazareth," which Luke calls his family's city (Luke 2:39), and the locals there knew of his mother Mary, his four brothers Jacob ("James"), Joseph, Judah, and Simeon (Simon), and his sisters (Mark 6:3). His father, whenever mentioned, is identified as having been named Joseph, but has no real place in the story of the adult Jesus. Yet the arguments against his name or existence are too weak to be taken seriously.[5] That his mother was named Mary no one doubts.

---

2. Cadoux, *The Life*, 27.

3. In Chilton's attempt to give the birth stories as much historical due as is possible for a modern scholar, he locates it in "another Bethlehem," in Galilee—an interesting move, but unconvincing.

4. Chilton, *Rabbi Jesus*, 3–7.

5. For example, we have Spong's suggestion that "Joseph" was invented for Jesus' unknown father because in the Greek of Zech 7:11 there appears "Jesus the son of Josedek." That assumes that Jesus was not known in Nazareth as "Bar-Joseph," and also that even Greek-speakers who knew Aramaic wouldn't notice the difference between Joseph ("He adds") and Josedek ("God is righteous"), especially when the two "s's" are two different letters of the Semitic alphabet, representing two different sounds.

There are a few strong hints that Jesus was rumored to be illegitimate—rumors not only reflected in the story of his birth in Matthew, reflected in Luke's account, and perpetuated in some early Jewish traditions,[6] but perhaps even hinted at here and there in John (7:27, 8:19, 41; but cf. 6:42). Jesus so identified himself with all sorts of outcasts that I'm sure he would not have been outraged by such stories for his own sake, though perhaps for that of his parents. But the church's use of claims of his birth from a virgin certainly would have called forth from critics the answer that they were just trying to cover up his illegitimacy.

Nevertheless, I believe, despite Chilton, that the idea Jesus was illegitimate cannot be maintained. Judaism had long developed a strong sense that those born of an illicit union were impure, *mamzerim*[7] (as Chilton admits), which not only threatened the purity of the society, but as a result also could not enter the temple.[8] Had there been such rumors in his lifetime, his enemies' use of them would most certainly have left more evidence than we find. Later critics of Christianity found such slander to be a fine debating tool. But those later Jewish Christians that other Christians called "Ebionites" simply considered Joseph to be Jesus' father.

On the other hand, even the hints of illegitimacy are all late enough to have arisen simply because Greek-speaking Christians, trying to explain Jesus in terms of the Old Testament, claimed the Greek translation (the LXX) of Isaiah 7:14, as "a virgin shall conceive," referred to Jesus' mother. The Hebrew original said instead, "a young woman is already pregnant," indicating the mother of Hezekiah, as Isaiah intended.

So long as it was assumed that the attributes ascribable to Jesus must be at least equal to the ones claimed for those numerous Greek heroes who were reported to have had supernatural births, it would seem quite normal to Christians of Greek background to find some evidence that Jesus had a supernatural birth, so that that particular Greek translation would be enthusiastically embraced.[9] Besides, it was the Greek Bible that for them was *The Bible*.

6. A survey of these may be found in Dunkerley, *Beyond the Gospels*, ch. 6.

7. See Gillihan, "Jewish Laws," 711–44.

8. Though it is admittedly possible, Chilton's extensive use of this idea to explain Matthew's birth account is difficult to accept.

9. It's interesting that the stories of the births of both Laozi and the Buddha have miraculous elements.

This, however, would hardly by itself explain Matthew's account. The idea must have been around before he wrote. Even though he wrote in Greek, His Jewish antecedents are far too evident for him to have invented the story himself.

Whatever the origins of the idea that Jesus was born of a virgin is of no concern at all to any of the authors of the New Testament except for Matthew and Luke. Outside Hebrew-reading Jewish-Christian circles, however, and even in Matthew, the need to authenticate Jesus from the Older Testament led to an emphasis on the LXX mistranslation of Isaiah 7:14 over against Jewish criticism and rejections. That sharpened the controversy with non-Christian Jews, who not only rejected claims that Jesus was "Messiah" but also quite reasonably held the Hebrew text to be *The Bible*, over against the Greek LXX.[10]

The issue became a point of fierce contention in controversies with Jewish critics, particularly in the second century, when apologists like Justin and Irenaeus made Jesus' birth one of the basic issues between non-Jewish Christians and others. By making "the virgin birth," and consequently the superiority of the Greek Old Testament to the Hebrew (a fundamental issue in the defense of the gospel against Jewish critics), those apologists completed the separation of gentile Christians from Jewish Christians. They also left an impress on subsequent theology,[11] wherein belief in the manner of Jesus' conception and birth was taken to be a *necessary* part of the creed.

It is important to repeat that these arguments on behalf of a supernatural conceiving of Jesus were *arguments against Jewish critics*. They were largely based on Christian claims that it was the Jews' own Greek translation, the LXX, that was divinely inspired, rather than the Hebrew Scriptures, which Christians, to defend their position, had to claim the Jews had altered. They emphasized the Greek "a virgin shall conceive" as over against the Hebrew and stressed that Jesus' birth was a fulfillment of prophecy, showing that Jesus was authenticated by divinely-given prediction *in the Jews' own Scriptures* (albeit in a Greek translation of much earlier Jewish origin. Later Jewish translations read the text differently).

---

10. A point emphasized by Hengel in his essay in Dunn, *Jews and Christians*, 39–83.

11. It also made the study of Hebrew almost disappear from Western Christian Bible study for many centuries. In the last century, some Greek Orthodox still maintained the superiority of the Greek over the Hebrew.

The Christian appeal to the Jewish Scriptures was inescapable, since Jesus was certainly a Jew and understood himself in terms of the Hebrew Bible. His first followers were drawn to him as the fulfillment of many images in it. Since he could not be understood except in terms of Jewish Scripture, any such scripture was fair game for use by Christians in trying to understand so puzzling a Jew as Jesus.

In following centuries, when defense against Jewish critics became unimportant, "the virgin birth" came to be something to be celebrated in its own light, as a special sort of miracle authenticating Jesus, and the emphasis tended to shift to Mary as quasi-divine. As the late-Medieval carol put it, "Mother and maiden was never none but she; Well may such a lady God's mother be." The early twentieth-century Fundamentalist movement made "the virgin birth" one of the six "fundamentals."[12]

Some arguments for denying the "virgin birth"[13] are more interesting than effective. A colleague told me his biology teacher argued that virgin birth did not imply "Son of God," since among some lower animals parthenogenesis—production of offspring without a male mate—can occur. The "scientific" response was that then Jesus must have been female, since there would be no source for a y chromosome. That was met with the claim that God, who invented chromosomes, could easily have produced an extra one. Such arguments are merely expressions of a denial of miracle. Grant that possibility, and the argument becomes something quite different.

Am I saying that the familiar Christmas birth-stories are to be rejected? Yes and no. They are indeed traditions whose content shows they ought not to be taken as literal history. But they are profound expressions of the church's perception of what was involved in Jesus' appearing in history. As one sensitive scholar has said of the Christmas texts,

> The tradition reflects the mature and realistic understanding of the Christian life, based upon the cumulative, year-round experience of the Christian community as a whole, in that, when people who knew the stories of Jesus' birth heard those stories recited in the worship service, they thought backward from the period after

12. When I was examined for licensure in 1941, the first question addressed to me was "Do you believe in the virgin birth?" The same question was asked a year later in my ordination exam.

13. In this Protestant use, "virgin birth" is limited to Jesus' conception. Catholic usage includes the birth process itself.

the cross and the Resurrection, and they frankly recognized that many of the implications of earlier events remained hidden even to Jesus' own family and closest disciples until after the climactic revelation of the Risen Lord.[14]

These were not fossilized ancient tales. They were soul-stirring poetry. Christians knew in their own experience the threatening opposition of established powers, the good news to the poor workers, the action of God in humans' behalf. The birth stories must be read as if the reader knows those things in his own deep self, too. They are deeply existential worship expressions.

Some have made much of the probable fact that in popular piety Mary replaced once-loved pagan mother-goddesses. This undoubtedly happened, but such goddesses are so normal and widespread in religious history that such emotional transfer seems hardly worth emphasizing.

I don't *deny* that Jesus was born of a virgin, but I can't affirm it. He may have been. Who knows? My father, a doctor, was interested in medical anomalies, of which there have been many. What, if anything, would follow from making Mary one of them? It might upset our obstetric science, but the sciences have been upset many times in their history.

Jesus was certainly a person worthy of celebration even without a birth-miracle. Everything that might be taken as evidence for it fails under close scrutiny. We just don't know anything about his birth, except, as Paul said, he was "born of a woman." That makes him one of us. Why add more to that than the fact that his life shows his parents must have been extraordinarily good people? For that, they deserve at least some of the honor they have received throughout Christian history.

Mark presents Jesus as "Son of God" without any evident problems about his birth, or any interest in it. But the classical view that one's "nature" comes entirely from one's father, as laid out in Aristotle, would not have taken long, once they took "Son of God" to be a literal description rather than an acknowledgment of status, to lead to the conclusion that Jesus could not have had a human father. That also contributed to the temptation to overlook his genuine humanity. Rather than *being* human, he was thought of as having "taken humanity upon himself," sometimes even as a disguise. To honor him as "Son of God," some made him to be a fake human.

14. Minear, *The Bible*, 91.

Later squeamishness about sex strengthened that attitude. At any rate, the rest of the New Testament seems to have felt no need to defend Jesus against a charge of illegitimacy, and the claim by some psychoanalytically-minded writers that Jesus called God "Father" because he didn't know who his earthly father was finds no basis in the evidence at all.

One can sincerely apply the title "Son of God" to Jesus—whatever one might mean by that—without assuming there was anything supernatural about his birth, but there is nothing askew if our common sense lets us consider his birth unique. We humans are in no position to lay down requirements as to how God should do what he does. But we do have an obligation to be as honest and consistent as we can.

The doctrine of the Trinity relates The Son to The Father as "begotten"[15] without any specification as to what that means except as an expression of the primacy of The Father, the Son's source and uniqueness, and the completeness of their unity in the Triune God. After all, we haven't the slightest idea what "begetting" might mean when applied to God. Terms that are surrogates for mysteries are demeaned when we make up non-mysterious theories about what they say.

Jesus was addressed in one story as "Son of David," meaning a descendant of King David. However, that someone could hardly have known Jesus' pedigree. Matthew and Luke do trace his line back to David or beyond, but they do not agree, and scholars doubt the reliability of their genealogies.

Still, since David lived a thousand years before Jesus and had a number of wives and many children, quite a number of Israelites could have legitimately claimed such ancestry. Many have asked whether Jesus' question in Mark 13:35–37 was his disowning of any such lineage, or whether it was directed against a claim that Messiah must come from the upper classes, or perhaps just a way of showing that the scribes didn't really have all the answers. Or it may have been his disowning that his ancestry (or parentage) had anything to do with his qualifications to proclaim the kingdom. Who knows?

15. It is possible that "only begotten," as we point out in Appendix C, is an English derivative from Jerome's Latin translation of the Greek *monogenes* as *unigenitus*, instead of the usual *unicus*, both meaning "unique" or "only." Creeds in English use either "begotten" without the prefix or simply "only." All of the verbs used can mean simply "to sire offspring" in some way.

Jesus' Davidic ancestry apparently was widely claimed in the early church (Rom 1:3). The fourth-century church historian Eusebius says that the emperors Vespasian (69–79 A.D.) and Domitian (81–96 A.D.) ordered the living descendants of David to be killed.[16] Jesus' "royal ancestry" apparently threatened the Roman throne.

Two of the very best known stories about Jesus tell of his birth. One tells of wisemen and the other shepherds (Matt 1:18, 2:19; Luke 1:26–56, 2:1–18.) They are quite inconsistent with each other, and neither of them is historically believable, but we will not enter here the long discussions about their differences and possible interpretations. We must limit this merely to noting that they give us practically no credible information about his birth and childhood, but have spawned many legends, traditions, and artistic representations.

His hometown Nazareth, so far as we know, was in no way exceptional, nor is there any indication his parents were not just typical, common Galileans. Apparently he was just another Galilean boy. But his character, interests, and commitments as a man must have had roots in his growing up.

Luke's pretty storytelling of Jesus at the age of twelve listening to and questioning "the teachers" in the Jerusalem temple appears to be more Luke than history, but may have been based on some actual incident. A piously made-up story would likely have had him teaching the teachers, instead of simply showing him to be a bright boy, which he undoubtedly was, one with an interest in and a gift for questioning interpretations of the Bible, as the narrative suggests.

One can assume that Jesus had problems understanding his calling,[17] problems that continued right into his ministry. Such confusions would undoubtedly have been troubling to his family. John reports in 7:5, "even his brothers did not yet believe in him." Mark 3:21 says he was taken to be "beside himself," even reading that to be his family's conclusion.[18] Some have interpreted Mark as saying his *family* thought him out of his mind. Pharisees said he was in league with the devil (Mark 3:22). Some have even maintained that Jesus was obviously psychotic, a charge that is

16. Eusebius, *History*, 3.12, 19.

17. Dale Miller's *The Adult Son* is a whole book on this possibility.

18. "Those closest to him," translated "friends" (RSV), can hardly mean his family, as some translations take it to do; they are not brought in until ten verses later (Mark 3:31–34).

not borne out by what evidence we have. Many a normal youth has had problems regarding his future.

All we can know of his upbringing we have to tease out of what historians and archeologists have dug up about Galilean culture in the first century, which isn't nearly enough, though growing slowly all the time. It appears much less homogeneous than was formerly believed. That's why I said that anyone who would understand Jesus must construct, at least roughly, his own narrative of his earlier life, as I did, by a gleaning from what is available. Each thus forms personal answers.

What, then, is the importance of the birth stories for our understanding of Jesus? First, that he was most certainly human—as Paul says, "born of a woman." Because his coming into the world as just an ordinary baby is something too everyday for one so unusual, later inventions, appearing only in Luke and Matthew, read his importance to believers back into the accounts of his origin.

Whatever the historical facts may be, Christmas is certainly an important Christian festival. One who did what he did, said what he said, died as he died, and was seriously reported as risen is one whose birth deserves celebration, celebration in story, drama, poetry, and song, as the church has done for centuries.

Luke struck several important notes of celebration in his birth story's poems. Mary sang that God, in Jesus' birth,

> . . . has scattered the proud in the imagination of their hearts,
> He has put down the mighty from their thrones,
> And exalted those of low degree;
> He has filled the hungry with good things
> And the rich he has sent empty away. (Luke 1:52–53)

When Simeon saw the newborn Jesus, he sang, to God,

> . . . mine eyes have seen thy salvation
> Which thou hast prepared in the presence of all peoples,
> A light for revelation to the nations
> and for glory to thy people Israel.[19] (Luke 2:30–32)

All of the above rejoice in the promise of a new age, an overturning of the existing oppressive power structures, something toward which

---

19. Usually "Gentiles," which simply means "non-Jewish nations."

the gospel has turned Christians' hopes in many ways through twenty past centuries.

Not many years after Jesus' birth, such things as these were being seriously proclaimed about Jesus, and have continued to be ever since.

In one of his Christmas sermons, Luther points out one further touch in the meaning of Jesus' birth. He remarks on how *small* God made his presence to be in the manger! Where others have proclaimed the overwhelming power of their god's appearance, the Christmas story celebrates God's willingness to humble himself for human's benefit, by making his entrance into human life as a helpless, vulnerable infant, responding from the beginning to humans' love. Both the stories, then, even Matthew's, remind Christians of God's self-abnegation for the salvation of human history.

The baby Jesus' importance to us demands that God's humanity, presented to us through him, should very properly be celebrated as unusual, and that's why those stories have been worth repeating over and over in the churches, not as history but as poetry and song within which deeper truths may be discerned.

The stories about Jesus' birth are miracle stories. The records of Jesus are filled with many more. The next chapter will take them up.

12

Miracles, "Spirits," and "Unique Events"

Upon the whole, we may conclude, that the Christian religion not only was at first attended with miracles, but even at this day cannot be believed by any reasonable person without one . . . . and whoever is moved by faith to assent to it, is conscious of a continued miracle in his own person, which subverts all the principles of his understanding, and gives him a determination to believe what is most contrary to custom and experience.

—David Hume[1]

There are two ways to live your life. One is as though nothing is a miracle. The other is as though everything is a miracle.

—Albert Einstein[2]

THE GOSPEL STORIES ARE full of miracle accounts. What David Hume said in 1748 represents, quite remarkably, an issue for many today. Though Christians may insist the faith began with miracles that are to be believed, skeptics assert that *that* is precisely the reason why belief is impossible, because "miracles don't happen."

Christians not only claim that unique events have occurred that cannot be described under the laws of nature, but also talk about "spirits" or "immortal souls" for whose existence there is no scientific confirmation. Science, it is claimed, has debunked the superstitions that are the basis for Christianity.

1. Insertion, in Hendel, *Selections.*

2. In a speech at Princeton. Personal reminiscence of Harold K. Kaser, *Monday Morning,* Apr 3, 2000, 28–29.

Miracles, "Spirits," and "Unique Events"

So we have to talk about "unique events." That doesn't mean we are talking about every miracle story. One can doubt many miracle stories without rejecting all of them in advance.

It made sense for Hume to say that Christianity "cannot be believed by any reasonable person" without a miracle. From his modern viewpoint, "reasonable" means that thinking relies on common sense "experience" as found in the sciences. It deals with what we can scrutinize or measure, and no one can do so with "spirits." So no rational person believes Christianity is part of science, or even "common sense." Something that isn't science has indeed gone on in the believer's thinking, causing him to believe "what is most contrary to custom and experience."

In Hume's day, intelligent people believed that "experience" would be very much the same for everyone, in all ages and cultures. And custom was simply funded experience. The world was the same everywhere, and "reason" characterized every human, though many made insufficient use of it.

Superstitions arose because people were moved by emotions, especially fear, and did not use their "reason" adequately. Religions that relied on miracles belonged to the unlettered, irrational, and gullible. So those like Hume claimed.

Many authorities in the church did appeal to stories of miracles to "prove" creedal beliefs—that is, to establish their own religious authority. So, for a hundred years before Hume, critics had claimed that miracle stories were fabrications of "priestcraft," to maintain the status of the clergy. This was partly true. Ever since the Roman Empire took over Christianity in the fourth century, ecclesiastical authority, which aims at order within the church, and political power, which aims at order in society in general, were often confused with each other.[3]

It was assumed that the church had a responsibility to maintain civic order by seeing to it that the beliefs and morals of every citizen were the same. How did the church get that power? Because it was the Christ's church, and Jesus' miracles testified to his authority over both belief and behavior! The church claimed status for itself on grounds of divine authority.

This meant that if one had doubts about the church's authority one had to have doubts about the miracles. The development of modern

3. See Richard Rubenstein's study of the Nicene controversy, *When Jesus Became God.*

science taught the whole culture that the cosmos ran by divinely established and unbreakable natural laws. Even the church bought in to that to
an extent. As one eighteenth-century hymn put it:

> Praise the Lord, for He hath spoken!
> Worlds His mighty power obeyed;
> Laws which never shall be broken
> For their guidance He hath made.[4]

If God had created the world to be ruled by ever-repeating and
unbreakable mechanical laws, then how could God be consistent with
himself if he made special exceptions to his own laws? God the supreme
heavenly engineer wouldn't disrupt the operation of his perfect machine!
Even salvation shouldn't upset Creation!

All of this is quite apart from the question of "the existence of God."
Students of Hume still debate whether he was an atheist or not (some
even argue he was really an intellectually baffled Christian, which seems
to me very questionable). And, although many have read him differently,
what he was arguing was not that miracles couldn't happen, but that
stories that report miracles are not a good enough *reason* for one to believe. By that he means we can't argue that a belief is true on the basis of
some miracle story.

One of the greatest of the old Church Fathers, Origen, put it thus:

> [Christians] charm demons away and perform many cures . . .
> But if we were to commit them to writing, although we were
> eyewitnesses present at the time, we would bring upon ourselves
> downright mockery from the unbelievers, who would think that
> we were inventing the stories ourselves.[5]

That doesn't mean we can't believe if we have an acceptable reason to
do so. But it is hard to define just what "an acceptable reason" includes.

So among the many problems Jesus' story poses for the modern
thinking Christian are several concerning miracles: What is the function
of the Christian miracle stories? To have faith, must one believe them? In
that case, what does "believe them" mean? Must "reason and experience"
be limited to what Hume took them to mean? And, most difficult of all,
what are the places of "reason and experience" in Christian belief?

4. "Praise the Lord, Ye Heavens Adore Him," *Foundling Hospital Collection.*
5. Hengel, *The Four Gospels*, 266n367, quoting Chadwick's trans.

First, let's limit the field to the events referred to in the gospels as either "mighty works" or "signs." The former term indicates they were impressive, the latter that they carried some important meaning.

Usual things rarely impress. Something is "unusual" only in contrast to what is usual, and "awe inspiring" only in contrast to the familiar and explainable. Therefore, "mighty work" implies "unusual," "unexpected," perhaps "awe inspiring." Events called "mighty works" in a gospel, occurring frequently enough to be referred to in the plural, suggest a change in the way the world is going. A "mighty work" then, may also be a "sign" that there is a "new order of things" confronting one.

Our modern scientific worldview, which Hume accepted in a rather qualified form, starts from an affirmation that there cannot be "a new order of things." That is the modern understanding of "natural law" (as distinct from the Classical, Medieval, and some "post-modern" understandings). Events such as tornadoes and earthquakes may be unexpected, but that simply means we don't yet have the precise knowledge to control them, or even to predict them. If we can't explain them satisfactorily, we take that to be a "not yet," not a "never." Like every other happening, they are "signs" of nothing but the same old order of things. They may be "unusual" in their occurring and "awe inspiring" in their power, but that is only a matter of quantity, and can be measured—even if we can't predict them yet.

"Predict" is the important word. We predict things on the basis of our past experience, and past experience is always, obviously, experience of the past. "A new order of things" cannot be the same old things that occurred in the past. But that would mean we have no basis upon which to predict them. Any events that we could predict simply couldn't be "signs" of some new state of things, so any such sign must be unpredictable.

But it is our ability to predict happenings on the basis of our customary habits of expecting and scientific theories. Even "laws" are still "customary habits of expecting," that is the ground of our believing in "the order of nature," that some things "*can* happen," and some things "*can't* happen." And everything that can happen can happen over and over again. That is, every happening can be put into a "class" with other happenings of the same sort that can happen anywhere, anytime, if the conditions are right. And the accurate statement of what those conditions are is a scientific "explanation."

What science means by "explanation" is understanding past or even current happenings in terms of collected scientific "reports" that are always *of the past*. We may predict the future, hoping it will turn out that way. But we know we may be proved wrong.

Yet, to be a miracle an event has to be "unique." It also is seen as something to be understood by its *purpose*. But purpose looks to the future, it is only understandable as showing us an unexpected future. It can't be classed as something that can happen anywhere, anytime, if only the scientifically stated past conditions for that class of event have been fulfilled.

That is why modern science, as it developed, does not deal with what ancient and medieval philosophers called "final causes," explaining things by their purposes for a future not yet observable. Instead, modern science relies on already observed past causes. If there are any "final causes," it can't deal with them, so, as strictly science, it ignores them. Only as "scientific" ideology can it deny them.

Even if we should grant the legitimacy of such happenings as "unique events," we would have to invent a separate "class" for each event, a class that wouldn't be part of any larger class or the happening wouldn't be "unique." Thus, I insist that the resurrection cannot be classed with any other "event." It's in a class by itself.

But if such a class can't be part of a still larger class, how can it be talked about intelligently? Yet there is no "scientifically reasonable" point of talking about such a thing at all unless there actually was at least one, there is a class we can put it into, and that class can be included in a still larger class of classes. And, as Hume would ask, can one be a Christian without believing in at least one miracle, The Resurrection?

Science seems to assume that no events are really unique. On the other hand, every event "is just what it is, and not another thing," so every event is "unique" in some sense. Thus we have a contradiction: every event is unique, but there aren't any unique events. If science says we have to be able to classify events on the basis of past events, and some can't be so classified but are genuinely unique, can we even think seriously, even though not scientifically, about them?

A recognized philosopher of science gives this answer, one we need:

> to escape between the horns of this dilemma... The needed escape hatch lies in noting that certain events are of such a nature that whenever we attempt to group them with others, such grouping proves scientifically uninformative. ...

Obviously all events can be put into classes . . . but for some events we cannot do this *fruitfully* or *informatively*, relative to the investigative purposes we have in mind. [This relativity] is, of course, a function of not only the events, but also of the aims of our inquiry, and of the development in the state of our knowledge of the domain of the phenomena involved.[6]

In short, the question of claimed "miracles" is made up of several questions: What are our "investigative purposes" as we raise questions about them? In what "domain" are we placing them? What sort of information are we seeking in discussing them? What is the state of our knowledge (not just our assumptions) regarding them and their context?

If we seek to use them to advance science's generalizations, its "putting into classes," there is simply no point in asking what *scientific* meaning a unique event may have, because it can't have a scientific meaning,[7] since the "uniqueness" that miracles must have to be miracles is absent. That is, if we find they "inform" us, the "information" they give us can only be *nonscientific*, such as "God's special action." It follows that "unique events," in so far as they really are unique, can have no place at all in science.

So even if we class Jesus' reported miracles as "healings," "exorcisms," "violations of known natural laws," etc., just what are our "investigative purposes"? Rewriting history? No, Jesus himself was a "unique event." History may record him as unique, but can it explain him? Or are we "revising medicine"? Our classifications aren't medically useful.

Does that mean they can have no truth of any kind? No, since truth needn't be scientific to be true. But it does mean that anyone who would accept a miracle story as recounting *a historical fact*, that is, a fact to be

---

6. Rescher, "On the Probability," Feigl and Maxwell, 229, 243 (italics in original, bracketed words added).

7. The logical difference between talk about the crucifixion or the Apostle's faith, as historic events, and talk of the resurrection shows up here clearly. Historical research can investigate the crucifixion and what the apostles believed those we have "classes" in which to file them. But we have no *class* of resurrections. "Resurrection" is primarily referential, not descriptive; it confuses any concepts we attempt to describe it with. So its reports give us no *scientifically useful* information though what it gives us may be much deeper in actually living life than many things typically scientific are. Nor does the hope of a general resurrection in the future open any doors for "possible worlds" arguments about its logic, since such "possible worlds" are always projected in terms of objectively defined descriptive concepts appropriate to this world. Of these, the hopeful believer has none relevant to science. He has only self-involving hope quite ready to be completely surprised and baffled, as the evidence shows the apostles were.

reported in secular history books, must be able to present just what kind of usefulness it has *as information about secular human life*. But if someone claims a present actual-life meaning for a miracle story, many would say he is "preaching" or "testifying," not at all a scientific activity.

So, what is the function of the miracle stories? This brings in a most relevant question: If what Hume was arguing against is one of the church's past uses of the miracle stories, is it the function of the miracle stories *in the gospels* to bolster the authority of the church? Hume, leery of the authority of the church, carefully took his examples from much later miracles claimed by churchmen.

Do the gospel miracles function the same way? Not quite. The ancients didn't argue that miracles couldn't happen. They believed them always possible. Many who followed Jesus expected miracles. In the records we find that the question was not, "Do or can miracles happen?" The serious question was, "Which miracles are divine, and which demonic?" That was the challenge the Pharisees raised about Jesus.

Jesus' answer was pragmatic: if genuine benefit to actual people results, no matter how high or low, how can they be considered evil?

Let's look at some of them. In Mark 5 we have the story of Jairus, who asked Jesus to come and heal his twelve-year-old daughter, who, he said, was dying. When Jesus arrived, Jairus was told, "Your daughter is dead." Jesus, however, announced that the girl was not dead, but asleep. He took her by the hand and said, "Get up," and she got up. "And immediately," the story goes on, "they were overcome with amazement. And he strictly charged them that no one should know this, and told them to give her something to eat."

As the story stands, it presents some interesting questions. Was she dead? Our legal standards for establishing death were certainly not fulfilled. But the bystanders thought so, and undoubtedly the story was repeated and preserved as a case of Jesus raising the dead, something ordinary humans couldn't do. Hence, a miracle that revealed that wherever Jesus was, divine things might happen. The girl's revival was thus taken to be not only a "mighty work," but also a "sign."

However, Jesus is presented in it as downplaying its importance in several ways: by his remark, "She is not dead, but asleep"; by his charge to them to tell no one; and by his insistence that things return to normal immediately ("Give her something to eat").

The girl's father hoped, even expected, that Jesus would restore her. Jesus already had that reputation. So a "miraculous" healing was anticipated. And afterwards "everyone was filled with amazement," since "reasonable" anticipations were violated, a very typical part of a miracle story. But what did it prove? That she had been dead? Jesus denied that. Why did he raise her up? Out of compassion—she needed to be restored to normalcy.

It needs to be pointed out that the miracle stories were passed down by word of mouth, and undoubtedly picked up decorations, as gossip does today.[8] But the gospel writers were not quite as naive as we are tempted to believe. There is no mention of "unclean spirits" in this miracle story. In fact, Mark is very careful to distinguish healing miracles from exorcisms; they are never confused in his language. For him, both showed Jesus' power, but different powers. And when Jesus sent his disciples out to preach, Mark reports he gave them both powers, mentioned separately.

Why then did Mark tell those stories? Apparently, in his judgment, they showed four things: that Jesus could produce remarkable results; that Jesus was interested in normal, happy life, not prodigies; that Jesus' healings were not signs of some private dignity on his part but anticipations and indications of the coming kingdom; and that Jesus was not out to "prove" anything. His motivation was compassion toward the girl and her family.

The first was what apparently made him famous and attracted crowds, most of whom cared little about the other three points, which were what Mark was interested in. Later, when the church had to defend its preaching of the gospel, it was used to emphasize his relation to God. The others were never forgotten, but often the prime issue became Jesus Himself rather than what God was doing through him, and affirmation of his miracles became more important than he took them to be.

Christianity has always incited criticism, so Christians needed answering arguments. When the Baptist sent to ask whether Christians should look elsewhere to see God's messenger, Jesus referred to his miracles, not as evidence of his own status but as fulfillment of prophecies of

8. "Most of the miracle stories were originally told by people who were interested, above all, in Jesus' healings and exorcisms, not his religious proclamation. This hypothesis explains their popular character and the relative paucity of specifically Christian themes." Allison, *Jesus of Nazareth*, 70, summarizing Theissen's conclusion.

what God would do in the "last days." He added, "And blest is the man who is not turned away by what I'm doing."[9]

Similarly, there is the story of the paralyzed man who was brought to Jesus but, because the house was so crowded, could not be brought where Jesus was teaching, so his friends let him down through the roof of the house (Mark 2:1–12).

> And when Jesus saw their faith, he said to the paralytic, "My son, your sins are forgiven." When the scribes present . . . [questioned this], Jesus asked, "Which is easier, to say, 'Your sins are forgiven,' or to say, 'Take up your pallet and walk?' But that you may know that the Son of man has authority on earth to forgive sins" he said to the paralytic, "I say to you rise, take up your pallet and go home." And he rose, and immediately took up the pallet and went out before them all.

In Mark, Jesus gives a reason, "that you may know that the Son of man has authority on earth to forgive sins (Mark 2:10)." Jesus did not ordinarily make any such claims for himself (and he often seems to distinguish between himself and "the Son of man"). The clause interrupts the Greek rather awkwardly, so even though Mark was quite capable of awkward Greek, I tend to believe it was added by Mark as his own theological comment, in which the "you" addressed was his future readers. It may, however, have already been added to the story in whatever source he got it from.[10] Nevertheless, Jesus' forgiveness of the man's sins (as distinct from any claim he made about it) was part of the story.

Here, Jesus treats sins, not some evil demon, as the cause of the man's paralysis. The scribes, who questioned his grant of forgiveness, undoubtedly, like most of their contemporaries, took paralysis to be a consequence of sins. But the man himself believed that, too, so Jesus' "forgiving of sins" *was itself the healing act.*

The real "divine act" was the forgiving of sins. It was an act that arose out of compassion for the sufferer, but in response to "their faith," the

9. Matt 11:7ff., Luke 7:18ff., (trans. mine). Notice that Mark does not represent Jesus as claiming any authority in his miracle stories. Jesus did not preach about what he did, but about what the Father does and will do. See Luke 7:18–23.

10. It appears Mark added such comments elsewhere, including 2:21 and 2:28 and possibly the last few words of 9:30, 10:34, and 10:45. This does not deny the truth of what is said. It only questions whether Jesus said it or Mark added it as clarification for his readers.

man's and his friends' *faith in Jesus' defining mission*, that is, not in some creedal statement about him. The evidence we have suggests that Jesus' forgiving or healing wasn't from any desire to make a point, but to direct the audience's attention away from himself to the new healed and forgiven state of the sufferer. Both the healing and the forgiving of sins were signs of what he was proclaiming: that the Kingdom of God, the Kingdom of healing and forgiveness was "at hand," which was what "their faith" was really faith in, even if they thought it was in the "magical" powers that came with his prophetic function.

It was not that the *healing* was offered as evidence that the sins had been forgiven, but the man's walking, the *result* of the already-accomplished healing. And the walking was not offered as evidence of Jesus' own power in himself, but as "the Son of man," representing the beginning of the new age, the "Kingdom (or realm) of God," one characteristic of which would be the forgiveness of sins. The "promised new order of things" was shown in the new kind of life for the man. The office of Jesus, of the "Son of man,"[11] was to signal the promised Kingdom's arriving.

Since the problems of history were then considered due to sin—as many of them have, in fact been sin, with its evil results of sickness as well as strife and moral disorder—both healing and forgiveness were signs of the new order. Jesus undoubtedly knew the promise of a "new covenant" in Jeremiah 31:31–34, ending with, "I will forgive their iniquity, and I will remember their sins no more," to go along with Isaiah's, "Then shall the lame man leap as an hart" (Isa 35:6).

Our modern medical questions about the seriousness of the paralysis, whether it was a result of nerve destruction, hysteria, or something else, are irrelevant. The story is not a story about the world, as *we* have to live in it, predict it, or try to control it. It is not a story about the most effective treatment for paralysis. It is a story directed to the question, "What are the indications that a new era, a 'new creation,' is upon us?" In Jesus' day, when immobility, isolation, guilt, and fear of disease were fundamental anxieties, walking, joining with faithful friends, relief of guilt, and restoration of health were significant signs that God was on the verge of doing great things, of changing the familiar way the world worked.

The miracles were not themselves the new world, so that one could derive a positive description of "the Kingdom" from them. They were

---

11. If it is Mark's insertion, his use of "Son of man" shows he well understood what that meant.

indications that it was beginning to show itself, *signs that it was coming, that it was near.*

At the same time, the "new order" was not to be *a new order of nature*, as the system of creation had been. What His "signs" announced was the destruction of "Satan's kingdom," the world in which disobedience to God had twisted the lives of humans.

Jesus' certainty that his miracles were God's promise of a new age to come and were not grounds for high claims for himself as an individual is shown elsewhere. As many shamans, witch doctors, and *curanderas* have reported, healing a single person takes something out of the healer. In Mark 5:30, when Jesus cured a woman He knew that "power had gone forth from him." So when he had a crowd to heal, as in Mark 4:20–30, healings must have taken quite a toll from him, so he needed to refuel his "power" by entering into an ecstatic prayer-state, like the early Old Testament "prophets"[12] (see 1 Sam 10: 5–6). But then, those close to him thought he was "beside himself."

The Pharisees claimed he was devil-possessed. Jesus' response was not to defend himself, but the promise of God he was announcing. He did it through two separate parables. The first was making nonsense of their claim: Satan would not shoot himself in the foot by setting his captives free.

The other parable suggested that his healings showed that God, the only one "strong" enough to do so, would destroy Satan's defenses and take over Satan's "treasure" of captives. So his power to heal was not his own, and certainly not Satan's, but had to come from God's Spirit. Thus, when the Pharisees suggested that releasing captives from bondage to disease or demon-possession was Satan's work, they were sinning "against the Holy Spirit," God's empowering presence, and thus changing the doing of good into an evil and cutting themselves off from real repentance.

We return to the miracles themselves. The miracle stories do not "prove" anything about Jesus or about the world. They do not suggest that natural physical laws were to be revoked or modified. They were signs, not natural events. Neither Jesus nor those who wrote about him were interested in denying the world as science describes, except in so far as science assumes a world in which unique signs never will occur. Science, to be science, must do that. But it does not follow that such is the essence

12. Each was a *roeh*, a "seer," not a *nabi* like Amos or Isaiah. Like them, Saul was "filled with the Spirit" (1 Sam 10:10).

of all that is, only the essence of what we can study in public and repeatable ways. And that doesn't include miracles. It just makes us very, very careful before we accept any miracle stories.

Beyond science, there is the awareness that we humans are not mere pawns of external physical forces. "Miracles" make no sense as data for natural explanation: science is correct in ignoring them, since its "method" allows no way to even describe them. As already pointed out, they can have no place even in the *language* of science.

One can acknowledge, however, that miracle and exorcism stories were, for their time, an appropriate vehicle for proclaiming the gospel: that in the appearance of Jesus, important things were happening in the history of the world of humans. Because we don't experience disease and "demon possession" in *their* terms, the stories have nothing to tell us about how to live our lives. But that means we mustn't insist that the experience-world in which whatever occurred must be rewritten to have been exactly like our own world of experience. The gospel says that fundamental things were happening in history, and faith is a response to that gospel, not to the miracle stories or exorcisms themselves.

If our sense of human precariousness involved us in deep fears of disease, etc. as manifestations of evil forces controlling our histories, healings might speak to us very deeply. But we are taught that disease, even emotional or psychological diseases, are just technological problems yet to be solved. "Believing" the miracle stories does nothing to alleviate our deepest anxieties. Nor is its challenge to our views of life able to break through our customary assumptions. Hence it says nothing to us about any "new state of things." We need no gospel about problems we believe we can solve.

The miracle stories need to be read not so much for what they say as for what they *meant at the time*. If we have different standards for reading meaning into them, we have to find ways to reinterpret the old stories to say things that will today challenge our comfortable sensibilities.

Some of them may ring no such bells for us. Frankly, stories like Jesus walking on the water, calming a storm, or turning water into wine are very difficult to develop a modern accord with. We don't consider large bodies of water as containing an evil being that can "swallow" us up, as they might have. We don't experience storms, not even hurricanes or tornados, as life-threatening evil beings, even though we may thank God when they have passed. (In Mark 4:39, Jesus "rebuked" the storm.)

Nor do we often thank God for the wonderful way he sends water down on the earth and then turns it, via grains and grapevines, into bread and wine, as they did at every meal. Those stories, as they stand, have no real message for us.

Because we see the world so differently from the way they did, many Christians now don't so much "disbelieve" such stories as sidestep the question of "believing" them. And this they can do, because even if one accepts that something unique might have happened at some time in the past, but won't happen again under apparently similar circumstances in the present, it is put into a kind of "fairytale land" that has no real significance for the present. They may be "believed," but they're not really *believed*.[13]

Who Jesus was and what his life and death indicate may confront us with important decisions, and so become a genuine part of our lives. But whether he walked on water or calmed a storm, as a distant-past event, is only something we can waste idle conversation on.

Further, it is likely that the same people who were interested in Jesus only as a miracle worker handed down most of the miracle stories. The stories often reveal that they have been shaped in their telling and retelling by such people. That Jesus became famous as a miracle worker is no reason that the stories of those who made much of that should be important to us. The gospel writers did receive them as tradition but used them for their own more significant purposes.

So no Christian is obliged to accept all the miracle stories. Every scholar is still stumped by the story of feeding five thousand men on five loaves and two fish. All sorts of hints can be pointed out, from folklore about a banquet associated with the coming Messiah, to church rituals, from prophecies about Israel being sheep without a shepherd, to the possibility that "thousand" should be read "family" or "clan" (a possibility in both Hebrew and Aramaic), and from the fact that they sat down in "fifties and hundreds," which is military language,[14] to what can go

---

13. Calvin somewhere comments that one can believe biblical miracles happened then, but must never expect one now.

14. The military overtones in Mark's account: ("five thousand men" 7:34–44) are glossed over by Matthew ("healed their sick" and "besides women and children" 14:14–21) and Luke (9:11–17), but appear in John's "take him by force and make him king" (6:5–15). Chilton, *Rabbi Jesus*, 186f., takes the military theme quite seriously.

on and on. Despite such attempts at how the story came to be, we really can't say.

And what the story means to us no one seems to know for sure, except some creative preachers. So what? We can't demand that *we* must be the judges of everything meaningful. Yet all four gospels treat that story as important! We are just not privileged to perceive what it meant in the first century. Why should we be? If we have no good explanation, that doesn't justify bad ones.

Perhaps if more of us were really worried about where "our daily bread" was coming from, not our daily hamburgers, pizzas, French fries, steaks, and dessert, but just our bread, as the main thing we have to eat, we might hold a different line of sight toward it. So, until I'm hungry enough to gain a deeper insight, I must treat it as a puzzling story; I can neither visualize clearly as happening nor can I say what it meant to its tellers at the time.

I am not so much lacking faith as just lacking credulity and possibly understanding. Faith is faith in the Christ, in his death and resurrection, in the "new life" he announces, the new situation God has promised to bring in, and in his faithfulness to do so. Faith is not "believing" in this or that prodigy or this or that miracle story.

As already noted, most of the miracle stories show signs of the natural expansion, even exaggeration that comes with being handed down from one storyteller to another.[15]

One thing further must be said. Ever since the development of Protestant Orthodoxy in the late sixteenth and early seventeenth centuries, faith has been tied to "believing the Bible" as being literally inerrant. "Faith in the Bible" became the answer to the Middle Ages' demand for "faith in the church." Both positions took the case backwards. One may hear the gospel from the church or from the Bible, but the faith that responds to the gospel is and has always been faith in God, whose Christ, Jesus was and is, not merely faith in the church or the Bible. Some level of confidence in them may underlie faith, but no formulation regarding

---

15. Straus, in his historically very important but widely criticized 1825 *Life of Jesus*, distinguished "history" in the gospels from "myth," "legend," and what "must be regarded as *the addition of the author*, as purely individual, and designed merely to give clearness, connexion, and climax." Reardon, *Religious Thought*, 124. Useful distinctions, even for one who disagrees strongly with how he used them.

either church or Bible apart from the Christ Himself can be part of the definition of Christian faith.[16]

Faith is an ongoing conversation that should involve one with the church and the Bible, but cannot be reduced to either one.[17] As Luther said, it is Christ Himself, first of all, who is "God's Word"; secondarily, the Bible *as proclaimed and discussed within the church* is God's word. And the church, to be honest, must discuss the Bible in terms of the world's best thought, scientific and otherwise, of its current age. God's Conversation with us goes on and on, and must always be kept up-to-date. The Bible is not just a museum piece.

But Luther said the Bible by itself, simply as a book, might be said to be "God's word" only at a third and still less significant level.[18] So unless a miracle story confronts the thinking and discussing church with the gospel, and in our day most don't discuss it, at least not obviously, then there is no obligation, and probably no motivation, for a Christian to grant them importance. One must grant that they are there, and honor the writers who tell about them, but they ought not become problems for faith, either one way or the other.

At the same time, we have to be careful not to fall victim to claiming too dogmatically that the way our modern world thinks about things is the last word. When a lady asked my father, "Doctor, do you believe in

16. The medieval innovation of "implicit faith," believing whatever it is the church teaches, even if you don't know what that is emphasized "believing in the church," but in a questionable way.

17. "Neither Jesus nor the earliest 'church community' constitutes the font and origin of Christianity, but both together as offer and response.... The primitive church reflects or mirrors, in its New Testament, the Jesus event in its effect on a group of people.... In that sense, as the church's "charter" or foundation document, there can be no substitute for the New Testament's authority.... Despite internal tensions the New Testament ... can be Jesus event in its effect on a group of people.... In that sense, as the church's "charter" or foundation document, there can be no substitute for the New Testament's authority.... Despite internal tensions the New Testament ... can be taken on one hand to be the result of the historical effect of the one Jesus at the source of the somewhat dissonant traditions, and on the other hand to be an expression of an "ecumenical" desire to marshal the original and diverse Christian traditions into a unity ... this ecumenical desire for unification ... is an indispensable element of the interpretative norm." Schillebeeckx, in Schreiter, *Schillebeeckx*, 131, 2.

18. I am tempted to say, "Our Bibles are nothing but carbon deposits on cellulose until they are seriously mulled over and responded to within the community of faith." The gospel was *proclaimed* by live people who risked themselves for it long before it was written down or printed.

divine healing?" his answer was, "I know no other kind." Healing is still a mystery. Every good doctor knows that it is either God who heals or the patient heals herself. Just what else was the most help is often unclear. It may even be the presence of unidentifiable gifts of special people with a "healing touch," rather than what is described as done.

There are too many credible reports of healings by medicinemen, *curanderas*, and people with such a "touch" for us to be pompous about the complete adequacy of our current medical theories—or even our ways of asking the relevant questions. (There may even be reports of exorcisms worth our attention.) We have to rely on the best knowledge we have, with all its limits, just as the gospel writers had to work within the knowledge they had. Neither we, nor they, have all the answers.

But it is inescapable that Jesus gained a great reputation as a healer and exorcist, even his fiercest critics admitted that, and equally inescapable that though he aimed at healing people, he did not aim at encouraging that reputation. And, as already pointed out, he viewed the healings as part of the promise that the reign of evil was on the verge of overthrow. These were not so much medical events as religious, even cosmic, signs.

In short, when we ask, "What really happened?" and seek an analysis of these stories in our modern terms, we're just acknowledging that we can't arrive at a reading we're willing to settle for. As a pragmatist philosopher would put it, our "enquiry arrives at no satisfying stopping point." That often happens when we are asking the wrong question. But if we read them in terms of the question, "What is the author trying to tell us about how Jesus was the promise of God to us?" some of the stories ring true. The ones that don't, don't, and each one of us has to let it go at that.

The gospels announce the promise of "the Kingdom of God," not the revision of our sciences or our common sense. But sometimes our common sense needs to recognize that genuinely new things do break into history, and when they do, they may upset our comfortably established habits of thinking.[19] After all, our culture is just another human culture. It will be replaced in its turn by other ways of thinking. And if we humans can do that, couldn't God?

---

19. That is not to say much of our science won't still be valid. Greek science was replaced along with the general outlines of Greek culture, but much of Aristotle, Euclid and Archimedes still stands, though within a deeply revised (and constantly being revised) context.

Before going on to the questions of belief, and what is required for belief, the question of "spirits" needs attention. In Mark's first account of Jesus speaking in a synagogue (1:21–28), he relates "there was in their synagogue a man with an unclean spirit; and he cried out, "What have you to do with us, Jesus of Nazareth? Have you come to destroy us? I know who you are, the Holy One of God."[20] We would probably call a "man with an unclean spirit" deranged and likely to say anything, so on that ground we could accept the story so far, while at the same time denying it any real significance. But Jesus ordered the "spirit" out of him, "and the unclean spirit, convulsing him and crying with a loud voice, came out of him."

A number of things about this story are interesting. Some years ago there emerged in the field of psychotherapy the theory and procedure of the "primal scream," referring to a climax in treatment wherein deep-seated conflicts that bedeviled the emotionally sick were resolved in a precipitate and painful manner, often accompanied by great rage and frenzied action. (There had to follow some time of "putting things back together," but an orally transmitted dramatic story would be likely to omit that.) A number of exorcism stories present a parallel pattern, so the difficulties in the story are reduced to two: the use of the phrase "unclean spirit" and the question of Jesus' agency in the healing.

It is quite evident that one of Mark's literary devices is to have "spirits" reveal what Jesus' own disciples were very slow to recognize correctly, that Jesus represented God's overthrow of the system of evil powers that oppress humans. Evil spirits could recognize Jesus immediately as their enemy *and hence as the liberator of humans*—two sides of the same thing, and they knew they did not have the power to resist him.

At that time, the language of "spirits" was the only one generally available to describe those distraught by the frightful conditions under which many were forced to live. That we prefer a different language demands only that we examine the grounds for, and the degree of justification for, our preference. In that day, Jesus' power to heal such disorders had to be stated in "spirit" terms—no other language was available.

---

20. "Destroy us," means "free humans from our power." Tertullian, a very early theologian, wrote "the task of demons is the overthrow of man: from the beginning, therefore, spiritual malice was foreseen as the ruin of man." Moore, "Demons and the Battle," 486. One cannot separate the ancient idea of "spirits" from the social experience of conquest, oppression and slavery, giving the need for 'redemption,' one of God's concerns.

Are we trying to say that "evil spirits" exist? Or, that they don't "really" exist? Neither. Do we moderns really know what we are asking about when we speak of "evil spirits"? Ordinarily we let them exist only in our imaginations (though some of us can remember the 1950's when something like evil spirits, we called them "communists," haunted many discussions, just as unidentifiable "terrorists" may today). Since nothing we undertake is directed toward coping with evil spirits, any ideas we might have about them have no practical function. Those who apparently can't help but be evil are simply called "psychopathic personalities," or, more popularly, "bad seed."

But the ancients knew what they were talking about: people who had lost their freedom, their ability to function normally, people who were way off base in the "things of the spirit." Such might cry out truths that others did not acknowledge as Freud pointed out, the paranoid person may sense deep antagonisms in people who don't themselves recognize they have them.

Many an "uncivilized tribe" recognizes "shamans" as in touch with things the rest of us miss. We simply don't have room in our ways of talking to deal with such things. So whether they "exist" or not is a question we don't know how to formulate effectively. To say they "don't exist" may be dismissing parts of actual human experience we don't want to deal with, because we don't know how we would.

Another way of saying the same thing is to notice that, since Newton, we only consider "things" to "exist" if they "occupy space and have mass" (or possess measurable energy). Things like that can be measured. We also assume that only such "things" can exist (except in something like mathematics: "How many prime numbers 'exist' between 10 and 20?" but numbers are only "countables." They don't have any other characteristics).

The tests we use to tell whether a thing "exists" wouldn't be relevant to "evil spirits," anyway. As a youth I read of the researcher who weighed bodies of dying patients to determine whether there was any measurable loss of weight at death. He found none, and announced that he had *proven* "there is no such thing as a soul." The counterclaim came quickly: he had instead *proved* that souls have no weight! Neither claim made any scientific sense, of course. All he had shown was that his instruments registered no measurable loss of weight at death. Anything beyond that isn't science, but theology or metaphysics, even if it might be true.

The point is that the records of Jesus' doings are the reports of his near contemporaries, couched in their ways of speaking. Any translation into modern terms is a quirky business, perhaps an arrogant one. Rather than worry about "What happened?" it is more important to ask, "What are the tellers of these stories trying to tell us about Jesus?" *That* is what really confronts us.

The stories of exorcisms tell of the authority "the Son of man" exercised as announcing that we humans would be rid of imprisoning situations we could not save ourselves from. This would happen at the arrival of a new state of affairs, a "Kingdom" in which we humans would not be so imprisoned.[21] They confront us with the impression he gave as the bringer of freedom. That becomes significant only in terms of the kinds of bondage we suffer from and the kinds of freedom we need if we are to be fully human. And that's where he is important.

If you gathered from this that I hold that problems about miracles and spirits are of so little importance they ought not to distract us from the more immediately relevant questions, you are right. But Hume also was right: miracle *stories* can't be used to *prove* anything. He should have recognized, however, that if they yield insight, if they jolt life creatively, they are not to be despised.

If a "miracle" were done before our eyes, we would be confronted with a challenge as to what happened and who it was that did it, and how? But an ancient story about some "miracle" comes to us as a *story*, a report, not the event itself. Our situation is quite different from eyewitness reports that were based on what they themselves were confounded by. Their report was handed to others who were not witnesses. So we may gather only the general impression such events made on those who were present at the time, without giving full credence to the reports as they finally get to us.[22] Their believing was a function of their life-experience. Our "believing" must be in terms of ours. Otherwise it isn't real believing, it is only the liveliness of our imaginations.

21. This may sound like Marx, but his Jewish background (though he was legally a "Christian") had deep roots in the same biblical prophets as did Jesus.

22. As already suggested, *kinds* of miracle stories may be usefully separated: some involve a saying by Jesus which may suggest a teaching, some involve an attitude or act on his part that may be revealing *to us*, and some may be just stories told by people who liked to gossip about prodigies. We can ask why the gospel writers used the particular stories they did. We don't know how many or what sorts of "miracles" they *critically omitted* from their accounts, as Luke did the second feeding of a crowd.

So having doubts about miracle *stories* is just being reasonable. Responding to the challenge and invitation of a gospel is not a problem of reason. It is much more a matter of openness of perception, noticing the world as the gospel calls it to our attention, catching glimpses of the saving will of God in history.

To summarize: We have no way to tell whether miracles have or have not occurred in the past. Science doesn't accept them, but science disciplines itself by setting limits to itself. Further, no belief can be *argued for* by a claim of miracles, but argument isn't the only reasonable basis for beliefs, since argument has to start with already held beliefs.

The miracle stories in the Bible show themselves to be of several sorts, handed down by different lines of tradition, and hence some are more worthy of attention than others. Belief itself must be based on something more than just the miracle stories themselves. Therefore, no Christian's faith should be based on nothing but a miracle story. And yet, though a Christian need not believe such of the stories as he finds reasonable grounds to reject, stories that illustrate or illuminate the faith are well worth mulling over.

However, there is one unique miracle that makes a claim on us today: the central event of the gospel story, the Resurrection. Its story was not to be told as a story, but to be proclaimed as world-shaking news, even today. Whatever "actually happened," when proclaimed, it has always come as a baffling mystery, and when truly accepted, as the ground for "a new creation" and great rejoicing, as millions testify not only every Easter, but every Sunday, and many every day.

Since there is no description of the actual happening, no ordinary "miracle story," whatever occurred needs some sort of unique elucidation, some way of connecting it to its present impact, and to our own experience. But before discussing those things directly, three thorny problems demand our attention: What did Jesus expect? What did he think he was doing? Why was he killed, and why did he allow it?

13

Jesus' Expectations, Trial, and Death

> A fundamental difficulty in every treatment of the Gospels, both
> as to their form and content, lies in the fact that the assumption
> behind our Gospels is the gospel of Jesus Christ, which in turn
> has its origin and its purpose in the person of Jesus.
>
> —Harald Riesenfeld[1]

JESUS DIED. HIS EXECUTIONERS were apparently successful, but their
expectations were mocked by what eventually occurred. Did that fulfill
Jesus' expectations? That raises four further questions: What did he expect? What did his crucifiers expect? Did they achieve what they sought?
Did he? Each of these has received more than one answer. In this chapter
we face the first three, in later chapters the fourth.

In chapter 13 of Mark there appears what has been called "the little
apocalypse," presented as Jesus' teaching about "the end of the world" in
response to four disciples' asking what signs would precede it. Luke and
Matthew present it in different and somewhat longer versions.[2] Though
these may contain some authentic sayings of Jesus, there are good reasons
for holding that none of the three discourses can safely be ascribed to
Jesus as they stand. I am quite willing to grant to Jesus Mark 13:32–37,
which constitutes an appropriate answer to the disciples' question in 13:4,
and perhaps verse 5. What lies between verses 5 and 31 seems quite inconsistent with what follows, but does represent a rather unified presentation
of some first-century Christians' apocalyptic ideas.

The three versions of this "little apocalypse" and their relationships
to one another present intractable problems. All we can say here is that

---

1. Riesenfeld, *The Gospel Tradition*, 52.

2. Mark 13:3–37; Matt 24:3—25:46; Luke 21:7–36 (see also 17:22–37).

Luke's version cannot be dated before 70, with Matthew's undoubtedly later, while Mark's seems to be earlier. Yet however strange those passages seem to us, they can hardly be very foreign to the attitudes and expectations held quite generally by Jesus' disciples. Some parts may even reflect beliefs of Jesus Himself.

In fact, Jesus probably said things about the coming "Kingdom" that could not be taken as anything but apocalyptic. If he did not, it is difficult to account for a number of things besides these parts of the gospels, such as his association with the Baptist and Paul's anticipations.

Jesus' more immediate earthly expectations, however, take first place. Mark reports Jesus speaking of the "Son of man's" death at least three times during his ministry, all of them after Peter's statement that Jesus was the Messiah. In 8:31, Mark says Jesus "began to teach them that the Son of man must suffer . . . and be killed, and in three days rise again." In 9:31 we find him teaching his disciples that "The Son of man will be delivered into the hands of men, and they will kill him; and . . . after three days he will rise again." In 10:33–34 Jesus says, "we are going up to Jerusalem, and the Son of man will be delivered to the chief priests, and they will . . . kill him; and after three days he will rise."

Three different ways of reading these reports are widespread. First, they are accurate reports of what Jesus actually said. Second, Jesus never said anything like that; all such reports are the church reading later ideas back into earlier history. And third, Jesus may not have said such things exactly as reported; they may have been somewhat modified, even added to, in being passed down (such as changing some vaguer assurance of God's vindication into "after three days rising").

I find myself embracing the third option for several reasons. First, in Mark, Jesus never says "I will be killed and rise again," but "the Son of man" will. In Mark he consistently treats "Son of man" as if it means someone else, or else a group, not just as a substitute for "I." Second, in Mark 10:32 he says, "*We* are going to Jerusalem, and "the Son of man" will be killed, and ten verses later asks James and John if *they* are ready to go with him through what is ahead. Third, He told *anyone* who would come after him to "take up his cross," which meant to face being condemned to servile death as an enemy of the powers of this world, Daniel's "beast." It appears that Jesus expected not only Himself, but also some of His loyal followers, to be put to death as part of a group "Son of man." After all,

Daniel equated "one like a son of man" to "the saints of the Most High," over whom "the beast" prevailed.

But that still leaves it quite likely that the "*after three days he* (the Son of man, not "I") *will rise*" (rather than "will be raised") were additions by the church tradition, to bring the statements in line with the church's job of proclaiming the Resurrection. Jesus very clearly believed God would vindicate Him, but apparently had no real idea just how. That was hidden with the Father, as His answer in Mark 10:40 to the two overambitious disciples shows. He said of their request for special places in the kingdom, it "is not mine to grant." He had no commitment to Himself, only to The Kingdom.

Whether Jesus expected drastic divine interventions in history has been much discussed. The Gospels certainly reflect such ideas—impending judgment, the need to be loyal under persecution—and many have held that they were added to His story later by followers who brought their ideas with them. Such ideas were certainly common in Israelite religion at the time. The number of "apocalypses" surviving into the present suggests that there were many more that have disappeared. So I'm not convinced that nothing of the sort goes back to Jesus Himself.

To understand Jesus as an apocalyptic thinker, of a sort, is quite reasonable.[3] Being immersed in His cultural situation, full of oppression under the invincible power of Rome, believing that the only possible rescue would be the one God had promised through the prophets, how could He not be. To free Him from His background is to deny His humanity. But what kind of apocalyptist was He, exactly? Just which of his sayings or actions are we to understand as pointing to some wind-up of history?

Jesus speaks of His fate as "fulfilling the Scriptures," so His theory of the future may have followed closely some writing that has disappeared, one we know nothing about (since the limits of "Scripture" had not yet been defined). To make anything out of that would be futile, since it could only give us back whatever we ourselves put into it, dug out of the records we already have. So we are reduced to gleaning what we can from whatever parts of those records we are able to interpret and are willing to trust.

3. Allison puts it very strongly: "Jesus, the millenarian herald of judgment and salvation, says the only things worth saying, for his dream is the only one worth dreaming . . . If there is no good God to calm this sea of troubles, to raise the dead, and to give good news to the poor, then . . . [history] is indeed a tale told by an idiot, signifying nothing." *Jesus of Nazareth*, 218.

My wrestling with the problem has been molded by the recognition of three things: One is Jesus' strange use of the title "Son of Man"; a second, the apparent differences between its use in Mark and its appearances in Luke, Matthew, and John. The third is its nearly complete absence from every non-gospel New Testament writing.[4] These complement the inescapable sense of coming judgment, generally preceded by persecution or even death, which is found not only in the Gospels that tell of Him, but also in the writings of His followers from Paul through the author of Revelation.

My (fictional) story of Jesus' earlier life emphasized the impression the already-mentioned figure found in Daniel 7 made on him. Against the "Son of man" the "fourth beast," a conquering "kingdom" (Dan 7:7, 23), would "make war," and would "prevail over" them (Dan 7:21), but only until "the Ancient of Days" intervened in "judgment" on their behalf, and gave them "the kingdom" (Dan 7:22) which would replace all previous kingdoms (Dan 7:27).

I find this interpretation of Jesus to illuminate some of the puzzling phrases in "The Lord's Prayer," which, according to Luke, Jesus did not formulate for everyone, but specifically for his immediate disciples. Thus, "Hallowed be thy name, Thy will be done" reflects God's eventual apocalyptic triumph.[5] "Lead us not into the time of testing" (Luke 11:2–4), anticipates the Beast "prevailing against the Holy Ones of the Most High" (Dan 7:21), and "deliver us from the Evil One" their final vindication (Dan 7:21–22).

"Son of Man" does *not* mean "Messiah." Horsley and Hanson say, "In pre-Christian times there was no general expectation of 'The Messiah' . . . [But] At certain levels of Jewish society, there was indeed some anticipation of a kingly agent inspired by God to bring deliverance to the people."[6] I believe Mark shows Jesus as *rejecting* the title for Himself, especially as "son of David." Instead, He identified Himself with His "true Israel,"

---

4. Except Acts 7:56 and possibly Rev 1:13.

5. Scholars agree it's to be read, "Hallow your name," expressing the expectation of God's "latter day" act of bringing all nations to obedience and worship. (Isa 2:2–3; Micah 4:1–2).

6. Horsley and Hanson, *Bandits, Prophets and Messiahs*, 90–91.

as "Son of Man."[7] As such, however, He had at baptism been "anointed" ("Messiah" means "anointed one," as does "Christ").

The story of three temptations that appears in Luke and Matthew seems to show Jesus' refusal of the role of Davidic Messiah, the "conquering Lion of Judah." In it He refuses three of the roles of a son-of-David Messiah: ending hunger, miraculous deeds, and ruling the world.

Jesus, of course, did not know what is now widely recognized: that what Daniel refers to are events that had happened nearly two hundred years before His time. Many Christians since then have found Daniel irresistibly inviting them to read it as predicting their own fearful expectations, so it should not be at all surprising to find folk doing that in the first century.[8]

Jesus was not a theoretical thinker, speaking abstractions in crisp concepts. He thought in images, historical images, images of intentions and consequences, images of deeply human concerns.

Jesus has been presented as believing He should continue the Baptist's work of calling all of Israel to repent—to become the true Israel—in the face of the coming earth-shaking events of persecution and the overthrow of evil. But, unlike the Baptist, who seems to have organized only a body of personal followers dedicated to repentance, Jesus felt called to be the organizer of the group of "the true Israel," the "saints of the Most High," "the Son of Man." He would appoint "twelve" to represent these "saints of the Most High," probably mirroring the "twelve tribes of Israel" (each named after a biblical individual and referred to as a tribe, by his name). These would fulfill the prophecy made to Abraham that through Israel, his descendants, all peoples will bless themselves.

7. Nowhere do I use the word "Messiah" of Jesus. On the basis of his resurrection Jesus became *for Christians* the "anointed one," ("Christ") but by Mark's time this no longer meant, especially for the Greek Christians, any traditional "Son of David" Messiah (except for some Jewish-oriented ones, like Matthew). Rather, it indicated one who has been elevated to a certain significant mission, as Paul suggests in Romans 1:4. There, Jesus was "appointed" or "designated" Son of God—a close parallel to being "anointed." "Jesus Christ" probably meant "the anointed Jesus" until usage turned it into just another name for him. Anointing, besides celebrating the crowning of kings and the ordaining of prophets in Israel, was a widespread mode of formally "appointing" in Hellenistic society.

8. Shortly before Pearl Harbor I heard a pastor find in the eleventh chapter of Daniel a detailed history of World War II in North Africa to date! He implied it would lead to the end of the age. It didn't.

The opposition Jesus faced came early from a small minority, the Pharisees, who claimed religious superiority and who wanted to recover the political power they had once briefly held. But the final threat came from the High Priest and the "elders," the Sanhedrin, who feared any disturbance of the existing power structures of the society.

They, with the Romans, clearly constituted for Jesus the "Beast," representing Satan's power over the world. For them, He was subversive of piety, culture, and political order. He had good reason to expect them to "make war" against Him, and they did. His confidence in God's faithfulness expected divine intervention to follow.

Mark 13 quotes Jesus as speaking of the Son of Man "Coming in the clouds."[9] That echoes Daniel 7:13. But there the "coming" is before the throne of God, not a trip from heaven to earth. There are a number of reasons for doubting that Jesus thought of Himself as some sort of apocalyptic "conqueror." He asked, "How can Satan cast out Satan?" with a parable about *binding* evil, ending its power, not destroying it.

His was not a vengeful "apocalypticism" in the usual sense. His expectation was rather that when God judged the earth (which He thought would be soon), the "Son of Man" would be signally honored by God with authority over all nations—a "Son of Man" made up of "those for whom it has been prepared" (Mark 10:40), prepared not by Jesus, but by the Father.

Even by the time the earlier books of the New Testament, such as Philippians, were written,[10] Christians had identified the glorified "Son of Man" as Jesus alone, since only He, not His followers, had been crucified and resurrected. As Mark remarks, they "forsook him and fled" (Mark 14:50). Jesus, knowing Himself called to be both a leader and a victim, showed remarkable humility. He didn't glorify Himself as being called to

9. In a part of chapter 13 that cannot be reasonably ascribed to Jesus. Though Mark 14:62 is presented as a genuine Jesus quote, 14:63 raises questions about that conversation, as reported.

10. See Philippians 2:10–11. "Jesus Christ is Lord" doesn't necessarily mean, "Jesus Christ is God," but "Jesus Christ is Ruler." The confusion between "Lord" and "God" goes back to the use of Greek *Kyrios* as the translation of more than one Hebrew word. (All of Paul's writings were earlier than the rest of the New Testament.)

be a unique triumphal figure,[11] but as a prophet[12] calling the true Israel together to be "given the Kingdom" with him, as "the saints of the Most High," however the Father might bring that about.

He did indeed end up alone, but only because the rest of His "Son of Man," His "saints of the Most High," His "true Israel," weren't true enough. They deserted him.

So I can't believe this "coming of the Son of Man in the clouds" idea goes back to Jesus' *teachings*.[13] Many deny all of it, attributing it to the apocalypticism of the members of the infant church. But we don't have any direct evidence of that, either. It seems more likely that Jesus did talk about a "Son of Man" coming in judgment, but left it open whether that would be the same "Son of Man" He identified with His disciples. Luke and Matthew do quote Him as saying that the Twelve would "sit on twelve thrones judging the tribes of Israel," which, if authentic, would suggest He expected them to be part of "the Son's" ultimate glory. Yet both those Gospels represent later stages of the tradition.[14] Further reasons for so reading "the Son of Man" can be found in Appendix B.[15]

That Jesus' views were not clearly understood by his followers— perhaps they didn't want to do so—is shown in the way that the title "Son of Man," though used in Mark in a way quite harmonious with my inter- pretation, loses clarity progressively in the later Gospels, and disappears entirely in the rest of the New Testament (except, as we said, in Acts 7:56 and perhaps Rev 1:13).

So we go on to the question as to what actually happened. On it there is significant agreement: Jesus ate the Passover meal with his dis- ciples (in John, dinner the evening before Passover[16]), and instituted a

11. All four accounts of the "Triumphal entry" suggest it was not the disciples, but the surrounding crowd who declared Jesus to be "Son of David." John 12:12–14 is most clear on this point, though Mark 11:8–10 certainly allows it.

12. Even though a prophet, he was too humble to have made the claim in Mark 13:31.

13. But Allison, *Jesus*, 119, argues for it doing so.

14. The "twelve thrones" saying is in "Q" material, so it may be later tradition than Mark.

15. A fine review of evidence and arguments about the phrase "the Son of man" can be found in Dunn, *Christology*, ch. 3, but discussion of its possible collective meaning is not relevant to his aims.

16. Rabbi Klausner is said to report a later Talmudic writing that says, "On the eve of the Passover Jesus of Nazareth was hung" (reported in Goguel, *Jesus and the Origins of Christianity*, 72). This could have been based on Christian reports.

bread-and-wine ritual "of the new covenant" (in John, washed their feet) by which he was to be remembered. This rite of "communion" has occasioned much discussion over the years, even violent disagreement and bitter antagonisms. It compresses so much richness into such simplicity, it is so central to the practice of the faith, but so full of profound overtones, that it permits no simple clarification or analysis.

Based on the Jewish ritual use of bread and wine, acknowledging our complete dependence both on nature and God's loving provision for us, and "showing forth" Jesus' faithful "obedience unto death," and God's acceptance and steadfast encouragement of us on that basis, it is better sung about and enacted than argued over. It is the church most deeply being the church, which is understood by us only as we, too, are deeply involved in being the church. Without that it is mumbo jumbo, or, historically, "hocus pocus."[17]

Whether Jesus thought thus, intended so, or anticipated all of the above, we have no way of knowing. But that is the way the "conversation" that is Christian history has proceeded. And there is no real alternative to that conversation. Christians are Christians because "communion" together as the church, "showing forth the Lord's death 'til he come," is not only a real plumbing of the depths of who we are, but a bond to all other Christians everywhere—ancient, modern, and still to come. Without it the church is not the church.

Attempts to adjust it to some philosophical theory, by mysterious "transubstantiation" or "consubstantiation," or Philistine "memorialization," may give us ways to talk more easily about it, but they yield no "explanation" that dissolves its mystery.[18] Without that mystery it is "only an empty ritual," which means a ritual that is not a real ritual at all, since it has no living content. It is then no part of the conversation, of which we are told "there was a livingness in it" which was the enlightening of life.

---

17. "Hocus-pocus" derives from the Vulgate *hoc est corpus meum*, "this is my body," which occurs in all four narratives of the Lord's Supper (in Mark, Luke, Matthew, and 1 Corinthians).

18. It does help bring about social solidarity, but sociology can only explain what sociologists can observe, so sacraments are classed with church dinners, camps and sports teams. Christians who sense the depths don't experience them as the same sort of thing at all. And Freud has led us to associate "ritual" with compulsive behaviors. Susanne Langer's insights in her *Philosophy in a New Key* are helpful here, though I don't find them to lead me to where she ends up.

"Mystery" is frustrating to me, as to any philosopher. But mysteries are mysteries. To claim we can plumb all of them is to be too boastful of our humanity, just as ceasing attempts to understand them is a surrender of confidence in ourselves, a surrender not to be made lightly, not until our struggles have sufficiently demonstrated our real insufficiency.

Jerusalem could not put up the huge crowds of pilgrims for Passover, so many slept outside the city. Jesus and His disciples apparently slept (with many others?) in the garden of Gethsemane, so Judas knew where He would be. As Jesus took His disciples there, He warned them that He foresaw them failing to follow Him through all that was coming. Once there, He prayed not to have to go through what He faced. (John has Him pray for His disciples before going to the garden; Jesus does not pray for Himself in John.)[19]

Those who discount this story of Jesus' intense prayer in Gethsemane with the claim that "the disciples couldn't have heard what Jesus was praying" make far too much of Luke's change of Mark's "a short distance" to "a stone's throw," and assume that Jesus prayed silently. They also ignore his reported intensely disturbed condition. It was a night the disciples, especially Peter, James, and John, would certainly have remembered and told about, no matter how sleepy they were. And their account would have been long remembered and deeply cherished.

Just why Judas sold Jesus out and led the posse to Him is probably unsolvable. As late as they wrote, Luke's "Satan entered into Judas" (Luke 22:3) and John's "the devil had already put it into his heart" (John 13:2) to love money show the tradition's lack of any useful rational explanation. All four Gospels indicate Jesus knew what Judas was doing.[20] This has led to speculations like that in *The Gospel of Judas* or Schonfield's *The Passover Plot*. Both suggest that Jesus directed Judas to "turn him over" and the meaning of the verb is usually translated "betray," but no account of Judas' motive or of when or how Jesus knew of his plan has been very convincing.

---

19. Unless one takes John 17:5 to be praying for himself. I doubt John meant it that way.

20. The recently discovered fragment of the *Gospel of Judas* shows that such a theory was extant among some Gnostics as early as the third century. That hardly constitutes historical validation, since Gnostic groups were very creative in their interpretations of many items in the tradition.

The theory that Judas was disgruntled at Jesus' not stirring up revolt as he supposed the Messiah was to do is rather lame. More intriguing is the idea that he understood Jesus' expectation to die in Jerusalem better than any of the other disciples, but assumed God's vindication would interrupt the execution. So he sought, on his own, to expedite it. Or Jesus may have sent him, feeling called to make sure He would be killed during Passover. No theory, nor the standard claim (based on John) that Judas was avaricious, seems satisfactory. (If he hadn't asked for money, wouldn't the High Priest have been suspicious?)

In any case, he could not bear the consequence. And the church had to blame him, even though all the other disciples ran away.

There are three things that are hard to escape. First, Jesus' knew He would die; that was God's will as He found it in "the Scriptures."[21] Second, His Jewish sense of God acting in dramatic historical ways like the Israelites' escape from Egypt made Passover the most appropriate time for His death. Finally, Jesus knew Judas would "turn him in" to the authorities (the usual translation "betray" is possible, but "hand over" is a more usual meaning of the word, and describes what happened, without moralizing).

To go back to Mark's account: Jesus is arrested there in the garden by a group guided by His disciple Judas, given a hearing before a hasty gathering of the council—hardly a legal trial—condemned, and turned over to Pilate for a Roman crucifixion. It seems over suspicious to claim that the accounts are based on no real evidence, but certainly naive to think they represent anything like an exact transcript of the proceedings. The expansions in Matthew and Luke of Mark's account are obvious and suspect, and hardly represent any firm additional evidence.

---

21. The Greek word *apechei* in Jesus' final speech in the garden (Mark 14:41) gives translators difficulty. It is often translated, following Jerome, as "It is enough," which hardly fits the context. On the basis of one authenticated meaning, "The deal is done," I find the suggestion neither outrageous nor easily dismissed, that Jesus either sent Judas to "turn him in" or set him up to do so, though one needs much better evidence to embrace it. If Jesus knew he was doing God's will by coming to Jerusalem to die at the hands of the Beast—the temple powers, the Romans and society's rich leaders—it would have been quite in the spirit of the Old Testament prophets to have made sure that what he believed the Scriptures predicted would occur, preferably at Passover. He was not at all just an ordinary prudent citizen. Judas would still have been overwhelmed by what actually happened. Yet to believe Jesus set himself or Judas up flies in the face of his usual selflessness. Much more evidence than we have is required. There simply isn't any satisfactory answer attainable on what we are given.

Many have doubted the report of the "trial," on the basis of Mark's account "they all forsook him and fled." But how far did they flee before they realized that the posse was after Jesus, and how long until they realized that they had gained some of the safety of anonymity?[22] Next comes the story of Peter following Jesus "at a distance" right into "the courtyard of the high priest." He gained entry, John reports, because "another disciple" who was "known to the high priest" got him admitted. That indicates two who weren't removed from the goings-on, two eye witnesses in the story itself, and there may have been more. That supports belief in the narrative.

Again, Mark's account of the trial comes off best. Matthew adds typical Matthean expansions, Luke rewrites the whole story to fit his aims, and John uses it for further theological and political affirmations. Mark also had intentions beyond a mere recital of events, but his earlier date gives less time for changes in traditional reports.

Two things seem clear: there were two interrogations, one by the high priest and one by Pilate (Luke's story about Herod is widely doubted, for good reasons), and Jesus made no effort to clear Himself. The high priest may have asked Jesus if he was "Messiah," since Mark reports Jesus was rumored to be the Messiah. There would have been no Jewish crime had He said, "Yes," though perhaps a Roman crime. However, I find I cannot believe Jesus was asked, "Are you the Christ, the Son of the Blessed One?"[23] That too obviously exhibits Mark's purpose in writing. But Jesus may have said, "You will see the Son of Man coming in the clouds of heaven," without clearly claiming to be that Son of Man yet or all by Himself.

22. The story in Mark 14:51–52 of the young hanger-on who ran away naked is tantalizing. That such an event was used in bawdy Greek comedies simply shows it was something that could really have happened. The other gospels omit it, so it wasn't deemed to be important tradition. It may indicate some eyewitness report (from Peter?), but is of no use in identifying Mark himself (or "the beloved disciple"!).

23. More probably what the high priest asked, sarcastically, was "*You* are the Messiah?" referring to the lone, beaten, low-ranking Galilean before him, abandoned by all his supporters. How could such a one even claim to be the conquering Messiah? That John 20:30 can be read as "that the Christ is *Jesus*" rather than "Jesus is the *Christ*" may indicate that, to Jewish audiences at least (though perhaps not to Gentile "God-fearers"), the difficult question was "We know what Messiah will be, but how can this *Jesus* be such?" (Klinghoffer, in *Why the Jews Rejected Jesus*, this as a major element in their rejection of Jesus.) Second Corinthians 5:16 with Romans 1:3–4, suggests that the switch from rejecting "Jesus is the *Christ*" to accepting "the Christ is *Jesus* (even though crucified)" was the overwhelming content of Paul's "conversion." See Appendix E.

He did expect God's final judgment and the vindication of His calling to be very near, otherwise He wouldn't have quoted Psalm 22: "Why have you forsaken me?"

The high-priestly court had already decided He was to be killed; they didn't really need evidence. One must remember that the high priest had become a political appointee, a collaborator with the Romans, distrusted and even considered illegitimate by many pious Jews (such as the Dead Sea Scrolls people). Mark, however, felt the affirmation appropriate to round out his Gospel, as indeed it does.

So we have to face the other half of the question: "Why did Jesus die?" in the form, "Why did the authorities kill him?" The Gospels tell of several charges against him. As early as his third chapter (probably far too early) Mark tells us that "the Pharisees" and "the Herodians," who were probably wealthy aristocrats that backed Herod's policies, discussed "How to destroy him."

At His trial in chapter 15, witnesses accused him of saying, "I will destroy this temple"; later the high priest accused him of blasphemy. Then He was taken to Pilate, who acknowledged that "many charges" were alleged against Him, but was interested only in whether Jesus claimed to be "King of the Jews," the charge posted over His cross. Matthew simply repeats what Mark reports.

Later Christian piety pictured Jesus' accusers as evil—he was "to wicked men betrayed." It is probably sensible to admit that any self-respecting government would have gotten rid of Jesus (ours would have found subtler ways than crucifixion). As was later said of Paul, He "turned the world upside down," subverting the established order of the "worthy" versus the "unworthy," of "keeping *them* down." The wickedness of His opponents was simply the normal wickedness that any respectable society demands of "law 'n' order" authorities.

As for Pilate, he would hardly have crucified Jesus except as a threat to Roman dominance, or at least as a possible mob-violence threat to civil order. John's report that Jesus was branded as "a king [who] sets himself against Caesar" is believable, as representing popular gossip of Him as "Son of David." So is Pilate's sarcastic sign, "Jesus of Nazareth, King of the Jews." There is no evidence Pilate tried to identify any of Jesus' followers, or that the two "thieves" crucified with Jesus were identified with Him in any way in Pilate's mind.

Except for an unbelievable appearance before Herod, Luke adds nothing to the Jewish trial, but says that the charge before Pilate was that He was "perverting our nation, and forbidding us to give tribute to Caesar, saying that he himself is Christ a King" (Luke 25:2,5). Further, "He stirs up the people." These were charges any Gentile would understand. But Luke, anxious to blame the Jews to escape suggesting that it was the Romans who crucified Jesus, insists Pilate wanted to free Him.

Matthew, going even further, has the people shout, "His death be on us, and on our children." He, like many Christians of his generation, saw the destruction of two generations of Jews in the downfall of Jerusalem in 70 as their punishment for Jesus' death. Later generations of Christians have unfairly—and tragically—interpreted "our children" to mean all subsequent Jewish generations, to the shame of the whole church.

All four evangelists report that the inscription above His cross, telling of His crime, read "The king of the Jews." Since later Christian writings don't refer to Jesus thus, it cannot be doubted that that was indeed the charge upon which he was crucified, adding further evidence of considerable historical reliability in parts of our records of His death.

Were the reasons He was crucified political or religious? To us moderns who "separate" religion and politics that seems a relevant question. Actually, it is not. Consider the following reference to the temple, from a discussion of the Hebrew prophets:

> The sacrificial cult was endowed with supreme "political" significance. It was the chief requirement for the security of the land and may be regarded as analogous to the cult of military defense in our own day. Both have their roots in the concern for security.[24]

The charges about the temple,[25] about taxes and Caesar, and about "stirring up the people," besides being threats to "national security," were also near blasphemy.

Jesus' recognition that God, in Jonah, saved the repentant Nineveh without any participation in temple rituals on its part, and His own insistence that the temple should be "a place of prayer for all peoples," so

24. Heschel, *The Prophets*, 196n4.

25. Neusner writes, "The most certain testimony of all to the enduring covenant was the Temple, which stood as the nexus between Jew and God. Its services bore witness to Israel's enduring loyalty to the covenant and the commandments of Sinai. They saw Jerusalem with the eye of faith, and that vision transformed the city." *Judaism in the Beginning of Christianity*, 18.

that the "court of the Gentiles" was not to be made a commercial area, undercut the legitimacy of the functioning temple. He was, thus, clearly subversive; He "turned the world upside down." By all earthly standards, He clearly deserved death. (But then, every government would feel more secure if God and all His genuine prophets were dead. It could then feel even more confident in its claims to be above moral and spiritual criticism by the people.) Unions of church and state have been engineered chiefly by the state, not the church, which has often, like Jesus, criticized the state.

Jesus certainly did not believe in the separation of church and state. He saw that both were fated to suffer together under God's just judgment.

As Jesus is dying, He cries, "My God, why have you forsaken me?" This is a saying that demands an interpretation, and has received a variety of them. Six other "words from the cross" were added in the later Gospels. Of these, only the three in John merit any consideration as historical, and there are good grounds for doubting every one. Though the three in Luke are beautiful, and tell us a great deal about Luke, they are so inconsistent with Mark, and so typical of Luke, that they engender huge doubt.[26]

In every account, however, Jesus dies. He was dead, dead, dead. He died not merely as a criminal, executed in the manner reserved for the very worst criminals. Even worse, those of the highest religion in the world, the Jews, following their Torah, "the Wisdom of God for which the world was created," knew him to be "accursed." Not merely condemned as subversive by political and ecclesiastical powers, but branded as vile by God Himself.

His crucifiers were, however, afraid to crucify him "on the feast day," for fear of "a riot among the people." Luckily, Pilate had already ordered two "bandits" crucified—a crucifixion that would not attract pious pilgrims but would draw the local low-life crowd that found executions entertaining. So Jesus was slipped in with those two "evildoers."

One can imagine an exchange like the following:

"Another crucifixion? Who this time?"

"A couple of terrorists—and some other guy not worth watching. He just hung there, hollered twice, and died. But the terrorists

---

26. In a paper read at the 2000 meeting of the SW Commission on Religious Studies, Daniel Wallace argued it was possible to identify two of John's "last words" as that author's version of (1) The one in Mark-Matthew and (2) The final one in Luke. One awaits further work along that line.

were a good show, cursing and yelling, and refusing to die. The crowd loved it!"[27]

Christians, of course, told the story as if Jesus had been the center of interest. To Mark, as to us, He certainly was. Whether to the crowd as a whole, we cannot say. Such usually made fun of the victim, so that they didn't need any of the Gospel's reported encouragement by the priests (who probably didn't attend).

One young Pharisee rabbinical student, Paul,[28] whom, I believe, had been warmly interested in the possibility that Jesus might be the Messiah, the "Son of David," was jolted to realize that couldn't possibly be so. The Messiah was supposed finally to cleanse the temple and establish Torah, but God, through Torah, in its embodiment in God's own people, had labeled Jesus utterly evil and rejected Him in the most awful way possible!

Though later "converted," Paul never got over the shock of Jesus being "cursed by God" by being crucified. His later theology shows this.[29]

Many since have considered Jesus primarily as a moralist. This may have been due to over emphasis on Matthew's account, based in part on the church's sense of mission among peoples who were seen as needing moral instruction to go with the Gospel. Careful reading, however, shows that Jesus' moralizing was always in the context of his apocalyptic expectations of judgment day. Such expectations have continued, in various guises, all through the Church's history, though too often confused with the same sort of cultural or political ambitions or hopes as killed Jesus.

For this reason, Jesus' "moral philosophy" will not be summarized. Anyone can do that for himself simply by reading the gospels—as, for instance, Thomas Jefferson or Gandhi did. His moral significance derives not so much from ethical dicta, but from what He was and did, His exhibiting God's humanity, presented in a historic human. That is what has been a tremendous moral force for many.

---

27. Marcus' recent article in JBL, "Crucifixion as Parodic Exaltation," sheds light on the humiliation of Jesus by the crucifying soldiers and many in the crowd. Those at the bottom of society, feeling oppressed by the ruling culture, might have rejoiced in the rebellion of the victims, as well as their suffering.

28. Luke, in Acts, has Paul say he was a pupil of Gamaliel. There are reasons to believe this a mistake. It certainly helped Luke's story. Possibly Luke knew the name of no other noted rabbi.

29. I extend this discussion of Paul in Appendix E.

Since His burial is later discussed under "Resurrection," this chapter closes with a summary.

Jesus' aim, despite His popular fame as a healer and miracle worker, was at first to be a herald of God's Kingdom soon to come. This developed during His active ministry into being founder of a preparatory group of the "true Israel," and educating them in what that meant. Anticipating the tragic element in the coming of the Kingdom followed: that "the Beast," the structures of power in the world, would "make war upon the Saints of the Most High" and would "prevail against them." This meant that the "Son of Man," the new Israel, must be willing to go to Jerusalem and die, confident that God would vindicate him (or them) in God's own way. The "Beast" saw to it that his expectations were fulfilled. What would follow was up to God.

Have I been saying that Jesus was so infatuated with Daniel's strange vision that He had lost touch with reality? That we should write Him off as a dreamer of no relevance to the modern or any other world? Not at all, because in that vision's terms He faced, as few others have, the deep reality of human existence: that human life creates institutions of power, which demean, suppress and exploit the weak, and lie to themselves to justify their doing so. He saw that the cure was not in countervailing power, he asked "How can Satan cast out Satan?" but lay with those few who become willing and capable of being "servants of all," and of spending their lives as a "ransom for the many."[30] True democracy, in fact, is not Libertarianism, but a way of enabling people to be "servants of all."

"Freedom of speech" and "freedom of the press" imply that each person listens to every other, who just because he too is a person, needs to be listened to, and as a "servant" is attentive.

We moderns would prefer to talk about such things in sociological or political abstractions. Jesus was a dramatic thinker, not a philosopher or social scientist. He was more a poet than an analyst, but most of all one who knew he was called to do what the world needed. He must be understood as such.

Poet Lowell put the matter forcefully:

Though the cause of evil prosper, yet 'tis truth alone is strong.
Truth forever on the scaffold, wrong forever on the throne.
Yet that scaffold sways the future, and, behind the dim unknown,

30. Mark 10:42–45.

Standeth God within the shadow, keeping watch above His own.
By the light of burning heretics Jesus' bleeding feet I track,
Toiling up new Calv'ries ever with the cross that turns not back.[31]

Institutions of power cannot heal themselves. Those who cried out for "liberty, equality, and fraternity" became the Beast when they saw their power threatened. Those who sought "a classless society" did the same. And when the church has courted power or toadied to it, it has not become a "servant of all" but one of power, wealth, and privilege—and has persecuted those who would call it back to discipleship.

"The many" have fared best where institutions of power ("this world") have been carefully limited in their ability to enslave and exploit. And one finds such places only where the Gospel has had influence without being wedded to power, where the church has kept itself free, or been kept free, from whatever powers there be. Thus history confirms Jesus' reading of Daniel's vision.[32] And it is evident that so deep a failing in humanity cannot heal itself.

In short, Jesus knew Himself to be a prophet—a smasher of idols—so he would die where idolatry was most centered—Jerusalem, the site of Rome's idolatry of power, the Pharisees' idolatry of their own tradition, the temple-idolatry of the priests, and the Son-of-David idolatry of the zealots.[33]

The idolatrous triumph of their power, crucifying him, was actually their defeat, since He knew God would vindicate Him some way.

---

31. Lowell, "The Present Crisis," *The Pilgrim Hymnal*, 441.

32. History has abundantly shown that attempts to establish a "Christian State" by political process—which is itself an instituting of power—have always shown themselves failures. It was to protect the church that the Pilgrims ruled that no clergy could hold political office. Roger Williams' "wall of separation" was between the "garden of the church" and the "desert of the state." Both aimed at saving the church from involvement with the state, the institution of power. They and Quakers, Hutterites, Moravians, and many other "free church" immigrants sought here "freedom for religion" *against their homeland governments*, not, as often claimed, freedom from the church. An "established church" is more often government seeking sanction and uniform concurrence than it is the church seeking power. If the church should do that, it would be seeking to be itself an institution of power, not of gospel and love, and would by that much have ceased effectively to be the church.

33. "Jesus' calling and work begins with his destruction of our idols; and the weapon which he uses to annihilate our false gods is the cross." Schlatter, quoted in Kasemann, *Perspectives on Paul*, 35n.

14

The Resurrection in General

But every passage has in view the same event, by which Jesus
who was dead passed into divine life. In fact the whole New
Testament is united in what it says about this event, which indeed in all the New Testament writings forms part of what is
fundamental to Christian life and to faith in Jesus Christ.

—Ulrich Wilckens[1]

FIRST, LET'S SUM UP where we are: Jesus undoubtedly existed, but the
records we have are limited, not contemporary with him, and ambiguous. Yet we have to rely on them in the absence of anything better.
The ambiguity results partly from the reporters' interests being various
and not our interests, but more from the historical facts themselves.

Jesus' disciples did not understand his aims, his teaching, or his heading to Jerusalem to die. They did not understand his death. But above all,
they did not understand his confronting some of them after his death in
a way describable only as "supernatural."

They did, however, expect that some day there would be a general
resurrection. This idea, with its accompaniments of immortal souls, a final
resurrection, last judgment, and heaven and hell, had entered their religion
while Israelites were part of the Persian Empire, from 539 to 333 B.C.

Such ideas fitted in well with and supplemented the religious ideas
already held. Pharisees taught they went clear back to Moses in their
claimed "oral Torah." Sadducees denied them, as importations. But most
Israelites just accepted them as tradition, as undoubtedly Jesus and His
disciples did.

---

1. Wilckens, "The Tradition-History of the Resurrection of Jesus," in Moule, *The
Significance of the Message*, 51.

So the records present various later attempts to make sense out of what happened. There were undoubtedly other attempts, as there have been in the church ever since, as it struggles to understand a gospel that beggars understanding.

As already pointed out, the storyline that has come down to us, filled out with other traditions regarding Jesus' sayings, seems chiefly to be that of Peter, James, and John. This is evident in the first three gospels and the early chapters of Acts, with some deviation in Matthew and much more in John, and is developed further in the thought of Paul. Of the other disciples, we know very little, nor is there evidence that other rival reporters or interpreters had any great following.[2]

In the very earliest Christian records we have, it was recognized that without the affirmation that Jesus was raised from the dead as "the Christ" there would be no distinctively Christian gospel. The first Christian writer, Paul, wrote sometime between 53 and 57 A.D. that, "If Christ has not been raised, then our preaching is in vain and your faith is in vain . . . If Christ has not been raised, your faith is futile" (1 Cor 15:14, 17). The Resurrection is the key item in the Christian gospel, certainly. But what was this Resurrection?

Consider four statements of the Apostle Paul:

> I repeated to you the all-important fact which also I had been taught, that Christ died for our sins in accordance with the Scriptures, that he was buried, that he rose to life again on the third day in accordance with the Scriptures, and was seen by Peter, and then by the Twelve . . . Afterwards he was seen by James, and then by all the apostles. And last of all . . . He appeared unto me also. (1 Cor 15:3–5)[3]

> [God] was pleased to reveal his Son in my presence,[4] in order that I might preach him to the Gentiles. (Gal 1:16)

> Am I not an apostle? Have I not seen Jesus our Lord? (1 Cor 9:1)

2. Some suggest that the "orthodox" church destroyed most of such evidence, but the church took centuries to decide what was orthodox. Disputants may indeed have wanted those who disagreed with them to be silenced, but evidence of any systematic suppression of "heresy" before the fourth century is lacking (except for the Donatists, whose heresy was hardly about Jesus). Nor is there evidence that the other traditions we have traces of lasted or amounted to much.

3. Weymouth trans.

4. RSV has "to me"; others translate "in me." The Greek preposition allows all three.

Paul, ... set apart for the service of his gospel ... about His Son: on the human level he was a descendant of David, but on the level of the spirit—the Holy Spirit—he was proclaimed Son of God by an act of power that raised him from the dead: it is about Jesus Christ our Lord. (Rom 1:1–4; REB translation)

One thing about this last quote deserves comment. "From the dead" is too easily read as "from being dead." "The dead," however, is plural: "from among all those who have died." Paul, like most Israelites, believed there would be a general resurrection at "the last day," wherein all would be judged, with the "righteous" being separated from the "unrighteous."

Jesus' Resurrection was unique, then, not in being "resurrection" a widespread expectation but in his being specially and uniquely certified as "righteous," hence fully resurrectible, *prior to* the general resurrection. He whom the official guardians of "righteousness" had condemned to crucifixion, an accursed death suited only for the most "unrighteous," God Himself had declared righteous.[5]

We have insisted that the Resurrection was unique, in the sense that it cannot logically be classified with any events that we can conceptually define. Nevertheless it was, for believers, an instance of what is going eventually to be more general. Does this negate its uniqueness? Not at all, since that uniqueness is its unclassifiability *as an object for our inquiry*. A general future resurrection is quite as much beyond our abilities to investigate as the unique one that occurred.

The "stumbling block" of Jesus' Resurrection was not the idea of resurrection itself, but of this special indication of his unique primacy. That primacy undercut both the primacy of Rome, guardian of civil institutions, and the "holiness" of the Jewish religious and cultural institutions, widely recognized as the most righteous in the known world. Jesus' kind of righteousness was seen as anticultural, contrary to "civilization."

I have given four of the earliest extant references to the Resurrection, all written less than thirty years after the crucifixion, but they raise many questions for us, somewhat different from the ancient ones. These must be faced.[6]

There are the "empty tomb" stories and the separate "appearance" stories, handed down by word of mouth, perhaps ritualized by use in

5. A further discussion of Paul's experience and testimony appears in Appendix E.

6. Despite the fact that Paul often wrote in controversy, where he disagrees with Luke's Acts he, rather than Luke, should be believed.

worship, and written down by the gospel writers later. They are more familiar to many, but are so incompatible with one another that they raise still other questions. Most people, whether believers or not, understand by "the Resurrection" a confused mixture of all of these stories. And when one asks, "What really happened?" one even gets into problems about what we mean by "really" and "happened."

To achieve some clarity before discussing problems of fact, the questions involved must be distinguished, not only in terms of what they are asking but also their degrees of importance. Consistently, in this book, I emphasize that gospel, which produces faith, comes before religion, which expresses faith in terms of some specific culture. Both come before theology, which orders and makes more consistent the language that religion uses to express faith, to proclaim faith, and, when under criticism, to defend faith. The most important questions, then, concern gospel. The others are secondary—still important, perhaps, but derivative and hence secondary.

Many would take the first problem to be the common sense one, "Did Jesus really rise from the dead?" A philosopher would then ask, "What does that question mean?", opening up the problem of "what is theological meaning?" There are good reasons for responding by asking, instead, "What is at stake in the church's proclamation of 'The Resurrection'?"

Why did Paul say that without it, the whole faith "is in vain"? In one quote above, Paul claims the Resurrection was the powerful designation of the Christ as "Son of God" (a phrase that needs unpacking), so as to be our "Lord" or "owner" (*Kyrios*). Paul has already identified himself as a "servant" or "slave" of the Christ, so he implies that it was the Resurrection that designated the Christ as his slave owner, That is, it gave Paul himself a new but derivative identity.[7]

To affirm "Christ resurrected," then, was to accept his authority over the believer and, in a sense, his ownership, as a more intimate expression of God's ownership of everyone.

He was now, in some cosmic quasi-legal sense, the Christ's possession. Or, as he put it elsewhere, his "citizenship" (*politeuma*), his identity, was now "in heaven" (Phil 3:20). His "slave owner," however, was also

7. He was quite graphic about this: "bought with a price," like a slave (1 Cor 6:20, 7:23). One must remember that slavery in the ancient world was not always as oppressive and degrading as was our enslaving of Africans. Slaves could be well educated and given positions of respect and even power, though only at the will of their owner.

the source of freedom, so being owned by the Christ was Paul's glory, his freedom, and his fulfillment. It was not a humiliation, because it was not a submission to mere power, but the embracing of promise.

This new status was reflected not only in his report of being "called to be an apostle" but also in his contrast between "on the human level" and "on the level of the spirit, the Holy Spirit." On the human level, where Paul had been before the risen Jesus "appeared unto me also" and where secular history is written, Jesus was "a descendant of David." On "the level of the . . . Holy Spirit," that is, the level of new knowledge given the church by Jesus' Resurrection, Jesus was known to have been declared by God to be "Son of God," "Lord Christ," our "Elder Brother."

Paul elsewhere describes the result of Resurrection as "God has highly exalted him (Jesus), and given him a name (that is, an office) that is above every name." This is the same idea Matthew reports in 28:18, wherein Jesus says, "All authority in heaven and on earth has been given to me." Jesus was condemned and executed by the highest civil and religious authorities of his time and place; Paul is asserting that Resurrection was a complete reversal of extant authority structures, which, of course, only God could basically subvert. But that also meant a relation to a different kind of authority.

The royal authority implied by "son of David" has been replaced by a higher kind of authority, "Son of God." But how can the Christ, as some kind of heavenly authority, be continuous with the Jesus who was crucified, dead, and buried? And how can that give new knowledge? Or offer us new identities? And how can those new identities be freedom? Such problems require much thought, and they cannot be avoided, but must wait.

To continue, then, when Paul must defend the authority he quite evidently had in the church, he asks, "Have I not seen Jesus our Lord?" (1 Cor 9:1), where his calling Jesus "Lord" clearly indicates he means the Christ *after the Resurrection.* Paul's authority did not lie in himself, but was given to him *because he was a witness to the Resurrection*—not to the event itself, which no one witnessed, whatever it was, but to the Risen Christ who had been raised.

We democratically oriented moderns find problems with this. We want to claim that our identity is in some way our own possession, and we acknowledge only such authorities as *we* have granted authority. But Paul has acknowledged that "according to the flesh," Jesus was just David's descendent; it is only "according to the spirit of holiness" that the Christ's designation as "Lord" is authoritative. That sets a troublesome qualification on what he says—if one tries to take it as a purely objective claim on his part. Just how is "according to the flesh" related to "according to the spirit of holiness"?

It is the Resurrection that makes the difference, he claims. His reference to "the Holy Spirit" means that it is *in the church* that we find the evidence of the Resurrection. That is a troublesome datum for the philosopher to handle.

The German scholar Wilckens points out that

> To have seen the risen Jesus when he appeared meant for one to whom this happened not merely that he thereby became a witness to the event of the raising of Jesus, but at the same time that as such a witness he also received special authority within the Church. The appearance of Jesus, the testimony to the raising of Jesus, legitimation as a witness and the commission to preach the risen Jesus clearly formed a single whole in the understanding of the appearance of the risen Jesus.[8]

According to Wilckens, then, the Resurrection meant four things: Jesus had been raised, witnesses testified to that fact, those witnesses were certified by what they witnessed, and they had been commissioned to proclaim "with authority" Jesus' return from death as God's promise of the world's salvation.

Problems with "the Resurrection" focus mostly on the first and third. The second is amply evident from New Testament texts, and the fourth was part of their witness. But it is the third that constituted the church, and always has. That Jesus had been raised was its message. At the same time, being raised has been an essential part of the "stumbling block" and the "foolishness" with which the gospel has been labeled, and for which it has often been quite understandably rejected.

The fourth has special relevance to the unanswerable question, "What exactly did those to whom the Resurrected Christ revealed himself *see*?" Though the later spinning of the "appearance" narratives stressed seeing, it is clearly evident in Paul, and in the result in the other cases, that the impact of an "appearance," whatever that means, was as a *commission*. The required response was *obedience*, not description.

---

8. In Moule, *Significance*, 59.

Jesus was not resurrected primarily as an appearance, but as Lord. He wasn't *observed*, He *confronted*.[9] And it is as *Lord*, commanding, not as some "appearance," that He was believed-in by those who brought about the church.[10]

In addition, "the Resurrection," in the Christian language, refers both forward and backward, but differently. Retrospectively, the Resurrection is affirmed to be a drastic judgment on all the institutions of power, piety, particularism, and pride that put Jesus to death, in short, the whole world system. But it is also said to be "according to the Scriptures," that is, it had significantly related antecedents, set down in the sacred writings: what John spoke of as "the conversation" that "kept shining in the darkness" (as we shall see in chapter XVI).

The Resurrection is also treated as God's stamp of approval on Jesus, His preaching, and His deeds, just as his post-death appearances were the validation of the witnesses to those things. In relation to the past, the Resurrection was both overthrow and fulfillment. There was that in the past which it overthrew, and that which it fulfilled. This implies that the fundamental tensions that the Resurrection bothers us with may be found throughout past history, and may be expected to continue in the future.

Further, the Resurrection, treated as God's validation of Jesus and his ministry, which established him as "Christ" and "Lord" as well as "Son of God," means that the new identity of the believer in being "raised with Christ" is the first part of fulfillment of Jesus' talk about "entering the Kingdom." But a crucial part of one's identity, "what it means to be human," is the identification of whom or what one must ultimately obey.

So, from the biblical point of view, one does not "obey" Jesus' teachings except in light of the "new being," participation in the new reality—presented in the Resurrected Christ. Only then is one in touch with "the Spirit of holiness."

9. The passive of the verb *ophthe*, translated "appear," is used "mostly of beings that make their appearance in a supernatural manner . . . God . . . Moses and Elijah . . . the triumphant Christ" (BAG 578); hence the element of transcendent *authority* is implied. Cf. Matt 28:17–18 and Gal 1:16.

10. There were undoubtedly a considerable variety of groups that claimed to follow Jesus, such as the "Ebionites" and those who produced the "gospel of Thomas" perhaps even the claimed "Q community" (if there was such). But it was those who *obeyed* his call to the Kingdom who produced the church.

This is not philosophy. It is theology, and only makes sense within the experience of Christians. That is something the Christian philosopher knows, but can't put into secular language satisfactorily. That can be taken as showing a weakness in theology, but can just as well show an equal weakness in secular philosophy. Each is its own kind of fideism—faith in how a serious and honest community sees things. But the two communities, though different, are equally serious and honest so they have difficulty communicating with each other.[11]

This, apparently, was why the gospel writers, and especially John, present the pre-crucifixion Jesus in terms deriving from the post-resurrection Christ. Can we parallel this undertaking by translating all this into modern ways of speech? The Christian thinker must at least try before he gives up on that project.

Prospectively, the Resurrection is called the "first fruits," the down payment, the first concrete certification, of the "life of the age of the ages." It is the promised fulfillment of human life, our part in the aim of Creation, the "new being," and spoken of also as pointing toward "a new heaven and a new earth." (That phrase immediately passes beyond understanding, because we can only imagine "heaven and earth" in images derived from this one. Yet we can use it to point to a genuine intimation of possibilities not yet experienced.)

Jesus "according to the flesh" was, as David's son, part of the human, historical order, the world system, the world system that killed Jesus, and of which he, as a man who died, was a part. "The Word made flesh" died just as flesh always must.

Declared "powerfully" to be "son of God" by Resurrection, he ceases to be part of the old world system, and becomes the first agent of a "new creation," a "second Adam," "Lord" of the new state of things. Just as the Resurrection is both a judgment on the past and its fulfillment, so Jesus, as part of the historical order becomes by the event of Resurrection, unique and revolutionary our link with the new order.

But this means that if there is no new order, if the old order is all there can ever be, there is no point in even discussing the Resurrection. And a *new* order can only be recognized as new by those who find them-

11. There are of course theologians such as Pannenberg and Schillebeeckx who are also competent philosophers, and some philosophers who are knowledgeable in theology. But many in the two professional communities fall short of such dual competence.

selves confronted by its radical novelty. To others, it is just a disturbance of the normal, probably to be ignored as deviant.

That is all implied in what Paul said. Can it be *verified*? No. But it can be *confirmed* by experience, bit-by-bit, as life has done for many a Christian. Such confirmation is what has kept the core of church alive, not just existing, all these years.

Those Christian apologists who claim to *prove* the gospel true are as off base as the critics who claim to prove it false. The gospel is too basic to be argued about; it must be responded to and obeyed. In this way, it can be found true.[12]

Such statements, even as metaphors, do not fit comfortably in our modern everyday language. But it is important to take note of them, for they demand that we think about the Resurrection not in terms of a few women being surprised at a tomb they discover to be empty, but in the terms that the rest of our sources and centuries of Christian experience alike have insisted are crucial. (It should be noted that finding the tomb empty is something one does not find anywhere in the New Testament after the incompatible stories that end the gospels nor in terms of a claimed resuscitation of a corpse.)

A second aspect worthy of struggle is that our critical historical methods deal with the "son of David" aspects quite responsibly, but what is there in those disciplines that are directed toward rendering what is "according to the Spirit of Holiness"? Isn't it a violation of our cherished habits of judging what is and what isn't?

The part of the problem that is "according to the flesh" is "what became of Jesus' body?" That is a question for historical method to tackle, and if it can, to answer. But "who or what it was that confronted the disciples after Jesus' death so that they were utterly convinced that Jesus who truly died was now present and had been 'declared to be the Son of God by an act of divine power'?" is a question we don't even know how to pose in a form amenable to historical investigation. It claims that what

---

12. This is something every pious Jew knows to be true of Torah, and every devout Buddhist knows about the Buddhist gospel.

happened was a *unique* past event,[13] unique in a way far exceeding the sort of particularity that every ordinary historical event has, and unique in a way that escapes the general principles under girding responsible historical investigation.

The problem is made more difficult because, in order to meet a variety of problems that arose very early, emphasis on "the empty tomb" became a useful defensive position for the church. And then, during its later history, the church tended to sanctify as "orthodoxy" some interpretations based upon philosophic positions no longer tenable, and to stress some aspects of the biblical references to the Resurrection while passing over others. But the neglected aspects are still part of the record, as we have it.

Further, there has arisen in the church a romantic piety that tries to treat the Resurrection as some sort of complete obliteration of the importance of Jesus' death, by claiming it made death no problem. During World War II, when death confronted many previously comfortable middle class people in a new way, there were, for instance, choir anthems such as Malotte's "*There is no death*," or one called "*Open our eyes*," which claimed that the Christ had made death "glorious and triumphant." (In my years as a choir director, I refused to use them, since they seemed to make an anomaly out of using the cross as a basic Christian symbol. If Jesus made death "glorious and triumphant" by any down-to-earth standard, then there is no Christian gospel, though there may be a Gnostic one.)

13. The SBL "Consultation on Ancient Myths and Modern Theories of Christian Origins" aimed at a "redescription of Christian beginnings" toward "the construction of a general theory of religion" on the basis of "a genuinely historical account of the beginnings of Christianity as a religion," by using "the discourses of anthropology, social history and religious studies" (Cameron and Miller, *Redescribing Christian Origins*, 15, 13). I have no quarrel with this as a purely academic enterprise (though I doubt its religious value). Since Jesus has no significance for faith except in terms of a *gospel* which claims *uniqueness* (as do those of Buddhism and Islam, etc. in their own terms), such a "general theory of religion" might enlighten one as to externally describable similarities/ differences with other religions, but, since it could not brook with what is "unique" it could provide no real *understanding* of Christianity as *faith* (or of Buddhist faith or the faith of Islam, or others). Though exclusion of the *uniqueness* of the resurrection fits our existing pieties of prosaic description and hence can contribute to a "general theory of religion" by excluding all "privileged" positions, it cannot give an account of *faith*, Christian or otherwise, that does justice to what it means for actual humanity. Hence it cannot achieve its claimed "humanistic" aims. Since a "method" can only deal with the sorts of data that gave rise to the method, it cannot make judgments about fundamentally different data. See Appendix D.

Jesus, however, took death very seriously, as anyone must who has any sense of the tragic dimensions of human life. The church, in its most fruitful times, has felt constrained to do the same.[14] Paul emphasizes the dire significance of death frequently, and in his chapter on Resurrection, written against the optimistic triumphalists in the church in Corinth, he maintained that "The *last* enemy to be destroyed is death," obviously for him a future event not presently in sight.

Paul, of course, like all our other sources, gives us problems rather than answers regarding death and beyond. But notice the four things Paul, in the first quotation near the beginning of this chapter (1 Cor 15:3–5), does stress as important: that the Christ died "out of concern for (*hyper* in the Greek) our sins"; that it was "according to the Scriptures"; that "He was raised the third day according to the Scriptures" (that is, the Hebrew Bible, probably in Greek translation); and that "He was seen by ('appeared to') Cephas (Peter), then to the Twelve."

This is a traditional formula he clearly states he was taught. It was probably the basic creedal statement of the Damascus or Antioch church, which, it is reasonable to believe, was closely related to that in Jerusalem. (Paul gives Peter and "the Twelve" the primacy of first mention.)

He continues the list of appearances with "to five hundred at once . . . to James, and then to all the apostles . . . last of all . . . to me" (1 Cor 15:6–8). That final item is undoubtedly his own addition; whether any of the others was his addition there is no way of knowing, though the clear stylistic parallel between "Cephas" (that is, Peter), "then to the Twelve" and "James, then to all the apostles" seems to indicate a traditional formulation, molded and stabilized by devout repetition. (By his order of mention, he may be playing down James, or at least "all those apostles" of the Jerusalem church who had serious doubts about his orthodoxy and some that may have been behind his troubles in Galatia and elsewhere.)

His report immediately raises the question that is the pivot of arguments about the reports of the Resurrection. "He died and was buried" is crucial to Christian language, so Jesus' dead body was an entombed corpse, part of the historical order of things. He died just like any other human being; his corpse was just as lifeless, and as subject to decay, as any other. What part did that corpse have in the Resurrection? And in what

14. Marius' recent biography of Luther emphasizes the place of death in Luther's thinking.

sense was that corpse still *Jesus*? Does "the Resurrection of Jesus" have to mean "the revivification of Jesus' corpse?"[15]

The return of Jesus' corpse to life would be an appropriate topic for historico-critical investigation, but would it constitute God's designating him as "Son of God" and "Lord"? And how would we go about investigating that latter possibility? To the strict historian, it wouldn't even be a "possibility," because critical historical method would have no way of even approaching the question.[16]

The only accounts of "the Resurrection" as a describable event are much later, more imaginative, and totally untrustworthy. There are no such accounts in the Bible. What we have there are later attempts to put together traditions about a very confused and confusing time, when the disciples lost their leader and had no idea as to what to do. But those accumulations skip from the burial to the empty tomb, and then to the "appearance stories." They tell us nothing of "what happened" to Jesus.

As Paul noted, Jesus "appeared" to them, but we have no clear or consistent picture of the nature or the order of those appearances (though, as noted, the word for "appeared," *ophthe*, is one used elsewhere for divine manifestations). At the first stage, what is clear is that what was important was the *message* constituted by the confrontations by Jesus, whatever they consisted in. The records we have show *that* to have been essentially a message of authority, a message of commission.

15. "The resurrection of the body" in the Creed need not mean "the revivication of a corpse," though one of the emphases in the founding literature of fundamentalism was that Jesus was raised *having the same molecules with which he died*. The same materialistic naivete is evident in the ninth century when two monks, Radbertus and Ratramnus, disagreed whether (1) the resurrected body of Jesus in heaven was identical to (2) the flesh born of the Virgin Mary and (3) to the "body" present in the Sacrament. They agreed about the first two, but disagreed about the third—though they didn't think in terms of the fundamentalists' molecules (or medieval "transubstantiation" either).

16. "There can be no doubt that the Easter *faith* of human beings is a historical event. But the reality to which it wants to point is no more "historical" than the creation ex nihilo, which can never be the subject of historical research on the basis of sources. Events in the realm beyond death are fundamentally removed from the historian's work . . . with the *Easter event* a Reality invades our world that is necessarily unavailable to historical relativism if it is what it claims to be." Theissen and Winter, *Quest*, 250.

But it also must have been a message of mercy, of compassion, and of forgiveness.[17] There existed no longer a compact assembly of disciples—they had denied Jesus by fleeing. They not only had no leader, they had been guilty of the most flagrant unfaithfulness. They had no excuse. Jesus had told them he was going to his death, and they all had promised to be faithful to the end. But they had run away, eventually, it seems, all the way back to Galilee.

Their attitude may well have been that expressed in the much later pietist hymn:

> Who was the guilty? Who brought this upon thee?
> Alas, my treason, Jesus, hath undone thee.
> 'Twas I, Lord Jesus, I it was denied thee;
> I crucified thee.[18]

The transition from such a state of guilt to becoming confident proclaimers of what the world took to be "foolishness" and "a stumbling block" can only have been a profound experience of forgiveness, acceptance, and commissioning by a Jesus who had to be much more than a mere wraith or revivified corpse.[19]

Paul's account of his own encounter that he parallels to the other "appearances," consists simply of "when he who . . . had called me through his grace, was pleased to reveal his Son to me (or 'in my presence'),[20] in order that I might preach him among the Gentiles" (Gal 1:15,16), plus "Am I not an apostle? Have I not seen Jesus our Lord?" (1 Cor 9:1). (Paul calls Jesus "Lord" only as the Risen Christ.)

---

17. "He is going to Galilee to see those who have fled from his death; Peter is mentioned by name. According to Mark's gospel, it is in the resurrection of Jesus, not in his death, that forgiveness is experienced." Dowd and Malbon, "The Significance of Jesus' Death," 297.

18. Robert Bridges, trans., *The Hymnal of the Protestant Episcopal Church*, 71.

19. Schillebeeckx: "What took place between Jesus' death and the proclamation by the church? . . . The reassembly of the disciples is precisely what has to be explained. Appearance stories and accounts of the empty tomb assume the fact of the reassembled community and its christological *kerygma*." Schreiter, *Sch. Reader*, 157.

20. Greek *'en* may carry this meaning.

Paul did not happen to come upon "the Risen Christ," as an object in the world.[21] The initiative was elsewhere. "God was pleased to reveal his Son" to Paul. And Paul equates his experience with that of all the others to whom the Christ "appeared." That God can reveal Himself, and can reveal other things, was a given in Paul's biblical Jewish background. What such a revelation consisted in was whatever God chose it to be. God's freedom was not to be restricted by any of the concepts or procedures of critical historical method. But Paul's experience was also his "conversion," and was the source of his deep sense of God's gracious forgiveness, since he had previously persecuted the church.

Even the much more concretely described appearances one finds in the later gospels of Luke and John carry an aura of strangeness about them that is quite different from appearances of a resuscitated corpse. Luke tells us that the two on the road to Emmaus who talked with Jesus for quite a while did not recognize Him; then, when "their eyes were opened, and they recognized him" He "vanished out of their sight" (Luke 24:13–31). When He appeared to "the eleven," "they were startled and frightened, and supposed they saw a spirit" (Luke 24:36–37). Later, "when He blessed them, He parted from them" (Luke 24:5).

These accounts hardly fit the Luke and John stories of Jesus appearing in closed rooms, eating, and displaying his wounds. And Thomas, who insisted he'd not believe unless he touched Jesus, believed without touching him. Confrontation was enough.

Under the circumstances, the confusion these "appearance" stories manifested might be taken as evidence they were made up, but equally well as showing that they weren't. They could be confused reports of events indescribable because without precedent, they are told in puzzlement and molded in being repeated within the tellers' frames of reference.

Many complain they can't imagine a resurrection that isn't either the resuscitation of a corpse or a hallucination, a "ghost." Such aren't any different from those disciples who were not apostles. They couldn't imagine it, either. That's precisely why it was so powerful. They already believed in spirits, "ghosts." But whatever this was, it wasn't something they already believed in. That is also the reason why later attempts to

---

21. Though much of Luke's three accounts of Paul's conversion in Acts cch. 9, 22, 26 are surely Luke's embroidery on tradition, it seems the tradition itself was based on what actually happened, since the Jerusalem church's acceptance of Paul's conversion would seem to have required a basically similar account. See Acts 10:26–27 and Gal 1:18–19.

defend its proclamation could only raise more questions. By all earthly standards, it was *impossible*. Only God could have done it. So, we can't expect to establish it rationally.

In short, secular philosophy must always hold the Resurrection to lack any real tinge of confirmability. Many other referred-to historical events may have little confirmability, but the philosopher can grant them a degree of probability, because we have criteria for estimating probabilities of clearly describable events. The Resurrection, however, is indescribable. When "described," it becomes only the resuscitation of a corpse, which is of course highly improbable, and hardly fruitful. That would not have founded the church.

The Resurrection resulted in reports by witnesses, reports that were given a privileged position by those closest to the situation, a position it certainly would deserve if it occurred. Those reports, and their intellectually drastic consequences, are what we have to go by.

A genuine miracle is a miracle, nothing less! But accepting a miracle requires a humiliation of the pride that tells us our past experiences, even shared or pooled, make us the judges of all that is, and that is very dangerous.[22] Jesus called his disciples to the danger of following Him, to death. But the death of "rationality" can be followed by a resurrection of a new rationality. As one Scripture writer put it, "It is a fearful thing to fall into the hands of the living God."[23]

The central issue is this: on what basis are we willing to question our commitment to the modern belief, dating only from the Enlightenment, that nothing can ever happen contrary to the basic assumptions of scientific method? To proclaim the Resurrection as a unique actual event is to see that science must be irrelevant to it and it to science. We can believe responsibly only if we are willing to grant limits to the universality of scientific censorship. That needs only a radically unique event, a defining event. For lesser events, repeatable events, science may be relied upon.

---

22. It was Galileo's fellow science professors who got him into trouble with the church: their science couldn't imagine that a telescope could give truth. I'm not saying here that we shouldn't investigate. Our obligation to doubt, investigate and suspend judgment does not assure that our ability to do so is adequate. "Ought," except in social duties, does not always imply "can." To say it does is to claim that we have no obligations to be anything more than a doer of public acts. That is a claim we have no a priori right to make.

23. Hebrews 10:31.

So the question is: Must we grant that the assumptions of scientific method determine the nature of every past event? Or only of those we can handle intellectually? That can be answered neither by science nor by historical method. It can be answered only by openness to the possibility of uniqueness and appropriately testified to.

How do we decide what is "appropriate testimony?" Only by faith: if our faith in scientific method is greater than our faith in those who have testified to the Resurrection and to God, who raised Jesus, we reject the testimony. If our faith in God and in the apostles outweighs claims of the utter finality of the metaphysical assumptions of science, we can believe. The issue cannot be decided rationally, since it is a decision about the nature and limits of rationality. But it is also a decision about the place of rationality in which we are.

Still, we have the two-pronged problem: how can one evaluate reports of a genuinely unique situation? Can it be maintained there never has been a truly unique situation? It is our habitual expectations of the world that are called into question, and our finitude made quite evident. We resist that.

In John's account, Mary Magdalene thought the risen Jesus was the gardener until He called her by name, but wouldn't let her touch Him, because He was "ascending to my Father." Later, He appeared in a closed room. In another story, He gave fishing instructions to disciples in a boat without their recognizing Him until they had caught a miraculous draft of fishes. Even in Matthew, Jesus met the women, greeted them, and they fell at His feet and worshiped Him. In each case, the initiative was with Jesus. However one may discount elements of the stories, it is Jesus' initiative that is central to them.

None of these are stories that commend themselves to a careful historian, or even to a careful common sense inquirer. They sound too much like reports beginning in confusion and stabilized by uncritical repetition. That doesn't prove they aren't, in some way, reports going back to actual occurrences. They do show, however, that we cannot confidently reconstruct those occurrences on the basis of the stories as they come to us. Only by leaving them in a sort of fairyland, safeguarding them from the hard questions, can we go along with their details. So we have to curb our imaginations.

Since every report of the church's coming-to-be hinges on the conviction that there was The Resurrection, the church and its literature, past and present, constitute the only sufficient evidence now available that The Resurrection occurred. But what was it that occurred? The thinking believer must settle for himself just how the various reports are to be put together.

That Jesus died and was buried seems not worth doubting.[24] That the church came into being on the basis of reports not just of His return from the grave but His exaltation to a new and high office and His giving commands that were received as divine instructions can't be doubted, either, since there is no other viable explanation for the arising of the church. But the stories linking those two historical facts leave us with so many unanswered questions, even questions we can hardly formulate satisfactorily, that we are forced to speculate about them.

The basic "stumbling block" for contemporaries who find this threatening them with loss of their rational self respect is just this: what do we risk if we also commit ourselves to something lying outside the familiar corral of things tamed by common sense, logic, and science? In such cases, the accompanying question is, "What might we gain?" Gospel offers promises; to accept them, we have to accept risk, or stay safe by giving up what is promised. But can we properly assay the risk while insensitive to the promise? (This is not to restate in disguise Pascal's "wager." He wrote for gamblers figuring odds, a thoroughly prosaic activity. Hearing a gospel and responding to it are anything but prosaic or calculative.)

Two of the problems pointed out above have been dealt with less than crisply: "What continuity can we establish between the Risen Christ and Jesus of Nazareth?" "How can that give new knowledge or identity?" The third, "How can such give freedom?" requires much more discussion, but later on.

Meanwhile we have at least four other questions to face regarding the Resurrection event: What happened to the body? What happened that led to the confused "empty tomb" stories? What happened that led to the conviction that Jesus had been "raised from the dead"? What happened that led to the conviction that Jesus had been designated "Son of God" and "Lord"?

The next chapter will further present my own understanding on these four questions, more or less in order.

24. That the soldiers were mistaken about his death, and he recovered from a coma and crawled out of the tomb, as in D. H. Lawrence's *The Man Who Died*, is patently imagination undisciplined by any serious study of the records.

15

The Resurrection in Particular

The elements in the New Testament which a non-Christian would not share are precisely the ones which alone account for the church's existence. They are those which relate to and depend on the Christian estimate of Jesus as crucified and raised from the dead, and of man's relationship to God through him.

—C. F. D. Moule[1]

FOUR QUESTIONS REGARDING THE Resurrection were given at the end of the last chapter. Let's begin with "what happened to the body?" and the "empty tomb" stories.

Jesus died rather late in the afternoon of Friday.[2] The next day was the Sabbath, but it began at sundown Friday. That gave sufficient Jewish reason for the dead body of Jesus to be taken down, so as not to desecrate the Sabbath, but (*contra* John) not time enough for embalming and a decent burial. So Joseph of Arimathea, a prominent Jew but not, I believe, as favorable to Jesus as later reports claimed,[3] found nearby an empty tomb which he commandeered for temporary burial over the Sabbath.[4] A stone was rolled over the entrance to keep out stray dogs, vultures, and jackals. Some women saw where Jesus was laid. (It would be their job to embalm the body.)

1. Moule, *The Phenomenon of the New Testament*, 11.

2. John says Thursday, but that may be to account for "after three days" rather than "the third day," or to make Jesus die on the day when the Passover lamb was killed.

3. He could have disapproved of the kangaroo court that condemned Jesus, without being a follower.

4. It was Catholic scholar R. E. Brown's *The Death of the Messiah* that first suggested this possibility to me.

I doubt that Joseph considered his burial of Jesus to have been in any way an honoring of more than the Jewish religious demand that a dead body must not be left hanging overnight (the two "thieves" crucified with Jesus were not dead yet, so they needn't be taken down). He may have had, also, some superstitious nervousness that Jesus may really have been someone special, which disturbed him because he was a member of the council that had condemned Jesus.

According to Luke, he spoke against killing Jesus, but that seems doubtful. How could Luke have known that? None of the other gospel writers did, and it sounds very much like Luke's pattern of dulling the sharp edges of the crucifixion story.

Jesus was "crucified, dead" thoroughly dead and, at least temporarily, "buried." That is the last thing we know about Jesus of Nazareth. Everything else refers to "the Resurrected and Glorified Christ," and makes sense only if discussed in those terms. If we will not admit them, there is nothing more we can say that has any importance.

Still, we can surmise. The date of Passover was always two weeks after new moon, so the moon was full. Since Sabbath ended at sundown Saturday, there was both moonlight and time during the night for Jesus' body to be removed from the tomb and buried elsewhere, or otherwise disposed of,[5] without desecrating the Sabbath. I conclude that Joseph of Arimathea was more concerned about the Sabbath, and, a day later, with vacating the temporarily borrowed tomb, than about Jesus or his followers. He undoubtedly had no intention of leaving Jesus in someone else's (as yet unused) tomb any longer than the Sabbath made necessary.

Who did it? Perhaps Joseph's servants, or possibly some temporarily hired hands, perhaps not even Jews, who cared only about being paid for doing what the Arimathean ordered. And with the body gone, there was no need to roll the stone back over the entrance.[6]

5. Those who find this sacrilegious are, I fear, just not willing to face the "stumbling block" of crucifixion: the full abasement suffered by the Christ. Being eaten by scavenging animals and birds or ending up in the garbage pile was a normal part of being a crucified human. The way the later gospels soften up Mark's account shows how hard it was for even the church of that time to accept the depth of Jesus' degradation by us his fellow humans.

6. One could argue that Joseph had the body removed to his own property, his own family tomb. This would account for the women not finding it where they had seen it buried, and for later tradition's putting the Resurrection in "Joseph's lovely garden." Because one would then have to account for Joseph's family neither corroborating nor correcting what the Christians later preached, I find such a suggestion utterly unconvincing.

John's account of Nicodemus bringing a hundred pounds of herbs for embalming is hard to accept. There simply wouldn't have been time. The story is so contrary to Mark's account that it invites suspicion. Embalming was usually women's work, and Nicodemus himself is often held to be John's fiction, representing the Jews who were confused about Jesus but unwilling to follow him. Therefore, I see no reason to accept as historical what John tells us. He wasn't writing history, but gospel.

The progressive attempt to make Joseph of Arimathea more and more into a follower of Jesus, evident in the later gospels, is too patently directed toward making the placing of Jesus' body in the tomb into a complete burial, rather than merely a temporary expedient[7]—an attempt to strengthen the claim that the disappearance of Jesus' body constituted *proof* of Resurrection.

Turning to Mark's account, which is clearly the basis for the others (though perhaps less so for John's), we are told that the women brought spices, which indicates they believed there had been no embalming. There, they found the tomb open and empty, and were told by a young man, "He isn't here. See where they laid him." At that, they became frightened, ran away, and told no one (except for John's telling us Mary Magdalene told Peter, whom Luke reports as going to the tomb to check it out, as we point out later). That the young man was robed in white, said "He is risen" and delivered Jesus' command to his disciples to meet him in Galilee all sound like later expansions of the story, but at the same time the last indicates that Mark took Jesus' first appearances to have occurred in Galilee.

I conclude that Jesus' body was removed from the tomb and gotten rid of, that the women did find the stone rolled away and the tomb empty, and that, if there was a young man, he just told them Jesus was not there, but they could see where he had been laid.[8] Then they fled in fear, at least

---

7. Wedderburn, *Beyond Resurrection*, 262 n.153: "There is a noticeable tendency in the Gospel accounts to claim Joseph as a follower of Jesus: for Mark he is merely one who was awaiting God's kingdom (15:43; cf. Luke 23:52), but for Matthew and John he is a disciple (Matt 27:57; cf. John 19:38: a secret one), and for the Gospel of Peter a friend of Jesus (2.3—he was also a friend of Pilate!)."

8. He also said, "Go, tell his disciples and Peter, that he is going before you to Galilee; there you will see him, as he told you." This reflects Mark 14:28: "But after I am raised up, I will go before you to Galilee." This belongs with the other predictions of Jesus' rising: it is quite appropriate as post-resurrection traditioning, but ill accords with the disciples' lack of expectation of the resurrection.

because with no body to embalm, they had no business in the tomb, and they knew that Joseph of Arimathea was an influential personage.

That would be especially true if they didn't know whose tomb it was that had been borrowed for the twenty-six-hour shelter of Jesus' corpse. There might well have been other elements in their fear, too; after all, Jesus' disciples had been afraid ever since he had headed for Jerusalem (Mark 10:32).

Such an account is a "denial of The Resurrection" only to those who claim to know more about exactly what is involved in a resurrection than we are told. The Canadian writer Morey Sullivan, in his novel *A time for Judas*, has Barabbas and his gang steal away the body of Jesus, hoping to play the disciples and the Sanhedrin against each other in an extortion game. But, when returning for the body to the spot where they had hidden it, they find that Jesus had in fact been resurrected, though not from the tomb. His story is fiction, of course, but it reminds us that there is nothing in the proclamation of Jesus' Resurrection that requires that it occur *at the tomb* (even though some of the stories mention grave clothes and "where he had been laid").

Mark ends with the women fleeing in fear. With a few elaborations of their own, both Matthew and Luke largely follow Mark to that point. From there they diverge, from Mark and from each other. Matthew had already reported the (quite unbelievable) posting of guards at the tomb at the instance of "the chief priests and Pharisees," and that an earthquake-causing angel had come down and rolled away the stone from the tomb door. He replaces the young man with the fierce angel, who tells the women that the disciples will see Jesus in Galilee. I find I can't accept as historical any of these Matthean additions, as he relates them.

In Luke, we find Marks' white-robed young man has now become two angels "in dazzling apparel," who, instead of ordering the disciples to go to Galilee, remind the women of things Jesus had said there. The women go and tell the disciples, *who don't believe them* (Luke 24:11). But Peter decides to take a look and runs to the tomb, where he sees no angels but some grave clothes, and leaves wondering[9] at what had happened (John 20:8 says that Peter did not "believe," though the otherwise unidentified "other disciple" did).

---

9. The translations that omit Luke 24:12 fly in the face of overwhelming textual evidence. But contra, see M. Martin, "Defending the 'Western Non-Interpolations,'" 269ff.

The most I can accept of Luke's additions are that the first reports of the empty tomb were not believed, and certainly not taken as evidence that Jesus had been resurrected! Peter in some way got word of the empty tomb, and went there himself, only to find it really was empty (John's account parallels Luke here somewhat), but that didn't give him the idea Jesus was resurrected, either. It is clearly a separate tradition that tells of an appearance to "Simon" (not "Peter") perhaps in Galilee, which might account for the "Simon" and would account for Luke's very brief mention, since it did not suit his theological account of things to place any appearances in Galilee.

In fact, Mark's report that Jesus would precede the disciples to Galilee, where they would "see" him, suggest that the "appearance" stories reported as occurring in Jerusalem may not have happened there. They may have been moved to Jerusalem in the church's defense against the later questioning of the Resurrection (not just by unbelievers, but perhaps by other followers of Jesus who did not accept the commissioning of those who became "apostles").

John reports that Peter and "the beloved disciple" ran to the tomb because Mary Magdalene told them Jesus' body had been "taken away" and she didn't know "where they had laid him."[10] (She seems to have meant by "they," those she observed burying him (Mark 15:42), Joseph of Arimathea or, more likely, his hirelings.) That disagrees both with Mark's story that the women were told "He is risen" and that the women "told no one." John may have preserved a tradition Mark knew nothing about—or ignored.

John also tells how Mary Magdalene stayed, after Peter and "the other disciple" had left, and asked an angel and then "the gardener" where Jesus' body had been taken. I take this to be evidence that when the other women fled, she changed her mind and found Peter to tell him that Jesus' body was missing. If, on the way, Jesus did appear to her, that might underlie both Matthew 28:9 ("they took hold of his feet") and John 20:15–17 (especially, Jesus' "Do not hold me").

However, I am uncomfortable with John's account that "the beloved disciple" accompanied Peter to the tomb. John may have drawn on Luke's account of Peter running to the tomb, but couldn't allow Peter to get ahead

---

10. Two of the "endings" of Mark that were added later state that the Magdalene was the first to testify of the Resurrection. There is no way to tell whether this represents a separate confirming tradition, or, more likely, just an echo of John's account.

of "the beloved disciple," whose literary function was to authenticate the account that John (the author) gives of things.[11] Still, he may have been a real disciple, not just a literary device, and perhaps things did happen more or less as John tells them.

If so, I doubt the "beloved disciple" was John, one of the Twelve though he may have been the "Judas of James" or "Judas not Iscariot" of Luke 6:16, Acts 1:13, or John 14:22, or one of Jesus' younger brothers (younger than James), or even the "another disciple" of John 18:15.

He certainly seems to have existed as the bearer of the distinctive traditions that characterize John's gospel. It was the "beloved disciple" who "believed." (Does this imply that Peter didn't, at least until later? Or was the "beloved disciple's" belief ascribed to him here to upstage Peter?). After all, chapter 21 of John seems to have been added by a later writer, after the "beloved disciple's" death, to persuade John's community to accept Peter's leadership.[12]

So, amidst all the doubts that the stories raise, we can with some confidence affirm several things: the women went to the tomb, but found it empty, then Mary Magdalene told Peter (and perhaps another disciple) that the tomb was empty. They then went to the tomb and also found it empty, because Jesus' body had been removed hours before, as soon as the Sabbath was over.

Those who removed it probably showed no particular care, and would hardly have remembered where they had put it (someone crucified was "accursed" under Jewish law and had lost all status under Roman, but the women couldn't feel that way). So the old question, "Why didn't someone settle the argument by producing Jesus' body?" has no point. It assumes that the argument over Jesus' Resurrection became a public issue immediately. It was the apostles' later preaching about his rising that was challenged, after they returned from Galilee. By that time whoever moved the body would have had no chance of identifying it, or even locating it. (They didn't have dental work or even fingerprint identifications, let alone DNA.)

If the young man told the women that Jesus wasn't there, they had every reason for leaving, and leaving hastily—they had probably come

11. Some scholars believe John's chapter 21 implies that the "disciple Jesus loved" represents a previous rejection of Peter's leadership.

12. The "miraculous draft of fishes" of John 21 seems to have been a part of the general tradition. See Luke's use of it in 5:1–11.

with great trepidation, though moved by deeply felt obligation to risk it. And even though they "told no one" (unless Mary Magdalene did), if their intent to embalm Jesus was known, or they were seen running away, or if they attempted to get a refund on their purchased spices, the other disciples could have become curious—as, apparently, Peter did, and saw that the tomb was indeed empty (Luke 24:12).

The important thing is that *the women did not take the empty tomb to have been evidence of resurrection* exactly why the "young man" had to be added. If they had, they would have done as Matthew assumed they did: told the disciples "with great joy." Thus even in Mark, the empty tomb becomes evidence of resurrection only when the young man says, "He is risen."

It makes most sense to assume that the story Mark drew upon did not at first include anything more about the "young man" than his remark "He isn't here" if the young man was even a part of the original report. The "He is risen" was probably added later, along with the speaker's white garb, possibly before Mark wrote. In that case, the women simply made the same common-sense assumption that John 20:2 and 13 report Mary Magdalene as making, "They have taken him away, and we don't know to where."[13]

If Peter ran to the tomb and found it empty, he would have thought the same—though, by the time John wrote, the emptiness of the tomb had become standard "proof" in the arguments about the Resurrection, so the "beloved disciple" "saw and believed." That is, the emptiness of the tomb had become an integral part of belief in the Resurrection. It wasn't so for Paul, or for anyone else in the rest of the New Testament. It was in a still later atmosphere that the other gospel accounts were written.

In Mark, earliest of the gospels, we find signs of the story's expansion. The women's lack of joy in Mark suggests that originally "He is risen" did not appear in the earliest tradition, but was added, though probably before Mark wrote.

---

13. Many conclude that Mark did not end with 16:8, but the rest has been lost. Imagination might suggest that the "ending of Mark" included the Magdalene's remark that "they have taken away my Lord" or other material in conflict with Matthew and Luke, so this was later removed from the manuscript, and the young man's message inserted, to "harmonize" the gospels. Since such would have to have occurred before any of the manuscripts or fragments now extant were written, it would have no manuscript support at all, and hence would be purely in the realm of speculation.

At this point it is useful to point out that the inconsistencies of the appearance stories in the Bible should suggest to us that the "appearances," whatever they actually were, did not happen right after the empty tomb was discovered. It would be quite natural for the time to have been collapsed in the later retellings. There is a strong implication that the earliest appearances, at least, occurred in Galilee. It not only took the disciples days to return to Galilee, but Jesus may not have appeared right after they got there (John 21:1–14).[14] Besides, there is a tradition that says the appearances lasted, not the "forty days" that Luke assumed, but eighteen months, though that figure may have included Paul's "conversion."

These facts throw into question the gospels' quoting Jesus as saying He would be raised "the third day." Those words were so well transmitted as to appear in Mark several times. If Jesus did say it, the question arises, "Why didn't the disciples *expect* Jesus' Resurrection?" It seems more likely that Jesus predicted only His suffering and death, and left up to the Father the details of His ultimate vindication. Even if He did expect a resurrection (eventually), how would He have known to date it precisely? And "after three days" or "the third day" could have been a locution for "not long after," perhaps influenced by Hosea 9:1–2—even though the context there refers to military threats to the nation.

After it happened, however, Jesus' Resurrection was seen to be an integral revelation of the meaning of His crucifixion. So much so, that the church could not resist adding predictions of His resurrection, even of a date, to predictions of His death. Doing so served perfectly the purpose of proclamation, the church's business, even if it didn't serve critical history, which was *not* the church's business (and is now so only on the basis of post-Enlightenment academic conscience).[15]

All of these points lead to a very important conclusion: the emptiness of the tomb had no real importance[16] until the apostles' preaching of

---

14. In John 21:3 Peter says, "I'm going fishing," a reversion to his earlier occupation, as if his following Jesus was something over and done with.

15. Verses like John 12:16, Mark 9:9–10 (= Luke 9:36 and Matt 17:9) suggest echoes of an awareness that some things reported came into the tradition later than the narrative indicates.

16. As already noted, John's statement that "the other disciple" saw "and believed" is subject to very strong doubts, since John's interest in writing accurate history is always subordinate to his theological interests, represented occasionally by "the other disciple."

Jesus' Resurrection met public disapproval, opposition, and questioning. *No one believed in Jesus' Resurrection because they found the tomb empty.*

I don't believe the apostles believed just because Jesus *appeared* to them, but because He *commissioned* them to preach of Him, to be the continuing "Son of man," the "Saints of the Most High." He appeared as *Lord*: the point of His appearing was to demand obedience. That was what designated them as apostles. *The others believed on the basis of the apostle's preaching*, and, indeed, called those who believed "saints." (Parallel to what the collective "Son of man" was called in Daniel 7:22.)

However, that preaching was what the opposition questioned, so it was natural for the church to emphasize what would have appeared in the imaginations of preachers and hearers alike. And ever since, believers, both preachers and artists, have dealt with the Resurrection as if its importance lay in its visibility. People's imaginations consist mostly of visual images, so that even though none of us can really imagine what exactly happened, we can construct our own visual images of it.

Only later, when opposition and arguments against belief piled up, the empty-tomb stories were used as "proof" of the Resurrection. That made the Resurrection much easier to imagine, and hence to discuss. The way the later stories expand on Mark seem to indicate that quite clearly. The more the Resurrection was preached, the more questions were raised about it, demanding "refutations," so defensive stories were multiplied. This is just what one would expect. What we would call "objective history" was no one's concern, but proclaiming the Resurrection and answering those who argued against it were very active concerns. So were the opposing attempts to refute it.

Since Jesus was held to have predicted that His death was to be "according to the Scriptures," the church searched for verses they could use in telling about it. Hosea 6:2 says: "After two days he will revive us; on the third day he will raise us up." If Jesus did predict He would arise "the third day," He may have been relying on that verse. I doubt that He did so predict. But it seems likely it influenced the church to make "the third day" part of the official affirmation of the Resurrection, even if all of Jesus' "appearances" were some time later. And "the third day" was when Jesus' body was found missing.

Since the precise day of Resurrection had importance only for its ritual celebration,[17] it is quite proper for the church to go along with "the third day." There is no alternative, just as Jesus' birth is celebrated on December 25, a rather unlikely date.

The more one studies the record, the harder it becomes to accept at face value anything that Matthew and Luke add to Mark's crucifixion and resurrection stories, except for possibly Peter's visit to the tomb, appearances to Peter and to the Twelve (or eleven) in Galilee, and that there were others. Their stories are useful indications that what happened between Jesus' burial and the otherwise inexplicable arising of the church was at least as confusing to Jesus' followers as we find their reports to be.

Mary Magdalene's "They have taken away my Lord,[18] and I don't know where they have laid him" seems a perfectly sensible response to the open grave. And, in light of the rest of the accounts, it was certainly not a speech the church would have put into her mouth. This means that the question, "What happened to Jesus' body?" was not yet particularly important to those sectors of the church that produced most of the New Testament, and probably shouldn't be important to us.

So, to summarize, the answer to our first two questions is, Jesus' body was carted off to some convenient disposal spot, and the women did find the tomb empty, and fled, perhaps being told by someone that he wasn't there. Peter may have heard of their flight, and went to the tomb himself only to find it empty. The "white robe" on Mark's "young man" was an understandable later decoration of the account, a step in the direction of the "angels" of Luke and Matthew.

The instructions to tell the disciples to meet Jesus in Galilee probably reflect the fact that the appearances Mark knew of, or took to be important, occurred in Galilee. So, just as Jesus' death was, to everybody else, an ordinary human death, his body was gotten rid of as an ordinary corpse, completing his identification with all the rest of us.

I have given my answers to the first two questions, "What happened to the body?" and "What happened that led to the confused open tomb stories?" We must now give a more complete answer to the third of our

17. There were severe arguments in the early church over just when Easter should be celebrated. See Eusebius' *History*, 5.23–25.

18. "Lord" here may not mean "God," but rather "boss," "leader," or elevated person of any sort. But "husband," as in *The Gospel of Judas* and *The Da Vinci Code*, is most unlikely.

questions: "What happened that led to the conviction that Jesus had been 'raised from the dead?'"

The records here are far from satisfactory, also. Matthew adds "great joy" to the fear of the women but Easter quickly became a joyous celebration. He writes that they run to tell the disciples, but meet Jesus on the way, and "worship him." Jesus tells them to tell "my brothers" to meet Him in Galilee. Later Matthew makes it explicit that He told them to meet Him on "a mountain," where He appeared, "but some doubted." There He commissions them to "go into all the world" and "make disciples," and that He was "with them" even to "the end of the age." Jesus' appearance was a commission to be apostles, ones sent out to proclaim, but to proclaim what? The continuation of Jesus' message of "the Kingdom," though Matthew, quite typically, makes it a commission "to make disciples" and "to teach."

It seems reasonable to consider the last as a tradition of a genuine Galilee "appearance." It is perhaps the one that Paul's tradition reported as "to the Twelve" (minus Judas, probably but Luke, in Acts 1:22 speaks of Mathias, Judas' replacement, as "a witness of His Resurrection"). What is notable about it is Matthew's comment that "some doubted" (possibly Thomas). Had it been a resuscitated corpse that appeared, or some private subjective vision, would that have happened? But one must remember that Matthew wrote some sixty years later.

As for Luke, he goes on to tell of a Cleopas and another disciple, who walked several miles with an incognito Jesus, who laid out Luke's theology of salvation history. When the three ate together, the two recognized Jesus, who then disappeared. They went back to Jerusalem and told of their experience, and were told "the Lord" had appeared "to Simon" (that is, Peter). But Jesus suddenly appeared in their midst. They thought Him a ghost (despite His having appeared to Peter), and were frightened, but He invited them to touch Him, and ate with them.

Later, they went out toward Bethany, and Jesus "was carried up into heaven." (Luke gives a significantly different account of the "ascension" in Acts 1, which, however, emphasizes Jesus' commissioning of the "apostles.")

"Thinking him a ghost" suggests a genuine tradition, parallel to Matthew's "some doubted," since it is too close to one of the chief charges that critics leveled against the church's preaching to have been an attractive addition.

Though Luke used the story of Cleopas (the "Emmaus story") as a fine medium for emphasizing his theology of history, many have taken it as suggesting a later presence-experience "in the breaking of bread." I believe Luke drew on genuine traditions of appearances of Jesus, but by the time they came to him, the original details had been thoroughly customized and probably expanded by retelling, and he placed them all in the Jerusalem area and used them for his own theological purposes. After all, he was writing for Theophilus, not for us.

The evidence points to the disciples returning to Galilee, and to the first appearances to Peter and the "Twelve" occurring there, one probably by the Lake of Galilee (John 21:1–14).[19]

The traditions Luke drew upon, however, center on Jerusalem, where he reports the disciples assembled. It seems natural that the confused period after Jesus' crucifixion, which may have been some weeks long, was collapsed in the retelling into the few days required by the appearance reports we have. No one collected them and organized them into the sort of standard account we would like to have. Each gospel writer simply presented them as he heard them, or wanted them remembered, in his own order.

Clearly, by the time Matthew and Luke wrote, there were a number of stories about Jesus' post-death appearances. Various traditions had traveled different paths, and came to the writers separately. Thus in Luke, Peter saw only grave clothes, but later Luke reports Jesus "had appeared" to him. We mentioned the fact that one account calls him Peter and the other Simon, which suggests different traditions, perhaps even different locales.

Some of the expansions undoubtedly developed out of controversy, like Matthew's story of the guards at the tomb, which clearly arose as a defense against the charge that Jesus' body had been "stolen by the disciples," or, like the stories of Jesus eating, having bones and wounds, etc. These were in defense against the charge that the disciples had "just seen a ghost" (though of course a wounded ghost is conceivable, and who knows for sure that ghosts don't eat).

Such arguments show those particular challenges had to be met, but hardly serve to authenticate the stories. Paul's arguments in 1 Corinthians 15, very early among Christian literature, show he had no place in his

---

19. But cf. Luke 5:1–11, Mark 1:16–20, and John 21:3–8. Did Luke resist reporting a Galilee appearance?

thinking for such tales. He sets "bodily" Resurrection over against "physical" as something quite different.[20]

These stories of touching Jesus and eating with him, as proof that He "wasn't a ghost" surely have their origin in later defenses of Resurrection preaching against unbelieving criticism. Such criticism would hardly have been significant until the Resurrection had been preached for a while, and we don't know how long it was before the apostles began their preaching career. (That Luke says Jesus appeared for "forty days" and the tradition existed that Jesus' appearances continued for eighteen months have already been noted.)

So to the third and fourth questions, "What happened that led to the conviction that Jesus had been 'raised from the dead?'" and "What happened that led to the conviction that Jesus had been designated 'Son of God' and 'Lord?'" one can only give a fragmentary and intellectually unsatisfactory response. However, it is a religiously profound one: Jesus confronted some disciples in a way we can't describe to our conceptual satisfaction, but which constituted a commissioning to preach a gospel that His death was not His final word, but His and history's new beginning. That is, we can't say exactly what happened, but we must admit *something* happened that produced an overwhelming change in those who had themselves been overwhelmed and dispirited by His death.[21]

---

20. In 1 Cor 15:44 he uses "spiritual" (*pneumatikon*) for resurrected "body" and "psychical" (*psychikon*, not *physikon*), for what is usually translated as "physical," as if intending our natural fleshly bodies. Classical Greek *psyche* was indeed perfectly natural, included by Aristotle under what was "physical," but the Greek distinction between "*psyche*" ("soul," a perfectly natural thing) and "*soma*" ("body") makes "psychical body" either "a living body," a resuscitated corpse (which the Christ wasn't), or an oxymoron, a sign that Paul was grasping for words, using what was available, no matter how unsuitable to what he was trying to say. In Philippians 3:21 he contrasts Lord Jesus' "glorious body" with "our lowly body," which Jesus of Nazareth once shared.

21. Those need to be heard who say that the early development of the church as a historically developing body must be understood in the terms presently useful for understanding how such bodies develop socially and economically as well as in *thinking*. But those tools of understanding have developed in history, and can never be taken as the last word, laying down rules as to what ought not be believed. The history of science shows that reality is much more complex than any ages' agreed-upon rules of understanding can lay final boundaries for. That the church appeared and developed in history is, of course, a sociological fact that can have sociological and historical explanations. The issue is simply: can the procedural limitations of such critical activities ask *the most important* questions about those events?

One cannot reach a genuinely satisfactory answer to the next and historically more important question: "How and why did the early church begin?" without asserting that *something unique happened and we can refer to it even if we can't describe it.* (Though the question may have more historical significance, it is perhaps religiously less important.)

That the Resurrection was to be proclaimed was not at all confusing. The Risen Christ, in His appearances, had commanded it. It was the essence of the church, as the continuation of Jesus' ministry, to do so. Therefore, the accounts of Resurrection had to have only as much definiteness as necessary for that proclamation. It is only our modern demands regarding history, forcing us to raise questions in our more critical mode, that make what has come down to us so inadequate as to be disturbing. To answer them we would have to have much more information than any existing records could offer.

Our intellectual disturbance arises from a demand we place upon ourselves: that there must not be any crucial information we cannot "in principle" uncover. Is that a claim of deity on our part? That is a question worth pondering.

To believe in the Resurrection is to believe the church's witness. That is not the same thing as believing in the church as a sociological fact. Or as something divine in itself. To believe the church is simply *to listen in depth.* It was the Christ who was resurrected. The church still looks forward to its own salvation, its own resurrection. And we don't really know how to talk about that, either. But one can listen.

The disciples' confusion does a great deal to explain why the records we have are so impossible to sort out satisfactorily. The appearances of the risen Jesus, which to us are such a problem, were actually what overcame the disciples' confusion as to what they were about.

They asked none of our questions about it. It was not a set of observations; it was a command to proclaim something overwhelming. When philosophers refuse to be overwhelmed, they are trying to play outside the Christians' ballpark, treating as hearsay what to the disciples was stupendous, not that the body disappeared, but that Jesus reappeared as their Lord, giving commands. And that's not something we are in a position to theorize about, or to question theoretically. We can only listen to their reports and the church's experience of responding to them, and decide how we will respond.

It is important to remind ourselves that only in things written long after the church was rolling with considerable momentum in Luke and Matthew, and John's "beloved disciple" story is there any hint that it was the empty tomb that gave rise to belief in Resurrection.

After we have reviewed the evidence and given due respect to our doubts, what have we left? Jesus was indeed resurrected but we don't know how to describe what occurred. What we are confronted with is simply the fact of the church's appearing in history, defining itself as being called of God to proclaim that Jesus was indeed resurrected. And it was *Jesus of Nazareth* who was resurrected as "Lord Christ." To base one's faith on a Christ so superhuman that He is no longer human is to cut us off from our own potentially fulfilled humanity. The Resurrected Christ is not a superhuman Christ, but a glorified *superbly human* Jesus Christ! But that means that "human" needs redefinition. And that we, as present humans, can no longer take ourselves as defining what "human" finally means. We need that humbling realization.

We philosophers like to say one mustn't believe anything one doesn't know how to talk about clearly. Yet, 2,400 years after Socrates, we still can't talk with sufficient conceptual clarity about life, freedom, beauty, goodness, or holiness, and Christians have found every one of those things in the Resurrection. No apology is necessary for the Christian philosopher who doesn't keep silent about that which no one can speak of clearly, but which has been found to be so very important for the understanding of the depths and prospects of human life.

The reader may have noticed that the only aspects of the Resurrection stories I have affirmed are that women found the tomb empty, Jesus "appeared" (whatever that means) to some disciples, and they began proclaiming his exaltation on that basis. The church had to struggle to find usable words, not words to describe it—there aren't such words—but words at least usable to communicate what they had been commissioned to proclaim.[22]

Those are enough to undergird the gospel. Texts "reporting" more than these three things are most likely later expansions, many of them

---

22. "There can be no doubt that the Easter *faith* of human beings is a historical event. But the reality to which it wants to point is no more "historical" than the creation *ex nihilo*, which can never be the subject of historical research on the basis of sources . . . with the Easter event a *reality* invades our world that is necessarily unavailable to historical relativism, if it is what it clams to be" (Theissen and Winter, *Quest*, 250).

answers to doubts about the reports or the authority of those who presented them.

Maybe so, but is all this believable? Many find it unbelievable, and they can give what sound like good reasons for their unbelief. What is needed, then, is to discuss what sort of strange knowledge or truth the "unbelievable" Resurrection proclamation offers, if any. To present groundwork for the eventual treatment of that problem, we must first return to the latest of the gospels, John, and deal with his much-discussed prologue.

16

John's Prologue

St. John's gospel, if considered by itself in isolation, is a riddle, but if it is regarded as the crown and completion of our gospel records, it falls into place . . . without St. John's gospel the earlier gospels are largely a puzzle, an unsolved problem, to which this gospel is designed to offer the key.

—R. H. Lightfoot[1]

ALL THE GOSPELS WERE written after and in the light of the Resurrection. But the gospel "according to John"[2] largely swallows up Jesus' humanity into a figure representing the Resurrected One, though as one rejected by "the Jews," which indicates a date later than the synagogue's expulsion of its Christian members. Where the other gospels are narratives in the service of theology, John is theology masquerading as narrative.

That is not to say that it denies Jesus' humanity, but it contributes little the honest historian can confidently accept in his account of Jesus' life. Nevertheless, it takes its place alongside the others as an important interpretation of the facts they report. It presents us with the question, "How should the Resurrection appearances affect our interpretation of the earthly ministry of Jesus of Nazareth?"

Each of the other gospels also presupposes the Resurrection, but it shows through their narratives only here and there, not systematically. From the beginning, John has Jesus speak and act as the resurrected Christ, not as the wandering Galilean herald of the coming kingdom.

---

1. Lightfoot, *St. John's Gospel*, 32, 34.

2. We have no way of knowing who "John" was, or even whether that was his name. The name seems to have been added later. The author of Revelation calls himself "John" (1:1, 4, 9), but his Greek shows he couldn't have been the author of the gospel.

John presents itself as a story of Jesus' teaching and activities leading up to his crucifixion, and tells it not as history or biography, but as a set of extended theological scenes. In it, however, the story serves only as a vehicle for the interpretation, something that it seems wrong to claim to the same extent about the other gospels. Hence, the evidence they give us for the so-called "historical Jesus" is more worthy of credence than can John's, no matter what bits in John might add to our evidence by reflecting genuinely factual reports. (John shows knowledge of Jerusalem's geography, and may even record some genuine details of Jesus' movements and sayings. The problem is which?)

John does give us many hints of controversies that developed within and on the edges of Christianity during the first century, as it was clearly written to dispute views it deemed unsatisfactory. Scholars note several different antagonists, including followers of John the Baptist, Jews who accepted Jesus as "Messiah" but as neither "Son of man" nor "Son of God," or semi-Gnostics (?) like those who eventually edited *The gospel of Thomas*, and no doubt others. It is, in short, a polemic gospel, polemic because, like Matthew, it was written in the midst of controversy and rooted in deep concern for the views it was defending. (Mark and Luke sound more interested in presenting affirmative views than in criticizing organized opponents.)

John was also eventually successful, for, despite early doubts, it was in time accepted by the church as the fourth gospel. The groups it opposed, except for the new Pharisee-dominated Judaism, eventually disappeared.

John, like the other gospels, was a product of the church. But that is true of nearly all of our information about Jesus. After all, who but the church was seriously trying to understand Jesus, or even remember him?

A basic issue obviously surfaces: "Was the church, in developing its understandings of Jesus, faithfully following him, or not?" Most of us answer the question primarily on the basis of our basic feelings about the church, what it is, and which parts best represent it. Those form the basis on which we interpret what little data there is.

The only intelligent answer is that we avoid being eager to interpret early deviations or later developments always as departures, while being wary and carefully selective in accepting them as genuine and serious developments in the evolution and expansion of Christian understanding.

Even less than the other gospels can John's meaning be read like that of a history or a court record. It's more like a sublime poem inviting us to dig more deeply into what things in the other gospels mean. Since the other gospels have a bit of the same character, despite their intention of presenting facts of Jesus' life, interpreting them is not just a matter of "plain language" and logic either. That they are so often taken "literally" has already required me to make some remarks about the inadequacies of literal, conceptual, prosaic language.

John's organization is argued about, but its main emphasis seems to me to be clear. His prologue ends with "grace and truth came through Jesus Christ. No one has ever seen God; the only Son, . . . he has made him known." Then John the Baptist calls Jesus "the Lamb of God, who takes away the sin of the world." The rest of the original gospel (chapter 21 was added later) presents how "the Lamb of God" "takes away sin," and that brings the "grace and truth" which is the knowledge of God, until he finally says, "It is finished." Even more than Luke, John is a gospel of forgiveness as gateway to knowledge.

John is profound interpretation rather than history.

Because confidence in John as a source of reliable historical material on Jesus is so weak (except possibly a few echoes), further discussion will deal only with its prologue, which speaks of "the Word" which was before the Creation and later "became flesh," and points toward the later inter-pretation of Jesus found in centuries of Christian thinking. It is a context within which we may understand Jesus. And since John appears to have had at least some knowledge of the traditions behind the other gospels, perhaps of the gospels themselves, the prologue offers a wider context for interpreting them, which the church has long followed.

Therefore, it is important to devote our time to the prologue. It has been traditionally translated "in the beginning was the Word, and the Word was with God, and the Word was God." I see good reason for ques-tioning the translation of all three clauses. I find my translation, which follows, and which translates logos not as "Word," but as Conversation to be a most justifiable interpretation.

> John 1:1 The Conversation was "in the beginning." Jesus was the Conversation made flesh, superior to its appearance in The Law of the Prophets. Equate it to the Son in the Trinity. It continues by the spirit in the church.[3]

---

3. I was interested to find that in the D'Ostervald French translation we find the word "parole" for logos. Perhaps other French translations do the same.

John 1:2–3 That Conversation was what God was concerned with at the very bottom of things. Everything that came about occurred because of that Conversation, and aside from it nothing came to be of all that did come to be.

John 1:4–5 What did come to be in that case was a livingness, and that livingness was the light of human living. And that light has kept on shining amidst the darkness, and the darkness couldn't do anything with it.

[*Here I omit verses 6–8, which are insertions that tell of John the Baptist*]

John 1:9–11 It was the genuine light that lights every human, a light that kept on coming into the world. It was present in the world, and the world came to be on its account, but the world did not realize it. It came to its own place, and its own lineage did not make it their own.

[*Here the shift from "it" to "him" is necessary, because English needs it, while the Greek doesn't.*]

John 1:12–13 But to all who responded faithfully to him, he gave the status to become children of God, ones becoming so not by ancestry nor by human history nor by human choice, but from God.

John 1:14 And that Conversation became a particular part of human history, and was our meeting-place-with-God-in-conversation. We have seen his imposing status, a status like that of a unique one originating from God, full of faithful lovingkindness.

[*Omit verse 15, also an insertion*]

John 1:16–17 And from his fullness we have all received favor replacing favor; for the teaching (the Torah) was given through Moses, then faithful lovingkindness came through Jesus the Christ.

John 1:18 No one has ever seen God. That one (Jesus the Christ), the unique Son,[4] the one closest to the Father, has made him known.

This last sentence summarizes the central significance of John's gospel.

Mark began with prophecies, but then went immediately to John the Baptist and Jesus' baptism, as if nothing earlier but some prophecies was needed for understanding the Baptist or Jesus. Mark has Jesus preaching by verse 14 of chapter 1. Matthew and Luke start with Jesus' birth, as though Jesus' life was significant from the moment of conception, though

4. Other readings found in ancient manuscripts would give "the unique God" or just "the Unique One."

they tell about it quite differently. In Matthew, Jesus doesn't preach until 4:17, in Luke until 4:14. Understanding Jesus, for them, required extensive preamble, but primarily about his antecedents and birth.

John goes even further. He puts the roots of Jesus' importance (though not his empirical individuality) as far back as it could be put—to "the beginning," when "God created the heavens and the earth." And it had to do with "what it means for God to be 'God.'" That is, what we finite humans can say about God. So that he (John) is maintaining that it is Jesus that makes everything understandable: not only human life, but also our whole context.

Further, that understanding is an understanding of God that is available through Jesus, who is the "Conversation" that became "a fact of human history," who is hence "our meeting-place with God." This implies that our understanding of 'God' depends on our immersion in "the Conversation."

To a philosopher, that is an amazing claim, one that flies in the face of most of the guiding principles of modern philosophy. Many Christian thinkers have, I think, explained it in ways that made too little of it in their attempts to digest it into common human reason. The usual move is to use the translation "Word" for the Greek *logos*, treating it as a fixed concept, fixed, and hence definable and manageable. "Word" became confused with the Platonic "idea" (bypassing Plato's dynamic sense of myth).

I take *logos* to be properly translated here as "conversation," since, as concerns God, it is an "it" involving the meaning of "God," but as concerns us, it is a "he/she" who appears for us in history. Translating it as "conversation" emphasizes that the *logos* comes to us not as a final authoritative *dictum*, but as an *invitation* to dialogue.

We have spoken of the many kinds of language. Language is fundamental to thinking, and conversation is the basic function of language, we learn it by conversing. It is easy to forget the relation of conversation to poetry. Both of them represent the language of life, of "livingness," of shared freedom, rather than of precision and control.

Translating *logos* as "conversation" is much more consistent with the way the Bible presents God as interacting with us humans and our history, especially in the prophets. Some pre-established blueprint that He must follow slavishly does not limit their God, who makes all things new. (Later rabbinical Judaism, with its emphasis on Torah as being "forever settled in heaven," developed in some tension with this view of the prophets, tending to reduce them to hardly more than footnotes to Torah, but Torah itself was seen as dynamically related to changing circumstances. It was never bound by a naive prosaic literalness.)

Every literalism forgets a crucial fact: the Bible, all through, is *the church talking to itself*. The Old Testament is the Old Testament church conversing and the New Testament likewise (joint prayer and praising are both forms of conversational agreement). As Luther said, "the word of God" is primarily the Christ (one pole of "the Conversation"), and secondarily the Bible as used and discussed within the church (the other pole), not just the book itself." And the church has a history, a growth, a self-correction.

John, in contrast to any such static idea, says flatly (1:4–5) that "in it was life," or, as I translate it, "there was a livingness in it." "Life" can also be taken as a fixed concept, but both the Greek *zoe* and the Aramaic *hayyin* ordinarily stand for what is ongoing, what is *being lived*, in contrast to the fixity of death. Only something ongoing can be what "sheds light on human living."

"Conversation" implies something living, involving constantly evolving relationships. One doesn't have to be a "process theologian" to recognize the Bible's understanding of God, "a consuming fire."[5]

It might be objected that by speaking of "the Word" as "the Conversation" we are making it impersonal, a thing, rather than as having the "livingness" we've already claimed for it. True, the word "conversation" is often used as if it is a thing overheard or reported, but conversing itself is an active relation, something that, far from being impersonal, is what makes persons into persons. Learning to converse is essential to a baby's becoming a person, and conversing is one of the most basic dimensions of freedom.

But crucial to conversing is *hearing*. Some years ago columnist "Dear Abby" spoke of being surprised that Helen Keller, when asked, "Which of your lost senses would you most want restored?" did not say "sight," but "hearing." Respondents wrote in to point out that "blindness cuts you off from *things*, but deafness cuts you off from *people*." Modern philosophy, like science, has focused very largely on seeing, but, as Paul says, faith comes by hearing. Whatever God is, to be known by persons

5. Interestingly, Rabbi David Cooper's recent (1997) book on Kabbalah is entitled *God Is a Verb*.

he must be *heard*. Hence Judaism, Christianity, and Islam alike stress "the *word* of God."

As John put it, "No one has ever seen God. That one (Jesus the Christ), the unique Son, the one closest to the Father, has made him known." Known not by seeing, but in the hearing that is one side of The Conversation, hearing that leads to harkening and obeying.

One celebrated historian of culture has said, "The finest achievement of human society and its rarest pleasure is conversation."[6] Saying of God, as I take John's gospel to do, that "The Conversation was what God was concerned with" is not a derogation of God at all, since "being God" meant that Conversation. It is a real improvement on statements that God is "a Substance" or "a Being," which, as we use those words today, say nothing very intelligible, or saying He is an "Ultimate" or "The Unknowable," which say nothing definite at all. Conversation is what has created us as humans "in the image of God." Conversation with God and His creation, shared among us, is what makes us more complete as humans.

The prologue says that it is the Conversation, the eternal internal loving give-and-take, that makes "God" *God*—so far as we can describe Him at all—and it is His give-and-take with humanity that makes Him "God for us" and "God with us" and "God among us," even "God before us" and, indeed, "God ahead of us," so that He is much more dynamic than merely being "the Absolute," "the Infinite," "the god of Theism," "the principle of concretion."[7]

Revealing conversation is closer to poetry than to prose. Earlier, poetry was defined as "an imaginary garden with real hedgehogs in it." I spoke then of God as "The Great Hedgehog" who hides in the poetic language of the Scriptures. Much of "the Conversation" on our part consists of looking, or listening, for the Great Hedgehog to show himself among the lesser hedgehogs we glimpse during our "conversing" with the traditional material. (Whether fundamentalists like it or not, the Scriptures function as part of the tradition. Without the tradition, the hedgehogs are most difficult to perceive.)

Further, one useful definition of humanity is "the conversing animal"; we are the "image of God" in our existence as conversing beings. We know who others are, and we know who we are, through conversation.

---

6. On the flyleaf of *A Jacques Barzun Reader*, there dated 1959. (Book dated 2002).

7. Or, as one Hollywood starlet has been quoted as saying, "God is a living doll."

Poetry is the clue to language, and any poem is an ongoing conversation of the poet with himself, with the world and with his hearers and readers, and reading a real poem leads one into conversation with the world, the poet and oneself at the same time.[8]

This suggestion that the "conversation" is an ongoing process indicates that the prologue must be interpreted from the end forward. That end states, "No one has seen God at any time" asserting the ultimate mystery of God; and goes on, "The Unique Son . . . has made Him known" through the "fullness" of the "faithful lovingkindness" of the conversation-made-part-of-human-history.

It is through the fidelity and compassion of Jesus that we find and enter the "conversation" that reveals "what it means for God to be 'God,'" so far as humans can speak intelligently of "God."[9] That "conversation," however, is the conversation which underlies the whole cosmos and all of history, so it cannot be the possession of any particular group, sect, tradition, or institution, or defined in any dogmatic definition, any conceptual idea of a "Word." God is in himself Conversation; He initiates the conversation with us, and we enter it by listening and responding.

What John is suggesting is that neither Jesus, the cosmos, nor "what it means for God to be 'God'" is to be understood apart from the "fullness of faithful loving kindness" that can be "seen" in the divine "favor" toward us with which Jesus fulfilled. And by which he clarified, the preceding divine favor of the Torah given through Moses—an earlier stage in the "Conversation" through which the faithful compassion which characterizes God can become "seen." Thus Torah was an event in "the light shining

8. In speaking of Paul as a "dialogical" thinker, Beker comes very close to what I very broadly call "poetry" when he puts the matter this way: "Dialogical thinking occurs within the 'covenantal' context of persons and involves all the human elements that make up conversation or confrontation. It is appropriate to oral discourse and is directly audience centered because it posits that the intent and thrust of Paul's thought is inseparable from the specific situation that evokes it" (*Paul The Apostle*, 38). In relation to preaching, this leads to Paul's claim that *faith* comes when one "hears" and "responds" in a self-involving situation.

9. As a most familiar verse (John 3:16) states: "That is the way that God loved the cosmos: he gave his unique son." (Not taking "God so loved" to mean "loved so much," but "loved thus." Greek *houtos*, "so," quite regularly answers "In what way?" It hardly ever answers "How much?" in the New Testament.)

in darkness,"[10] a favor, a "grace," and Jesus is the further illumination by the same God, an illumination of which Torah was a precedent, part of the same conversation.

This suggests a familiar philosophical problem: if I say, "the light kept on shining in the darkness," that "religion" springs from something essential to every human, am I echoing what many philosophers of religion have been saying? Thinkers such as Herbert of Cherbury in the seventeenth century, Schleiermacher in the eighteenth, and Feuerbach in the nineteenth? They argued that all religions arise from one single source, and by the same process, which implies there has never been a human who understood himself but who did not have a religion.[11]

Do I echo that? Not at all! No one is in a position to pontificate about the "origins" of religion. Every such theory simply projects something the thinker thinks about himself or his fellows. "The light kept shining in the darkness," yes, but "the darkness couldn't do anything with it." Nothing is said about the essence of humans; it may be just as human to be blind to the light as to perceive it. "The light" need not mean "the light of "reason," but quite as well the active light of God "lighting every man," whether they respond or not. Paul said faith is "the gift of God," not some essential gift of humans as such.

Thus I cannot see that the "logos doctrine" commits one to a conclusion that "All religions are at the bottom the same." When revelation is made universal, it is no longer revelation but just discoverable fact. And of no religion I have ever studied can it be said that it deals only in "dis-

10. This is not to be taken as reflecting a supercessionist Christian rejection of Judaism, but rather as an assertion of essential kinship, as Paul in Romans. Like many Protestants, I was raised on a "two-covenant" theology that set "law" against "grace" in a way quite foreign to what Paul was really saying in Galatians and Romans, and which helped perpetuate the evil caricature of Jewish faith (and the evil caricature of Christianity which Christians' behavior led Jews to develop) that have so tragically marked Christians' relations with Judaism. The differences between the two are important enough without being misrepresented. Recent restudies of Paul have clarified the history and the relationship of both significantly. The basic issue in Jewish-Christian relations is whether Torah is to be related to Jesus in terms of the Jewish cultural interpretation of Torah or in terms of God's "gracious loving kindness" in Torah as revealed in Jesus and revised in both religions. Neither side, I believe, has as yet satisfactorily worked through this problem.

11. Augustine's "the Christian religion existed of old and was never absent from the beginning of the race" (*Retract*, I.13.3) has been quoted as saying this. But he was just explaining that in an earlier book (*De vera religione*) he did *not* say that there was no genuine faith before Jesus. He was certainly not saying that Christianity was in some way universally implied just by being human.

coverable facts." On the other hand, to identify things in one religion with those in another unrelated to it historically is to set for oneself an impossible task of verification, confirmation, or even accurate description.

Regarding interreligious relations, John has been roundly criticized for making "the Jews" the villain in his story. At the same time, he presents Jesus as being what the Torah was about. The Pharisee rabbis treated their traditions interpreting the Torah as "the oral Torah," having the same authority as the written one—and hence as equally "the word of God"; they claimed to reject Jesus on that basis. That made them the (unbelieving) "Jews" for John, Jews who did not believe their own Torah,[12] and he responded by saying that Jesus was a continuation of the "genuine light" that "kept on coming into the world."

That light graciously gave the Torah and then, continuing its work, fulfilled it with the appearance of Jesus, who, John claimed, would be followed by "the spirit of truth," the "advocate," who would eventually "lead you into all the truth." This truth is still the truth in the Torah, carried further in the truth of Jesus, but for which in its still further fulfillment the disciples were not yet ready (16:12–15). Nor, apparently, are we.

I find the ongoing character that John ascribes to "the conversation" illuminating his strange story in 8:56–58: "Your father Abraham rejoiced that he was to see my day; he saw it and was glad." The Jews then said to him, "You are not yet fifty years old, and have you seen Abraham?" Jesus said to them, "Truly, truly I say to you, before Abraham was, I am." (Much has been made of "I am" as an echo of God's reply to Moses' request for His name in the burning-bush story in Exod 3:14. It is often translated as "I am who I am," but more probably as "I cause to be whatever I cause to be," which is a statement of complete freedom and ongoing creative activity.) John is not presenting Jesus here as one who claims that he as an individual existed in Abraham's time, but affirming that the "Conversation" that was "made flesh" in him was the same conversation into which God drew Abraham, since it was "what it means for 'God' to be *God*."

The whole of John is to be understood as a poetic, dramatic, and narrative commentary on the previous gospels, presenting Jesus as being concretely what the prologue claims. Like many a poem, it may contain historical fact here and there, but its thesis is that we should "do the truth" by entering, as part of the whole cosmos, into the Conversation, which is

---

12. John 6:45, "It is Moses who accuses you, on whom you set your hope. If you believed Moses, you would believe me."

what God can mean to us. Only then can we make sense of what Mark was trying to tell us: that "Son of God," properly understood, can be a meaningful title for Jesus. But that very fact should warn us that there could be many ways of taking the title "Son of God" wrongly.[13]

This brings us to the chief emphasis of this book: Jesus has been called 'the Lord Christ,' expanded as "Son of God" and also "Son of Man"; he has been labeled "of one substance with the Father" as regards his Godhood, and at the same time "of one substance with us" as regards his manhood, but always "in accordance with the Scriptures." That is, rooted in the Israelite tradition, which stresses both the gulf, the *difference*, between humans and God, but also the profound parallel and affinity between them. One scholar labeled both the "two substances" of the Nicene Creed "as incomprehensible as they are incompatible" to the modern thinker. What kind of sense can one make of such statements?

Further, the story of Jesus is not complete with his dying and resurrection, since he is presented as "sending the Spirit," which is equally God, but which in some sense functions as Emanu-El, "God with us," and also as "the Spirit of Christ." Thus we end up with the Trinity, not in terms of some theologian's "the Father incomprehensible, the Son incomprehensible, the Spirit incomprehensible, and yet not three incomprehensibles, but one incomprehensible,"[14] but as an inescapable way of stressing the unity of God as "God for us" in a complex interactive unity. No matter how much we link religious language to poetry, such statements are pretty baffling stuff.

So the question, "What will you do with Jesus, who is called the Christ?" demands several questions in response: "'Jesus' we know from history, but what do we make of this 'Christ' label?" "That old language was trying to say something, maybe something important; how are we going to say it today? "How do 'God,' 'Christ,' 'church' and 'Holy Spirit' fit together, and what do they really have to do with the Jesus of two thousand years ago?"

John's prologue gives us some hints. What "God" can mean to us is the Fatherly but beyond-the-horizon pole of an ongoing conversation, the conversation that deals with the tragedy that the cosmos, of which we are a part, is as it is. God is the conversation partner in response to whom we catch glimpses of the "livingness which illuminates human living," and

---

13. For instance, in 1837 Hon Xiuquan, a Christian convert, dreamed God had named him God's Second Son, and led the great Taiping rebellion, which lasted until 1864 and cost the lives of at least twenty million Chinese. See Jonathan Spence's *God's Chinese Son*.

14. A formulation I met many years ago in W. T. Stace.

which maintains the morale that we have to have in order to allow the healing and liberating power offered to us in the Christ to overcome the destructive forces we are too readily caught up in.

What this amounts to is that John invites us to think about Jesus as embodying in himself both sides of the conversation. On the one hand, we see God's initiative in inaugurating and maintaining it: we can receive Jesus as "sent," both as God's message and as the invitation to us to respond—a message about us as humans (Son of Man) quite as much as about God (Son of God). On the other, we recognize our obligation to respond and continue it: Jesus was freely "obedient." As John quotes him, "My teaching is not mine, but his who sent me" (7:16), and "I seek not my own will but the will of him who sent me" (5:30).

Jesus is, in a way, the medium of the conversation as well as some of its content, though what he points to beyond himself is at least as important as what he is in himself, as Jesus of Nazareth. He points to the *pastness* of the Conversation in his reliance on the Torah and prophets, the *livingness* of the Conversation when John presents him as saying "I am the way, the truth and the life" and "I am the resurrection and the life," "I am come that they may have life, and have it more abundantly." Also, in the *ongoingness* of the Conversation when we hear "receive the Holy Spirit," "who shall lead you into the whole truth" as your "advocate."

Historical criticism tells us that Jesus did not in fact speak as he speaks in John. If he didn't say these things, what part should they have in our interpretation of Jesus? They should apply only as it becomes part of The Conversation.

That is similar to the question: "If Jesus is God's Conversation with us regarding the ultimate questions, who else do we allow into our conversations?" If the questions really are the ultimate questions about our humanity, then we can hardly shut any serious discussant out. But that doesn't mean we must accord everyone's voice the same importance. Then how do we assign various degrees of importance to the myriad voices that may fall on our ears? We have to sort them out, because some are more relevant than others. For instance, in an earlier chapter I suggested that many Christians confuse their readings of the other gospels because they impose John's portrait of Jesus on the others' accounts. In this chapter I suggested that John links up and completes the others. Isn't that an inconsistency?

No. Each of the other gospels is primarily a narrative interpretation of the Jesus of history, colored in each case by a particular theological understanding of the Christ of faith. John presents a developed understanding of the Christ of faith in giving us in narrative his full-fledged theology of the Christ. We don't have to *accept* the interpretation of John or of the other gospels, but they must be *taken into our account*. They are part of The Conversation. To consider Jesus is to wrestle with the question of just how the basic Conversation became in Jesus "a part of human history" as "flesh," not as words that could be engraved on stone tablets or typed into a computer.

To summarize, then, John's prologue gives us a framework for talking about both Jesus and our situation and context. Most basically, he sets some ground rules: whatever is not a participation in the ongoing Conversation of the compassionate, liberating God in his faithfulness to His tragic cosmos, is inadequate with respect to Jesus. But participating in the Conversation is a demanding thing. Even "his own" did not receive him. And crucifixion was part of the Conversation. Mark tells us Jesus said, "If anyone would follow me, let him deny himself, take up his cross, and follow."

That is a focal point of The Conversation. If no Crucifixion, then no Resurrection.

So we are back at the resurrection. Without it, Jesus was only another individual in the history of the Conversation. Then, if he revealed God at all, it was bounded by the same natural historical limits within which Abraham, Moses, the prophets, and John the Baptist (and possibly even the authors of the Suras, the Quran, the Gita, and other such things). But history slew him in disgrace, ended his involvement in history as it was. Resurrection shows drastically that God creates something from nothing, and brings good out of evil in ways beyond history. Thus he can save the world from itself.

That is, the Conversation continues beyond history.

That's not philosophy, but theology. Philosophy is tempted to place everything within history. Theology requires that we consider the Resurrection, the focal point of faith, as not limited by history. Faith requires that we consider how the Conversation involves our lives today. That means we must go beyond past history to discuss what sort of knowledge the Conversation, up to but now including the Resurrection, gives us, if any. The next chapters wrestle with those questions.

17

What Jesus Means to Us, Part I

> He comes to us as one unknown, without a name, as of old, by
> the lakeside, he came to those who knew him not. He speaks to
> us the same Word: "Follow thou me!" and sets us to the tasks
> which he has to fulfill in our time. He commands. And to those
> who obey him . . . he will reveal himself . . . And, as an ineffable
> mystery, they shall learn in their own experience Who He is.
>
> —Albert Schweitzer[1]

A T THIS POINT IT might appear that "a philosophical estimate of
Jesus" or a "philosophical assessment of his ethics" should appear.
That both could be a waste of time is the main point of this book, since
my understanding of Jesus is that he neither understood himself nor
presented himself as primarily interested in ethics, save as preparing
the body of disciples for being the "Son of man," heralds of the coming
kingdom of God.

Jesus was a prophet declaiming that God was about to restructure
the human world. He urged the common people to repent in commonly
understood Jewish ways in preparation for whatever was going to happen. What they would become would be up to God.

To the few special followers he called to be the "Son of man" he gave
special instructions, summarized as "being like a little child," "taking up
your cross," and being "servant of all."

Jesus' teaching occurred in a world organized and dominated by the
relation of patron to client, as many of his parables show. His requirements
for those who would be the "True Israel," the "Son of man," he summarized in two "commandments": "Be nobody's client, have no patron but

---

1. Schweitzer, *The Quest of the Historical Jesus*. Cited in Scott, *Sources*, 251

213

God (fully obey the *Shema)*"; and "Treat no one as a client" ("Love thy neighbor"). Jesus had no new creative ideas, except in his knowledge of what he was called to do. He died an ignominious death, and what few followers he had apparently evaporated. But, as Paul pointed out, Jesus was declared the "Son of God" by virtue of his Resurrection. Before that, he was simply "Jesus of Nazareth," even though perhaps one of David's many, many descendants. How we speak of anything beyond that we can only construct on the basis of metaphysical theories.

From the beginning I have maintained that since Jesus' teachings, critically examined as those of the historical man of Nazareth, have no real significance for philosophers using contemporary ways of critical thinking. They, whether immersed in the Enlightenment view of what it means to be a human or in some secular revolt against it, work within basically theological (even if anti-theological) but often unconscious presuppositions.[2]

Objections can be raised that for centuries Jesus has functioned widely as a moral teacher, and is still frequently quoted in moral discussions. In John 2:6 Christians are told they "ought to walk as he walked," some late medieval wrote *The imitation of Christ*, and novelist Sheldon introduced the question, "What would Jesus do?" to American piety. The question of what Jesus was, is one question, while the results of his life, death, and resurrection is quite another. Those results are basic to thinking about Jesus himself. We can get a deeper understanding of Jesus by considering what he brought about.

Jesus is a very puzzling figure, so Christians have found themselves profoundly defined by a number of aspects of him and his work. Thus there are Christians whose piety focuses on the apocalyptic Jesus, who cry, "Come, Lord Jesus!" (Rev 22:20; 1 Cor 16:22), and there are

---

2. I have already noted that scholars may start from some impersonal methodological theory, whether theological, sociological, or some other, and then treat the evidence as being no more than an embodiment of that theory. This is but another instance of the imprisonment of intelligence within conceptual language. The sociological theory of "patron and client" is of course such a theory. Jesus dealt with it as a good analysis of evil. Jesus was a unique person, in a strong sense something that theory can neither establish nor refute and the proper response would be to let the effects of Jesus the unique person get into us, however that may come about, and let that temper our previous commitments to intellectual theories. If that is "pietism," it can yet be a pietism both humane and intellectually honest. Honesty does not always require following some "method" wedded to literal language.

Christians who mainly sorrow over poverty and criticize exploitation, and are devoted to the kingdom.

There are Christians who trust him as a miracle worker, one who labored at cures; and Christians who look to him as a key to understanding the universe (Col 1:15–17). There are Christians who concentrate on his death and resurrection as answers to the world's sin, and Christians who are absorbed in celebrating him ceremonially and artistically.

In the introduction, his importance for understanding our humanity was invoked. Each of the above represents some aspect of that. As humans, we live toward the future, and need a more-than-everyday ground of hope. We sorrow over the personal and social structures that limit human's freedom. The universe pleases, threatens, and puzzles us, and it moves us to awe, wonder, and a need to understand. We know we sin, we hate as well as love ourselves, and we need justification, reconciliation, and purity. Also, we feel deeply our need to express what goes deeper than words can express.

Jesus, the strange executed but resurrected first-century Galilean can touch us, excite us, and confirm us in all these areas. The vast Christian literature bears this out. Its best products have resulted from seeing the story of Jesus as confronting us as the "Conversation that is the meaning of 'God-for-us,'" the conversation that can impact every one of the aspects of being human.

Though hardly anyone today follows Schweitzer's exact interpretation of Jesus, his famous quote, at the head of this chapter, touches on a most important point: as the Lord Christ, Jesus comes to us, he *confronts us*. Jesus is the actor; he has the initiative. He is no longer the vulnerable one, and we the judges. He questions our whole life-project of escaping vulnerability. What does he confront us as? In the first chapter, the connection between our ideas of humans and our idea of God was pointed out. But who are humans? We are hardly just ourselves. We often divide humanity between "us," whom we identify with, and "them," whom we distinguish ourselves from. Then there are "the rest," whom we ignore, or use, as we will.

Those distinctions aren't stable. I understand there is an Arab saying, "I against my brother, my brother and I against the family, our family against the clan, our clan against the world." The course of life is often a story of shifting commitments, shifting enmities, and shifting unconcern, adding up to shifting identities.

There are people who see God as an enemy, to be feared or flouted. Some see him as unconcerned, to be ignored. Others look at him as friend, to be manipulated and used. Still others think he is to be honored and enjoyed. Jesus' God was the last, and he knew that the love of God the Father was grounds to "rejoice and be glad" even when "men revile you and persecute you" as "their fathers did the prophets."

Jesus confronts each of us, as he confronted all those who heard him, with the question, "Who am I, ultimately?" The Jesus who appears in history knew who he was. He was the human act of God, presenting the world with the presence of God in a thoroughly human life (hence he prayed to the Father), and thereby confronting us with our own genuine humanity and with God at the same time. He was part of nature, as human nature, and part of history, the herald of God's new act in history (as Moses had been in his time), and at the same time himself. Both the church and the world have been troubled thinking about him ever since. But just who are we?

Back when the University of Colorado still had "Religious Emphasis Weeks," as a professor there I was on a panel with a noted priest, president of a Catholic college. I forget the topic of the panel, but a student asked the priest a typical question: "What right do you have to go to another culture to persuade them to believe what you believe?"

His reply was, "If I know you have inherited a million dollars, but you don't know it, should I tell you?"

As the son of missionaries, I well understand both the question and the answer. There are, unfortunately, missionaries who have considered their task to be to make "them" as much like "us" as possible. There are others who are so aware that the gospel is "good news" for every culture, that they know it as something to be shared. The gospel, that is. Not our western culture, but "the good news for all people" *where they are.* Good news, which can deliver us from thinking of our culture as "us," and theirs as "them." And that even though our culture is in many ways historically dependent on the Christian tradition, theirs may not be. When it becomes a Christian culture, it will still be different from ours.

Jesus confronts a hearer in his own culture, not that of some speaker or of some ruler, theologian or philosopher. He confronts anyone with his own humanity, as the judgment on his humanity, and the transcending of that judgment. Otherwise Jesus is not "believed *in*."

Part of the church's fault in this area can be traced to Matthew. Ever the moralist, he said our mission was "teaching *them* to observe . . ." instead of inviting them as if they were already "us," equally human, equally sinners to be confronted with the loving judgment of God which Jesus presents to them. One can contrast Luke's loving "be ye merciful as your father in heaven is merciful" (6:36) with Matthew's moralistic revision: "be ye perfect as your Father in heaven is perfect" (5:48).

So it is time to contrast what has been going on so far in working out the relation between what we can believe *about Jesus* and what it means *to believe in Jesus.* Or, as the Greek puts it, to believe "*into* Jesus the Christ."

So far, what I have been doing is to look *at* Jesus, while the believer looks *to* Jesus. Or, as the Schweitzer quote above puts it, to hear Jesus' call, to respond to it, to obey, perhaps best put as "to hearken." (The Greek word often translated "to believe" basically means "to be faithful," "to trust," or "to be trustworthy.")

To hearken to Jesus is to find him, as Schweitzer suggests, revealing himself. Not propositions or laws, not moral rules, not traditions, but himself.

This, of course, cannot be achieved by simply relying on critical history. As Dibelius said almost a century ago,

> The methods of critical historical science can indeed deal with human activities, but the act of God is not something that can be investigated by such historical methods. *Critical scholarship can thus not deal with the revelatory act of God, but only with historical events.*"[3]

By "historical" he meant, "available to the methods of the critical historian." But having one's whole outlook challenged by Jesus is not doing critical history. Instead, it may well be described as "the revelatory act of God," which such history has no relevant test for evaluating.

To be confronted by Jesus is to recognize that before reality, that is, before God, we have no defense. All our claims, all our arguments, all our theories, all our self-aggrandizing power ploys, are insufficient.

Also, it is to recognize what it is we have no defense for: our culture, our history, and ourselves. And then to recognize that God is our only real defense against our contemporaries and ourselves, just as the Father

---

3. (Italics in original.) Quoted in Theissen and Winter, *Quest*, 102.

was Jesus' defense against our whole human race, including himself. That is the meaning of the Resurrection, and of Paul's response to it.

Jesus becomes important as we surrender our habitual stance as questioners with him as the questioned, and instead allow him to call us into question. That is the fundamental point. In the Resurrection he becomes no longer anyone's object; as his crucifiers had taken him to be. We are the objects whom He confronts in the church, though sometimes we don't respond.

He calls, "Follow me!" We don't validate him by our belief; he validates or invalidates us in our response, our obedience. Both our self-validations and the cultural ones we share become ludicrous. The great evils in Christian history arose just because "Christians" tried to use the Christ (or their theologies about him) as a means to their own or their culture's self-validation. Constantine's combining Christianity with the state is a tragic example of this.

The problem we are facing is that the records of him are, as mere texts, objects upon which we can sit in judgment. Indeed, to be intellectually honest, we must. But the texts are also *testimonies*, items in a conversation, in The Conversation. They reach out to us; they invite us.

They are past testimonies, with much human experience between their time and ours, so being critical may put ourselves in an intellectual dialectic or polarized argument with the texts, rather than listening to them and responding, no matter how critically. That may shield us from the genuine conversation they invite us into, the ongoing discussion that is the church when it is most alive and most truly itself.

On the other hand, the texts, as the "other" of the Conversation which confronts us with Jesus' call to follow, may draw us into themselves and into that Conversation, where we may find what it means for God to be "God-for-us." That is the "revelatory" act.

The problem with *language about* Jesus, put briefly, is that genuine conversation can be disrupted when we critically analyze and judge our own and others' language. What enables the conversation is listening, openness, and "hearkening."

The Resurrected Christ is not available to us for intellectual analysis or criticism, only reports about him are. He Himself confronts us only when we enter seriously into the Conversation as it proceeds within the

community who listen to him and respond, that is, obey.[4] That obedience is not to rules, but to a confronting Person, presented strangely in
the collective presence of the whole believing community, which is itself
continually confronted by the Christ, the Conversation.

I have implied from the start that, apart from the Crucifixion-and-
Resurrection taken as one complex sign, and the existing church that
resulted from it as an echo of that sign, Jesus has no positive historical importance. One must admit that many terrible historical acts have
been done in the name of "the Lord Jesus Christ" by powers that in his
name, but to their shame, over-lorded, fought, subjugated, oppressed, exploited, degraded, and even killed other humans, sometimes even their
own members.

These acts were quite contrary to what Jesus proclaimed the will of
God to be,[5] the will of God "done in heaven and to be done on earth."
A little thought, however, attributes such misuses of Jesus' name to our
human ability to twist and degrade any good thing, making it something
that Jesus announced God would, in His own time, cure—and which only
God can, though he may use us in the process.

In terms of secular history, the crucifixion was just another event,
and one of hardly any importance in itself since Roman forces crucified thousands of Jews. But history must face the question: "How did
the early church come into being, and why did it take the shape it did?"
The existence, growth, experiences, and influence of the church and the
distinctive Conversation that is its inner life demand discussion and deep
reflection even if critical history has nothing positive it can say about
The Resurrection.

History, written according to scientific standards, can give no satisfactory account of the church's origin. Attempts to do so must downplay
the distraction and depression that marked the disciples, every one of
whom had abandoned Jesus in crisis, and had scattered, apparently, to
their Galilee homes and occupations. The noble experiment had collapsed,

---

4. It's only responsive obedience, not sociological characteristics, that makes a
"church" a *church*.

5. In Mark 10:35 ff., James and John ask to be Jesus' second and third in power in his
kingdom. His response was that power over others, the heart of the world system, is not
obedience to God. God is fundamentally a God who fosters goodness and freedom. He
is served by our being "servant of all," not by us wielding power, even if that be done in
his name.

deflated by Jesus' apparent failure and the triumph of both religious and civil powers, the ordinary definers of our human existence.[6]

Yet the church exists because something beyond the crucifixion and burial happened, something more than women visiting an empty tomb. It was a series of events, events overwhelming to those who were confronted with them, a series of "appearances." These events were received as commands to obey, and seen as having roots in the forgiving love of God and His concern for the liberation of mankind, a concern going back to the beginning of things, that is, before there came into existence any of the temporal evils which constitute blights upon the world.

Those events were found to have promise reaching to the very end of things (the Kingdom of God, characterized as "the life of the Age of Ages"), that is, the final age, heralded in the New Being the approaching of the Kingdom promises.[7]

Most important, the "appearances" of the Resurrected One, whatever they were, is evidence of a fundamental ground of both Judaism and Christianity: *that God is faithful to his creation.* This unanimous declaration of the whole Hebrew Bible was reaffirmed, not displaced. Neither the death of the leader nor the cowardly failure of his followers could interrupt God's lengthy (and unbearably drawn-out) process of bringing in his kingdom of freedom and righteousness.

And that, it must repeatedly be emphasized, does not mean some final "triumph of the church," any more than it meant, both in Jesus' time and now, a final triumph for Judaism. It will be God's suffering with us, but will eventually be his triumph, not ours.

Its coming has indeed proven to take much longer than either prophet or Unique Son expected, but the church, like Jesus himself, has learned to be patiently confident of God's even more patient calendar. Even when tempted to ask why we have been forsaken, we can still trust we haven't been.

---

6. I readily grant that historical explanations of the success of the gospels of Buddha, Confucius, the Rishis, and Muhammad have similar difficulties. That simply shows that comparing such things solves nothing. Though they show similarities, they are not "similars" that we can classify with each other or bring under some general theory. Mysteries can differ in mysterious ways. But it remains we must do all we can to understand them in their differences as well as similarities, knowing we will fail.

7. The past was the Israelite past, and the hoped-for future was the vision of Israel. It is a shame that different interpretations of both, by Jews and Christians equally, were so disruptive, and have been ever since.

Whatever happened, whatever Jesus' resurrected "appearances" were, they were imperative. They laid upon the disciples a charge to continue Jesus' preaching that "the Kingdom" was on its way; history was in God's hands. It was also a charge to live as Jesus himself had lived, and perhaps even die as he had died. Until God brings in His Kingdom fully, we are to behave as the ongoing evidences of the kingdom's certainty and as increasingly conformed reflections of its freedom and righteousness—and its present character as rejection and even suffering.

Many unbelievers hold secular views of our overall moral obligations that are similar to Christians'. The difference between cultures little influenced by the gospel and those permeated with it suggests these agreements are positive secular results of the church's mission in the past.

These ideas are all, of course, non-literal ideas, but no more "symbolic" than many others that figure in any understanding of history as living rather than merely mechanical. The gospel has never been just an intellectual challenge, though it has its intellectual dimension. Neither has it had merely an emotional appeal, though it can be deeply felt. Its appeal is its invitation to take the drastic step of allowing oneself to be caught up into the nascent New State of Things and living according to its embodiment of God's self-giving love, which is both the fulfillment and the correction of the old state of things and its perversions.

Paul put this perception very tellingly:

> that I may know him and the power of his resurrection, and may share his sufferings, becoming like him in his death[8] .... one thing I do, forgetting what lies behind and straining forward to what lies ahead, I press on . . . for our identity is in heaven [the Kingdom of God] . . .[9]

The crucifixion-resurrection event was an end, and also a beginning, a beginning so unlimited as to be cosmic. Unless the invitation of Jesus is heard as what theologians call "eschatological," that is, dealing with dimensions of life that cancel out and replace our familiar past-historical dimensions, it is just another moral, metaphysical or practical appeal. And such appeals lie within history, as we write it, based upon the past.

---

8. Phil 3:12. Translation amended from "conforming myself to his death," with Beare's *Philippians*, 24.

9. Phil 3:13, 20 (RSV trans., alt.: for *gar*, replacing "but" with "for," for *politeuma*, "identity" rather than "commonwealth" since one's ancient "city-zenship" was his identity).

They can be dealt with philosophically, even scientifically. That is, they can be dealt with in prose. But heard eschatologically, history transcends dead prose, because "there is a livingness in it," a harmony, an echo of Jesus.

Millions since have heard Jesus' call to his disciples, "Follow me," and become "fishers of men," which announces the new freedom based on the graciousness of God. Many of us, unfortunately, have fallen far short of the expansive loving fellowship presented by Jesus' form of life.

So what's to be done? If a critical thinker hears Jesus' command, "Follow thou me!" and is caught up in its promise and moved toward obeying, what then? One must identify in some way with the community that has faith in Jesus and enter into its "conversation." Then one must define just where in the morass of "modern thought" one is to stand, so as to locate a starting-point for thinking about Jesus.

Specifying that morass is too complicated to go into here. It will have to suffice simply to confess that I take my stand on the natural sciences and technology, as developed in our western culture, as the most effective way at present to describe, predict, and control physical events, but without the Enlightenment's idol-worship of it. And on literature and history as necessary to prevent the biological, psychological, and social sciences from reducing human beings to mere collections of concepts. I also take the fine arts, too, as entries into qualitative reasonableness.

All of the above are acknowledged to be relative to, but not limited to, their cultural contexts. Religion may make use of, influence, and even produce all these, but its roots are prior to them and must be to a degree independent of them. As Paul Tillich put it, "religion is the substance of culture,"[10] not its form. Culture gives it its form, more or less.

Why religion is prior to those other elements has already been indicated more than once. At the most basic level we have to face our human frailty in the face of our situation, the ground of what Paul Tillich has called our "ultimate concern," the sum of threats to which a gospel promises an answer. Faith arises as response to that gospel, religion emerges as expressions of faith, shaped indeed within some culture, but such expressions of the faith work either despite the culture or they reshape it.

Then doctrine and theology finally emerge as the formulation and clarification in words of what the faith means as expressed in the attitudes, relationships, and active involvement in the religion. But these can

---

10. *Theology of Culture*, 42. He goes on to say, "Culture is the form of religion."

be Christian only as they do express the genuine founding faith, by being an authentic response to the gospel of the resurrected Lord Christ.[11]

As regards the basic threats to us as humans, consider this from Psalm 103:3–5:

1. Who forgives all your iniquities,
   Who heals all your diseases,
2. Who redeems your life from the abyss,
   Who crowns you with steadfast love and mercies,
3. Who satisfies your hunger with good things,[12]

So that your youth is renewed like the eagle's.

Here God is thanked for alleviating five fundamental anxieties: guilt, disease and death, meaninglessness, lack of love, and lack of food. There may be others, but these will suffice. Our human situation presents us with these threats quite regularly, but they vary in intensity from person to person, culture to culture, and age to age.

Many of us middle-class moderns have never really known hunger, hunger that is painful and persistent. We know nothing more threatening than appetite. Guilt is for us rarely a deep threat. We tend to hold our ancestors, our neighbors, our government, or other peoples guilty for our social wrongs, and Freud taught us to doubt our personal guilt feelings as neurotic (though some evangelists assume that the weight of guilt our ancestors labored under is still widespread among us). Diseases, we are rather too confident, have been conquered, or will be. But meaninglessness and lack of love mark our current culture, and questionable cures for both sell well.

What does this have to do with Jesus? Paul Tillich reminds us that

> Christianity is what it is through the affirmation that Jesus of Nazareth, who has been called "the Christ," is actually the Christ, namely, he who brings the new state of things, the New Being.

11. I revered Paul Tillich as a teacher and as a man, but had serious disagreements with him and, therefore, I did not become a disciple. I largely share the very serious questions about his thought raised by Dourley in "Towards a Salvageable Tillich," 3–26, and others, though I do not share that author's apparent Process Theology.

12. Hebrew here is unclear. KJV follows LXX. RSV has "satisfies you with good as long as you live." A. Weiser, *Psalms*, translates, "Who satisfies your longing with goodness." JPS's *Tanakh* has "He satisfies you with good things in the prime of life" with a footnote "Meaning of Hebrew uncertain." For the next line I follow KJV.

Wherever the assertion that Jesus is the Christ is maintained, there is the Christian message; wherever this assertion is denied, the Christian message is not affirmed.[13]

As I have emphasized, Jesus is important only if he "is actually the Christ," if he "brings a new state of things." But the message within which both "Jesus" and "Christ" find their contextual meaning has to do with God "the Father."[14]

Contrary to the philosophers' artificially constructed concept of "theism," with its metaphysical predicates, the biblical characterization (not a "definition" and hardly a "description") of God, as Jesus found it in the prophets, is, as summarized by Jewish theologian Heschel:

> To the prophets, the gulf that separates man from God is transcended by His pathos. For all the impenetrability of His being, He is concerned with the world and relates Himself to it. The divine pathos is like a bridge over the abyss that separates man from God ... The fact that the attitudes of man may affect the life of God, that God stands in an intimate relationship to the world, implies a certain analogy between God and creature ... The disparity between God and man is overcome in God, not in man.[15]

What God is in Himself we cannot know. What we can know is God-for-us, "He who brings something out of nothing, whose compassion for His creation brings life out of death, replaces bondage with freedom, and

13. *Systematic Theology*, vol. 2, 97.

14. Basic to the Christian is the affirmation "resurrected Christ = historical Jesus," which is a philosophical outrage. Which predicates applicable to the man Jesus are applicable to the risen Christ? Which of the risen Christ's are applicable to Jesus the man? The gospels successively and piously built up a list; and subsequent theology, and even more popular, piety, have much extended it. The same is true of Jesus' birth. What predicates of John's eternal "Word" apply to the newborn human Jesus? Multiple heresies have arisen over these questions. Christians do not agree as to which predicates are common and which aren't, and no method for sorting them out, except, unfortunately, the exercise of bald authority, has succeeded in achieving widely accepted answers. The question follows: "How did the apostles identify the resurrected Christ who appeared to them, if there were no predicates he shared with the human Jesus?" *He identified himself to them!* But what led them to accept his self-identification? We are in no position to investigate that. Self-identification is a thorny problem for philosophy. A mystery is a mystery precisely because we can't sort out the predicates, or even find them, with which we might describe or question it. This problem is another instance of how inadequate language is for describing the deeper dimensions of what is, and the inescapable place of the facing of mysteries in living deeply.

15. *The Prophets*, vol. 2, 8–9.

reconciles an alienated world," all of them "new states of things," endings to the threats that make the present world run.

Existentially, God is the super-context of all our intellectual and experiential contexts, whether space, time, energy, consciousness, identity, society, sensibility, everything to which or in terms of which we have some relation. All point beyond themselves to their "ultimate context," however dimly. So our existence is a relation to God, our life is a relation to God, our identity is a relation to God, our freedom is a relation to God, and our aesthetic taste is a relation to God. Else "God" is not *God*.

God is for us not a concept, an idea, an object, but That Which or He Who is the actual living relationship that underlies all other actual relationships.[16] He is the other pole of The Conversation. Our alienation is our violation of that relation and of our relations to ourselves and to each other and to God's creation so that reconciliation is required.

Jesus is "the Christ" if he does indeed remove guilt, relieve disease, end meaninglessness, offer and enable love, and end hunger and privation, *wherever each of these is the fundamental existential and alienating anxiety of humans.* If he does not do those things in such situations, he is not "the Christ," since he does not bring "the new state of things," the "promise of the kingdom of God," which evidences God's bringing something out of nothing, life out of death, freedom out of bondage, meaning out of meaninglessness, reconciliation out of alienation, justification out of guilt, and so on.

What is our deepest anxiety? Not "what are we at present most worried about," since that may be our income tax, or our teenager's first date, or pleasing our boss. Those arrive and pass. At the bottom of all our deep anxieties lies the fact that we are both determined and free. We are limited as to where and to whom we were born, and to the gifts we were born with. But we know ourselves to be responsible for what we become, what we are, what we do, what we think, and what we worship.

Our thinking is largely circumscribed by the limits of our native language. We live in a world which functions most effectively by cause-and-effect. We may live seventy or eighty or ninety years, but we will die, and be no more significant than our great-great-grandparents are now. The Psalmist knew this well. "As for man, his days are as grass; as the flower of

---

16. This may sound like Aquinas' "pure act," but Aristotelian language is not being used here.

the field he flourishes, and the wind passes over it, and it is gone, and the place thereof shall know it no more (Ps 103:15–16)."

Yet we are responsible for what we do with what we are given. We are fallible, but ought not fail. We plan, and are frustrated. We judge and misjudge; sooner or later we must judge ourselves; eventually we will be judged. The best we can do as we approach death is to pray with another psalmist, "Establish thou the work of our hands upon us, yea, the work of our hands establish thou it (Ps 90:17)." Even our "footprints on the sands of time" will progressively fade, but, while they last, they may still show some meaningfulness to our earthly lives.

But how can the life, death, or even resurrection of a strange Galilean Jew of twenty centuries ago be an answer to any of these anxieties? To speak of Jesus as "the Christ" is to claim that he is, in some fundamental way, involved in their answer. Of course, if we are not aware of any such "concerns," then we have no ear for any genuine gospel, and Jesus' relevance to us would seem purely academic. Even so, we may have some religious curiosity, some emotional need for a "religion" to express our religiosity through, some consumerist desire to "get something out of" religion, or some superficial practical or social need to "belong" to some religious party.

Søren Kierkegaard spoke of Jesus in a paradox, as "our eternal contemporary." That is, it seems, a genuinely Christian way to talk, but like any paradox, it can be understood, and probably misunderstood, in more than one way. Certainly Jesus, if he was just the onetime Palestinian individual who grew up in Nazareth, cannot be effectively relevant to our anxieties today. The creating, life-giving, liberating, reconciling efficacy of God necessary to clear up problems implicit in our existing as creatures free, responsive, responsible, and yet finite and in part determined and hence essentially tragic, requires some element of the "eternal," whatever that means. Yet the deepest contemporaneity with us is also required. It is *our* anxieties, *now*, that need meeting.

God's involvement in us, however, is much broader than merely healing our anxieties. Basic to the prophets' understanding and Jesus clearly understood himself as in the prophetic tradition is the fact that God is involved in both the overall tragedies and the overall promise of history, the history we add to by our responses, our innovations, and by our selfishness and foolishness. His interest in the fulfillment of history goes beyond our desires. We have to talk about this broad scene in eschatological symbols and riddles precisely because while we may see dimly some likely results of our foolishness, our hopes can only be formulated in parables and poetry that rest on God's involvement, not just ours.

The problem has long been stated as that of the relation of "the temporal" to the "eternal." This I find unsatisfactory, just because of the words used. They have been treated as synonyms for "the corruptible" and "the incorruptible," "the things that perish" and "the things that abide," "the earthly" and "the heavenly," and "the corporeal" and the "spiritual." These oppositions may have made sense to St. Paul, but none of them make much clear sense to the modern mind.

"Eternal" is appropriately applied to numbers and other mathematical terms, because we have invented them precisely to have ideas freed from time, corruption, change, and facts. They can be "eternal" because they don't refer to anything until we temporarily assign them such a reference. As Bertrand Russell put it, "Mathematics is the science in which we don't know what it is we are talking about."

Our language has been deluded by the "eternity" of mathematics for centuries, making all sorts of problems for theologians. God is not "timeless" in the sense that "eternity" is "timeless"; God *loves* time. He invented it. Time is precisely what makes the universe a functioning universe, and humans functioning humans. To say that time is the opposite of what God is, is nonsense—unless we are just saying that God is not limited the way the cosmos is limited.

We have assumed that eternity is prior to time, and then proceeded to assume that because God is prior to time, He must be "eternal" (a clear example of the classic fallacy of "undistributed middle").[17] But the only content we can give to "eternity" is either the empty negative one of "timelessness," or the assertion that it is what characterizes mathematics and clearly defined concepts—which are our human inventions, developed in history.

We are time-beings. We are who we are by remembering the past, anticipating the future, and teetering on the indistinct and moving fence between them. Any gospel that affirms our significance as humans must confirm us as time-involved beings.

Some have spoken of God as "the eternal Thou," because we are confronted most deeply by "thou's." But our relation to any "thou" is a relation

17. "Times" can be logically distributed, "prior to time" can't.

in time, no matter how continuous or continuing it may be. We, as time-bound humans, find ourselves confronted in time, so God may be for us the "ever-continuing Thou," the "ever-accepting Thou," the "ever-renewing Thou," but "eternal" makes God too static. As Deuteronomy puts it, in typically Hebrew functional terms, "The God of past ages is our dwelling-place, and underneath are the ever-continuing arms."[18]

I'm not objecting to the Bible's use of "eternal." Many ancient folk considered time to be "the destroyer" of our accomplishments, and the world to have always been as we find it. We instead are convinced that time has allowed us to produce progress. Yet God's response to our "progress" is his free choosing, not something we bring about.

Nor can one object to calling God "eternal" if that expresses His difference, supremacy, mystery, and our wonder and awe. But the "eternity" we ascribe to numbers and logical concepts is just a reflection of our development of very fixed habits of finite thinking. A great deal of theological nonsense has emerged from taking our most stable mind-habits to be a blueprint of what can be or must be, just because they establish limits to *how we can talk and think about things.*[19]

So what relation can a first-century Jew whom the Romans executed as a criminal have to our present deepest anxieties? None, except as in some way he is incarnate today in our own involvement in the world, its history, and the sharing that makes up our own lives. When discussing the Resurrection, we acknowledged that the claim for it was a claim of bridging the past and the future. The "Risen One" is both the "Crucified One" and the "Coming One," the "Judge," and both "according to the Scriptures." As Paul put it, the "son of David," Jesus, had been, as a huge occurrence, declared to be "Son of God," the Christ, *by his resurrection from the dead*, his transition from the vulnerability that characterizes history to an ongoing, unending present, and a promised unending future as the invulnerable "Coming One."

---

18. Deut 33:27, translation mine. Other translations may use "eternal" and "everlasting" here for *qedem* and *olam*, which obscures the difference between "from the beginning" and "ever-continuing" (though *olam* is ambiguous as to past/future—compare Mal 1:4 with 3:4, Mic 5:4, or Psalm 136). Neither of them originally indicated static timelessness.

19. The debate concerning "absolute truth," pro or con, is often foolish. We are *creatures* who live by *our* languages and in *our* institutions. Whatever "absolute truth" may be, it is mere hubris to claim we have it in our formulations, especially when such a claim has often been used to gain or to hold power.

How can any reasonable person make sense out of that? St. Paul himself called it "foolishness" and a "stumbling block." There is simply no way to get from good, solid, reasonable secular common sense to such claims by respectable, logical step-by-step argument. So the Christian philosopher must start somewhere else: with good, solid, reasonable *faith-full* common sense, justifiable as *common* sense only by the centuries of Christian experience and thinking.

Jesus did not live "once upon a time," or in "never-never land." The simple fact that we number our years by referring them to his time shows that our knowledge of who we are puts us in a concrete historical relation to him. His world was our human world, and still is. The connections have been real, and continuous. The years from him to us make up a significant part of history, the same history we know we are now living in. To be a Christian is to live in that history, while taking him to be the culminating point of it, though, of course, not yet its termination.

Some fifty years ago, H. Richard Niebuhr, in a book entitled *The Meaning of Revelation*, pointed out that each of us has more than one history. Most of these are "outside" histories. We acknowledge them but they don't define who we are. What I know of the history of Russia or of the Mayans or Aleuts is to me "history," all right, but not in any deep sense "my history."

There are histories, however, that we find ourselves to be "inside," but which are also "inside" what we are. Who I am is much more tied up with American history, English history, Scottish and German history, and even Chinese history. One of my grandfathers was born in Germany, the other in England. One grandmother was conceived in Scotland but born aboard a ship just about to dock in New Zealand. And I was born and went through elementary school in China. Like many Americans, my roots lie in more than one place.

But there is more to it than that. My father was a doctor, and understood himself in part in terms of medical history. As a philosopher, I feel a kinship with Plato, Aristotle, Augustine, Descartes, Kant, Dewey and Wittgenstein and Confucius that I don't feel toward figures important in most other fields. And as an educated member of our Western culture, I know my deep debt to Greeks and Romans, even to the Arabs, and especially to the Hebrews. But my deepest "internal history" reaches back to the Bible, by way of the continuity of the church.

The train of events recorded and responded to in Scripture define me more deeply than anything else, except perhaps my being a native English-speaker and English-thinker and having had the particular parents and other loves in my life. And the continuous line between Bible history and the present or at least one of them, the one important to me is there somewhere in the church. Not all of the church, or in all of the history of the church, but don't ask me to make too confident judgments as to what parts of each. Our judgments of the past are far too fragile.

As Augustine pointed out, the church is a *corpus mixtum*. Not everyone in the church is part of his City of Light, nor are all members of the latter within the empirically identifiable church. One traditional way to put this is to say two things of "The Holy Spirit": that he (or she) works "ordinarily within and through the church" but also "when and where and how he (she) wills."

St. Justin the Martyr, about 155, said, "those who live according to reason are Christians, even though they are accounted atheists. Such were Socrates and Heraclitus among the Greeks, and those like them." One doesn't have to agree with him in detail, but what he acknowledged early needs to be constantly reaffirmed, that it is not for us to claim to be able to draw a clear line of separation between those through whom the Spirit works and those who resist. To do so is to be sectarian, not faithful.

The main point here is that one can only be a human being in terms of some vision of the past, because in living the present towards the future, one works from the past that is one's defining past. But one cannot be fully a human all by himself; one comes to be human in relation to others, particularly by conversation and joint participation. So one's internal history cannot be purely individual, private, or unique. To be human is to be part of a largely shared present which reaches toward a largely shared but undefined future on the basis of a largely shared and relatively defined past.

"Largely," but only largely, each of us is an individual, and each brings different things to that sharing. Sharing is never complete; each of us holds back something of what we are. Sharing is also never perfect, because what we do bring doesn't always fit in with what others bring, and we often find it difficult to accept what others offer as their share. The relationships upon which our humanity is based are strained, even broken. But however stretched and warped, they are *there*.

Once one thinks of it this way, one sees that free individuals, who must define for themselves who they are, cannot be expected to relate to one another without things that produce alienation. That is part of what Christian theology has called "original sin." "Sin" is much more than immorality; it includes everything that makes questionable one's being a genuine human being, which means anything that disrupts our relationships among humans or between humans and our widest context. And the context beyond all contexts we call "God."

Free, finite, short-lived beings, constantly saddled with creating their shared humanity, always on the way to becoming themselves together but never quite achieving it, cannot be anything but tragic. Our finitude makes us anxious about life's necessities and death, our temporariness confronts us with meaninglessness, our illusions about each other and ourselves disrupt our relationships and produce alienations. The limits to our ability to communicate with one another produce enmities and lack of love. And all of them together show us incapable of straightening the deepest problems out by ourselves, though most of the time we just delude ourselves into thinking we have it made.

There is goodness in us, too, goodness that can respond to the goodness in Jesus, the "Christ," inaugurating new good in us. The writers of the gospels did not say, as we do, "Jesus is the Christ," but "the Christ is *Jesus*." They knew what "Christ" (Messiah) meant; the new thing that had to be said was "The Christ is not what we expected, "David's son," converter, or destroyer of the Gentiles, but Jesus of Nazareth, who laid down his life as a "ransom," that is, a liberator, for the "many" (which can mean "all," even though not all allow themselves to be liberated).

For us to say "Jesus is the Christ" is to say that we define God's loving will in terms of the resurrected Jesus of Nazareth, that in some way we find in him the promise that all these things are to be overcome, but the roots of that promise lie in the past, and in the timelessness before that. The point of studying and musing about Jesus is to *see* that the promise in him is in some way guaranteed by God's faithfulness to his entire Creation, as manifested in the Resurrection.

That means he must be talked about in the present and future tenses as well as the past tense. The next chapter does that.

18

What Jesus Means to Us, Part II

> When we speak of Christ we take what Francis of Assisi or
> Martin Luther King learned of Jesus into our relationship; we
> take over the treasures which people have gathered in their re-
> lationship with Jesus. He is the Christ . . . who goes before us
> and continues to be active, from whom we can learn.
>
> —Soelle and Schottroff[1]

JESUS' OPENNESS TO ALL sorts and conditions of people, his compassion
and hospitality, and his courage, but also his refusal to separate himself
from the evils of human life: homelessness, poverty, rejection, and finally
death—all these reveal the *grace* or graciousness of Jesus. Put together
with his centeredness on fulfilling what God intended his function in life
to be, these become what Christians affirm is itself a revelation of the
grace or graciousness of God.

This has always challenged Christians to face up to what is involved
in truly being a human being. And that means living as images of God,
and hence as Jesus lived, focused on everyone's need for freedom and
love, for relatedness, while all the time trusting in God's faithfulness toward good for his creation.

The basic Christian benediction is "May the grace of our Lord Jesus
Christ, the love of God the Father, and the fellowship of the Holy Spirit"
be "with you" or "upon you." These taken together [2] mean "moving you to

---

1. *Jesus of Nazareth*, 140–41.

2. This is a statement of the *unity* of God, not of three gods. Since very early, there
have been disputes as to just how the Trinity is to be expressed, always affirming God's
unity but under the necessity to speak of it three ways. Frege's distinction between *reference* and *meaning* leads to the suggestion that the three names are not descriptions
of three separate beings, but three pointers to God, ways of addressing Him that are

accept being changed toward a more gracious, more loving, more warmly sociable way to be," that is "more truly human," more in line with God's will to goodness for all,[3] as Jesus showed true humanity to be.

But just as human relatedness depends on the character of the persons related to, our discovery of our deepest humanness involves our relation to the most important of our contemporaries—the living, resurrected Christ, present in those who are accepting this promise of being changed. This experienced mystery has always been spoken of in Christian circles as "the presence of Christ through the Holy Spirit," which works primarily "in the church," the people who join with us in living with that mystery. (When this is lacking, a "church" is hardly a *church*.)

The Christian language of Jesus' "sending the Holy Spirit" is the other side of the paradox of "the living Christ" both "having ascended into heaven" (as "Lord") and being "with us always, unto the end of the Age," as our "Elder Brother," but always as the Crucified, the one destroyed by our human piety, so requiring New Creation.

The church has always recognized both the necessity of so speaking and its logical difficulty. As the Apostles' Creed puts it, "I believe in the Holy Ghost (the "Lord and giver of life," which is what makes) the Holy Catholic Church (into) the communion of saints, (by the proclamation of crucifixion and resurrection, and amidst which occurs) the forgiveness of sins (and hence the promise of) the resurrection of the body and the life everlasting."

Such language has always cut across the grain of philosophy. As the second- and third-century Church Father Tertullian said of it,

---

required by the threefold ways He enters history and our lives. This escapes Sabellianism by making no use of Greek metaphysics. The mystery is a failing of our language possibilities, not of what can be.

3. Here philosophers will likely bring up "the problem of evil." Free and responsible beings bring both good and evil upon the cosmos, as children bring to earthly parents, and it is better that they be confronted with the possibility of evil, both moral and physical, that they may become agents of good rather than of evil. We humans evolved very slowly, and undoubtedly with many failures, toward more of an image of God, just as children learn very slowly (and some never) to be free, responsible, and to produce good rather than evil. To assume God's intention was to produce human consumable pleasures rather than genuine good would be the same kind of insult to God as would to charge parents with having the same aim. The "problem of evil" became a *philosophic* problem, rather than a theological one, with the Enlightenment's fascination with hedonism (as in Paley's *Ethics*).

> It does not shame (us), because it is shameful . . . it is absolutely believable, because it is absurd . . . it is certain, because it is impossible,[4]

that is, we are attempting to express experientially known truth which logical, prosaic language is not capable of stating.[5] My discussion of poetry was to show that doing so is a perfectly normal, indeed the most basic, functioning of language.

In Christian language, Jesus is called "The Son" because he called God "Father" (he may also have spoken of himself as "the Son," though we have no way of knowing what exactly he would have understood that to mean). As Christians' theology developed, it was seen that to speak of "the Son" says that he is connected in some essential way with "God" (that is, the Father and the "Holy Spirit"). Just how they participated in each other was a point of great dispute.

His participation in our lives, however, was also seen as the reflection of his participation, as the Son, in the Father. Just how one is to spell out these relationships is still a problem. But talking about God and the things of God has always been a problem, a logical problem, a linguistic one, and an expressive one as well as being in still other ways an intellectual one.[6]

The experience of being Christians demands that we find ways to talk about it, while acknowledging that such matters are beyond our ability to speak clearly. But when we humans can't even talk clearly and crisply about beauty, why one great artist or composer is "greater" than another, what else should we expect? Christians have always recognized

4. *De Carne Christi*, ib. v. Translation mine.

5. In a widely-read essay, Bernard Williams, taking off from Tertullian's remark, says there is "a sort of inherent and necessary incomprehensibility, which seems to be a feature of Christian belief," but goes on to argue "If, then, the Christian faith is true, it must be partly incomprehensible; but if it is partly incomprehensible, it is difficult to see what it is for it to be true" (Flew and Macintyre, *New Essays*, 187, 211). But a creed is an *expression* of what is already known to be true, not a *statement* to inform someone who does not know what that truth is. If one says, "I love you" to someone who does not know what love is, it *is* "difficult" for the hearer "to see what it is for it to be true." The Creed makes sense to the Christian because he already knows what it is trying, however incoherently, to say.

6. Schweitzer usefully discusses this problem, which I revert to several times, as involving the difference between *explaining* and *understanding*. Following Dilthey, he says "under-standing" "can be defined as thinking that recognizes reality greater than the human mind can encompass in explanatory terms," which seeks to know something as communication rather than as thing, leading to comprehension of meaning, which involves the knower in participation, and that at a cost. "The dialectic," 53.

that talking about such things is a confusing problem, while at the same time recognizing that if it weren't a problem, we wouldn't be talking about *the deepest things in life.*

To say "Jesus is the Christ" is to say that in some way we find in him the promise that all these things are to be overcome, but the roots of that promise lie in the past, his past. The point of studying and musing about Jesus is to see that promise in him as in some way guaranteed by God's faithfulness. But that means we find ourselves forced to talk about him in his present relevance.

In the present, the world may refer to him as "the church's 'Christ,'" or, intending something perhaps a little broader, "the Christians' 'Christ,'" with multiple quotation marks. But to the Christians he is "God's Christ," without the single quotes. How do we get from one to the other?

For modern thinking, we don't do it by just appealing to "incarnation," or "Son of God," or "two natures." Each of those statements becomes a problem, not an answer—if we find them making any sense at all. So let's go back to our problem of defining ourselves as humans. Sartre tried to describe us as if each of us was an isolated locus of undefined freedom who must decide, as his own project, just who to be. He stated half the facts correctly. As over against all ideas that would limit who we are to what nature has made of us, he made an important criticism. And he was insightful in talking about extreme or revolutionary moral choices.

But, as beings in history, we are not entirely of our own making. One of my cousins was a professor of medicine and father of two sons. He spoke of newborns as "human larvae," because they were still so far removed from being persons. A newborn has already been defined not merely by its genes, its DNA, but by its mother's diet and exercise, and also by its mother's voice, which it has heard in her womb for weeks. It already has a singular relation to her it has with no one else, a relation not of its own making.

And it becomes a human being, in any adequate sense, by several things: being cared for, being loved, being invited to talk, to walk, to respond, and to accept both its powers and its vulnerability. A "new-born" can be rather fully described in biological and medical terms, terms also applicable to most animals, but a "person" can be described only in terms fully appropriate to persons.

The transition from being the first sort of being to the second sort involves attention, invitation, compassion, sensitivity, responsiveness, courage, dedication, and valuing love, on the part of the parents. On the part of the child, it involves response, acceptance of roles, and in some sense, obedience, but every one of these is not just a choice. Each is a discovery that arises out of being responsive to an invitation. Becoming a human is becoming related. Becoming related is responding to invitations and in return learning to invite.[7]

Two recent authors put it thus:

> "The baby . . . reaches out toward that world to interact with it . . . Around their (the caretakers') personalities, the baby models its own personality . . . In a sense, it takes their personalities into itself. Thus . . . the other person, in effect, becomes melded with the *self*."[8]

Only as loved and related to does one become a potential person, and only as loved by God did humans emerge as humans. Only in being members one of another are we parts of humanity, but it's a matter of more or less. That's why we can speak of some as "real persons," "real human beings," comparatively, and sense that others, and ourselves, fall short. But since the ultimate context of all relations is God, and every other relationship is to something in creation dependent upon God, the question of being human is also the question of our relation to God, who stands behind the love that reached out to us and created us as persons. Being human means one learns to love, and only by becoming related does one become an actual person.

To be a Christian is to find one's own potential humanity presented to one in Jesus as "The Real Person," the one whose relation to other persons showed him to be "the real humanly-related person," and whose relation to God showed him to be "the real God-related person," and, as a result, one whose relation to himself (so far as we can discern it) was integral to the other two.

In short, Jesus becomes for us both the Most Loving One and the Most Lovable One,[9] the one to whom we might respond without any reservation at all—if we could respond to him wholly, and open ourselves

---

7. In the ancient Japanese folklore of the *Kojiki*, the primal "human" pair, the parents of Japan, are named Izanami and Izanagi, "he-who-invites" and "she-who-invites."

8. Ashbrook and Albright, *The Humanizing Brain*, 83f.

9. An important early psychologist of religion, Pratt stated, "In many cases getting converted means falling in love with Jesus." *The Religious Consciousness*, 160.

up to him completely. He is the one who can love us toward being truly human, embodying the New Being, entering the "Kingdom of God." He is the one who calls us to "walk as he walked."

At the same time, he shows us how carefully and strenuously we organize our lives, our institutions, and ourselves in order to ward off those dimensions of genuine humanity we find uncomfortable. And we attempt to make a virtue out of doing so, often claiming a relation to our institutions, and even to God, that involves violating our relations to other humans. By so doing, we align ourselves with those who crucified Jesus.

Taking Jesus seriously makes us aware how deeply we have done just that. Beyond that, however, we may also take seriously that he "came to seek and to save that which is lost," us. "Jesus' calling and work begins with his destruction of our idols; and the weapon that he uses to annihilate our false gods is the cross."[10] Idols are always enslaving. Not to recognize the falsity of our gods is to not take Jesus, or our humanity, seriously enough.

To save our false gods, we might take Jesus simply as an ideal, a role model, and many have tried to do so. But the "imitation of Christ" either becomes merely a more or less strenuous moral discipline, entirely in our own hands, and likely conducive to pride, or it finds itself growing into more than mere imitation. Why? Because Jesus held himself not to be "entirely in his own hands." He was focused on God, the Father; in terms of obedience to a will not his own that was nevertheless a will to his real fulfillment. He was called to discover and fulfill himself in being absorbed in his relation to God. And that meant a relation to others, to history, to the whole world.

That raises problems if we assume we already know what "God" is like. A Fascist dictator demands that every citizen be "absorbed into his re-lation" to the state, or to the leader himself, as, say, "the Fuehrer," and some have pictured God in that image. Others have thought of God as aloof, distant from the world, utterly dignified in his untouchable otherness.

But the testimony that Jesus bears to God is to the One he found behind the Bible narrative, the loving and compassionate Father, the be-stower of existence, life, freedom, and significance, as illuminated by Jesus' own devout life of prayer, which, as already noted, may be spoken of as "complete defenselessness before God." But complete defenselessness be-fore *What Is* means the abandonment of all our clinging to *what is not*.

10. Schlatter, quoted in Kasemann, *Perspectives on Paul*, 35n.

Limited by Greek metaphysical categories, the church in past centuries has spoken of the Christ as "of two natures," formally one-hundred-percent divine but formally one-hundred-percent human at the same time. That is the language of the creeds, language thoroughly foreign to the language of the Bible, the language of Jesus, the language of his disciples, and our language. And too often the "divine" tended so to obscure the "human" in the church's teaching that it hardly lived up to its own commitment, except verbally.

Jesus' death on the cross was his ultimate identification with God and God's ultimate identification with our humanity, and hence is our ultimate invitation to face up to the truth about how what *we try to make ourselves be* may contradict *what we more basically are* as the "image of God." Kasemann comments that "Jesus' cross is essentially directed against all religious illusion and it relegates man to man's humanity."[11] Our "humanity" is not to be defined empirically, by science or by "common sense," but by "looking to Jesus."

Karl Barth said in his *The Humanity of God* something that we have already quoted in part:

> It is when we look at Jesus Christ that we know decisively that God's deity does not exclude, but includes His *humanity* . . . . Is it not true that in Jesus Christ, as He is attested in Scripture, genuine deity includes in itself genuine humanity? . . . In the mirror of this humanity of Jesus Christ the humanity of God enclosed in His deity reveals itself. Thus God is as He is. Thus He affirms man. Thus he is concerned about him. Thus he stands up for him.[12]

And Canadian Douglas J. Hall: "the Christian gospel has more to do with the humanity of God than with the divinity of Jesus," and also the Dutch Catholic theologian Schillebeeckx: "God is more human than any human being."[13] That makes sense only in relation to Jesus as the Christ. But it is we who are to be more fully in God's image, even though our ideas of God are constructed in our own inadequate present image.[14] To believe is humbly to subordinate our mental pictures of God to The Conversation.

11. *Perspectives*, 35.

12. Extracted in Wm. Scott, *Sources*, 318, 9.

13. Schreiter, *The Schillebeeckx Reader*, 287.

14. 1 John 3:2, "we are children of God now; it does not yet appear what we shall be."

The problem of how Jesus is related to God—the involvement but also the distinctions that still demand intense theological discussions about the Trinity—might be given in terms of the "humanity of God" already mentioned. What Colossians gives as "He is the image of the invisible God, the firstborn of all creation" and Hebrews puts as, "He reflects the glory of God and bears the very stamp of his nature"[15] might today, I suggest, be said as, "though our humanness falls short of real humanity, Jesus was a human who in presenting us with genuine terrestrial humanity presents God's humanity also."

We may refer to the much-quoted verse of John 3:16, "this is the way God loved the universe: He sent his unique Son, that whoever is faithful to Him should not perish, but share in the life of the final age."[16] "Whoever" is an open reference to any human, of any race, sort, tongue, or kindred.

The Christian Gospel starts from two things: the precariousness of the human situation, and God's loving concern for all of it, indeed the whole universe. It goes on to tell of Jesus as God's involvement in human life—all our lives, our history, even our death—and God's involvement in (not merely authority over) the life of all of us.

Our interpretation of John's prologue identified Jesus as "the Conversation which is God-for-us become a part of human history." His death was an erasure of his significance, an erasure that the Resurrection nullifies, and gives us the contemporary Christ as the continuation, in subsequent history and into the future, of that Conversation he embodies.

"God's Conversation" that involves us includes all the interactions recorded in the Bible, all our interactions with those records, and much more.[17] But it isn't "conversation" at all except to the extent that we immerse ourselves in it. It is no mere casual conversation; it requires complete involvement.

15. Col 1:15, possibly written by Paul, and Heb 1:3, certainly written by someone else.

16. Translation my own.

17. I am not ready to deny that "the Conversation" also figured in some way in the lives of Buddha, Confucius, Muhammad, or Nanak, but believe we Christians and Jews are not capable of judging rightly just how that may be, and should not self-righteously attempt to do so, or allow them to do so for us. Christian humility requires that we resist the temptation to tell God what His relation to those other faiths is. *Testifying* to our own faith to them is the missionary imperative. *Judging* other faiths is not. We have much more pressing problems with ourselves in the light of the ways our own limited backgrounds and assorted stubbornnesses limit our witness.

To respond to the Christian Gospel is to find Jesus to be the embodiment of what it means to live a human life *coram deo*, "before God," and since we exist "before God," we have no other realistic alternative.[18] But as we also exist "among humans" as Jesus did, how we do that is also part of "the Conversation."

This means that "the imitation of Christ" is not defined by his statements as "a great moral teacher," but by accepting his promise to embody in our lives his openness to every kind of person, particularly those society passes by, his seriousness in listening to every indication of what God's love for the universe called him to do, his confidence in living within that love, and, above all, his profound assurance that God is faithful to His own loving aims, even when one has to face death for being obedient. And to commit ourselves to an institution within which those who are faithful find their individual and corporate unity.

That means the facts of his life are important when they help reveal *him* through what he did, said, and suffered, rather than the reverse, and show what we do and suffer in obedience to his charge. There is more. It means imitating as best we can his deep, constant private life of prayer. It also means that his embodiment in his own life of deep critiques of power, pride, piety, and particularity should illumine our whole social world, and so should his perception of the tragic dimensions of existence which we humans must face together with the Father.

Such commitments may be so subversive of our established habits that the best of institutions, even religious ones, may be tempted to turn against the genuine prophets of the Lord in their midst, and slay them for overturning the world's apple carts—as they did Jesus and many who have followed him.

In short, to "believe in the Christ" is to discover him to embody what it means to be a human being in the light of our widest context, to accept his offer of a transformed humanity, to be faithful as he was faithful to the Father, and to look forward to the promised future he presents. That's what finding the humanity of God in him means.

All of the above boils down to the question: what would be our maximal authentic fulfillment as humans, as images of God, over against

---

18. Jews too. The medieval rabbi Nachman told his son to do everything he did as if in the presence of *The Shekinah*, God's mode of being present.

the many *inauthentic* "fulfillments" we invent and seek?[19] How are we to be made, together, as human as possible? (A single human, like Adam, could not be really human.)

"As human as possible" assumes "the image of God," and that is the Christ. The social embodiment of this the church calls "the communion of saints." To be a saint is to be as human as one can become, even though knowing that one has not yet arrived.

The "offense of the cross" that made Jesus' crucifixion a "stumbling block" to young Paul and his Jewish contemporaries lay in the impossibility they saw that God could be so self-demeaning as to send anything less than a conquering Messiah, one who establishes Jewish Torah-culture everywhere. Our stumbling block is much more our difficulty in accepting that God would be so innovative (and so critical of our self-worship as humans) as to depart from our beloved "laws of nature" and our self-defined human standards to resurrect as "Lord" one who was, as one subversive of our established institutions, despised, rejected, and executed.

Our difficulties in believing lie in the cross's demand: it is *our humanity* that requires us to look to that despised, rejected, and "criminal" failure for the model of fulfilled humanity, who in his turn fulfilled the humanity of those around him.[20] The resurrection is a "stumbling block" as the demonstration that when we live as truly human, the world makes failures of us, and, in the last analysis, it is only God who can unmake our failures and carry us further.

How can any reasonable person face that? Ever since Jesus' resurrection, whatever that was, believers have found the deepest invitation for their humanity toward its fulfillment in the announcement that God, who presided over the original emergence of humans upon earth, certified Jesus as human's fulfillment. But he did this by negating the rejection, the criminality, the demeaning execution we humans laid upon him, and the reasons we did it and still are doing it. In answer, God made him the living Lord of human living, "the Lord Christ," the one to be followed and obeyed,

19. The Italian existentialist Abbagnano developed his philosophies of both science and life in terms of the difference between "authentic" and "inauthentic" possibilities.

20. Confucius got but a glimpse of this possibility when he characterized the "truly human man" as "If he wants to stand tall, he makes others stand tall; if he wants to succeed, he makes others succeed." "Analects" 6.28.2, trans. mine. He also admitted he had never found such a person, 4.6.1, 2.

one given a transcendence over the shared limitations of our self-centered humanness, a transcendence that promises a less limited humanity.

How did it happen that Jesus, who identified himself with "the Son of man," came progressively to be called "Messiah" (God's special appointee), then "Lord," then "Son of God," the title that later Christians interpreted in terms of Greek thinking as a metaphysical mystery, that Jews considered blasphemous, and that Muhammad, in the Qur'an, rejected by "God has no son!"?[21] What sense can be made of "Son of God"?

In the Bible, we find a distinct pattern of the son-father relationship. A son

1. Is acknowledged by his father,

2. Learns from his father,

3. Is obedient to his father,

4. Identifies himself with his father's aims and interests,

5. Is recognized as continuing his father's presence in the world, and

6. Inherits his father's realm.

He need not be descended from his father he may be adopted,[22] but he must function as a son in those ways. The Apostle Paul spoke of believers as being "baptized into Christ" (Rom 6:3; Gal 3:27) and as being "adopted as sons" (Rom 8:15–6, 23; Gal 3:27),[23] a theme echoed by other writers in Ephesians 1:5 and Hebrews 12:7 (most experts doubt that either was written by Paul, the former by a later disciple or associate, the other by one somewhat influenced by his teachings).

Whatever else the title "Son of God" may mean, it is evident that Jesus, in his complete commitment of his life to coming to know God's will for him, his obedience to that will, his identifying himself with God's Kingdom, and subordinating his private concerns to it, learned from God, obeyed God, and identified himself with God's aims, and so fulfilled numbers 2, 3 and 4 above. His resurrection was perceived as number 1, God's acknowledgment, apparently read back into several stories in the gospels.

21. Qur'an 5, 75; 19, 35; 43, 59.

22. In the Israelite "levirate law," a dead man's widow could give him a son by his brother, and the child would legally be the dead man's "son." See Mark 12:19; Deut 25:5–6; also Psalm 2:7.

23. In 9:4 he also speaks of "The Israelites" as having been adopted as God's "sons." Some early Christians believed Jesus had been "adopted" at his baptism.

What is reported as his "giving of the Holy Spirit," interpreted as "I am with you always," shows his recognition as continuing his father's work, and the church has never separated "Thy kingdom come" from the fulfillment of history spoken of as "the Christ's return," the fulfillment of the Father's intentions. It seems to me that anyone who insists on attributing some further kind of "Sonship" to the Christ claims to know more about both the Father and the Son than either the texts or Christian faith require. Do we really know enough about God to dictate what "Son of God" must mean exactly?

Philosopher Alfred Whitehead spoke of "the fallacy of misplaced concreteness." Christians have tried too hard to make God "concrete" in Jesus. The concreteness of Jesus' *humanity* is his divinity; otherwise we are denying John's assertion that it is *Jesus* who "makes God known" as *the Conversation made flesh*. This is one of those places where philosophy has often corrupted theology by tempting it toward achieving conceptual clarity where that can't be done.

The concreteness of "incarnation" just *is* Jesus, not some further set of concepts we want to extend his confrontation of us by.

If the most basic dimension of human life is our relation to God, Jesus' devoted sonship confronts us with what a human being can be, and what we should be, while by his failure and death, he shows that the final obedience is not something we can achieve for ourselves. That constitutes his fullness of humanhood.

At the same time, his resurrection, and the constant presence that Christian experience testifies to, confront us with *what evidence there can be* of God's steadfast promise to fulfill our humanity as He fulfilled Jesus'. What more of "God with us" and "God for us" can we hope for or desire? That constitutes what, within the limits of our finite human formulations, we can mean by his "divinity." God's humanity, shown in Jesus, we can not only at least partially understand, but also can seek to enter into.

Am I denying the title "Son of God" to the Christ? Not at all! The problem isn't accepting the title or rejecting it, but determining, "What do we mean by it?" Rejecting the Christ or following him is not a matter of titles, but of looking to him, relying on him to save us from ourselves. It is also learning from him, identifying with him as he identified with us, and being faithful to him as he was faithful to the Father. And that may mean somewhat different things to each of us. Each one of us is called individually to be saved into his obedient flock, his Kingdom.

By this time the philosopher is saying, "So what? How can anyone believe such theological cant, such pious daydreams? How can he be "Our contemporary"? He can't be seen, examined. There's no evidence he's still available. Why should we believe on no evidence?"

No one tells you you *should* believe. Believers aren't better than unbelievers; they don't *deserve* more. They just have received more, more than they deserve, and have responded because they were helped to respond. The question isn't, "What *should* we believe?" It is, "Have we heard the invitation, and, if we have, what *may* we believe?" If considering Jesus draws us to him as the revealer of what we are and what God is, there is no reason we *shouldn't* believe. We are free and responsible persons, and don't have to justify ourselves before those who have not heard the invitation, or before those who have heard it and rejected it.

And it isn't true we have no evidence. The evidence is ambiguous, as everything deep about us humans is, but it's real. The evidence is the church, not so much the church of the hum-drum believers, but the church of the saintly (who may be hard to identify). We are called to be more human by those whom we see to be more human, and hence more Godlike, than we are. And those are the ones who are most like Jesus, who is the most Godlike because he is most human. They confront us with Jesus as God's Christ, God's Conversation, into which we are invited.

Then what of the cross? Why did Jesus have to be rejected, shamed and crucified[24] to fulfill his mission? The Bible points toward a variety of ways of answering that question, and the church has experimented with several types of theories about it. Mark quotes Jesus as saying that the Son of man came "to give his life as a ransom for many," which led to the idea that the cross was a deal with Satan to buy his human captives back. That was quite popular centuries ago, but is not much heard any more.[25]

Paul said, "Christ died for (or 'because of') our sins"; this, with similar verses, led to various substitutionary theories, many of them bypassing the biblical overtones of "redeem" as "keeping in the family."

24. "[decapitation] was 'the least painful and degrading form of execution' . . . in contrast to crucifixion, one of the slow, spectacular, and painful . . . [ultimate punishments] inflicted on slaves and other imperial denizens of low status. Josephus gives multiple accounts of imperial crucifixions of Jews . . . Philo also attests to the crucifixion of Jews, describing the torture and crucifixion of Alexandrian Jews." Berkowitz, "Decapitation," 747–48.

25. Last century the Swedish theologian Gustav Aulen worked over this idea in his *Christus Victor.*

The last thousand years has seen widespread popularity of the idea that Jesus was the Father's whipping boy for the whole naughty human race: "the slave hath sinned, and the Son hath suffered," as one hymn puts it. That idea of a vengeful God, rather than the compassionate Father, whether demanding that his besmirched feudal honor be satisfied (the Medieval version) or his anger at disobedience be bought off (the more modern version) has, at the same time, put off many and has often misrepresented the biblical presentation of God.

Under Capitalism, that was changed into God as the Great Creditor, to whom our sinful debts must be paid, and "Jesus paid it all" another possible misrepresentation of God. And theories that make Jesus' sufferings simply a model of faithfulness for us to copy or a sorry tragedy for us to be sentimental about are much too thin.

As often happens when one spends time and effort on any profound matter, thinking about the cross shows how complicated our human situation is. One could say, it shows how difficult is the task that God's love for his creation set for Him. Even the unlimited power that could create free beings could only do so by limiting itself. The unlimited love that willed freedom for those beings in their self-contradictions could do so only by accepting upon itself the tragic contradictions caused by their relations to one another. The unlimited patience that could wait eons for free beings to appear so they could look forward to promises to be kept would have to endure patiently those who undercut such promises. But love capable of tender compassion for the entire cosmos and concerned with healing its alienations without destroying its freedoms must suffer the strain of identifying with the evil as well as the good.

The great biblical epic presents God not only as he who brings something out of nothing, freedom out of slavery, meaning out of meaninglessness, life out of death, but also as he who "justifies the ungodly." Such characterizations may be true even when every theory we can form to explain them is woefully unsatisfactory.

One problem is that the question some Christians are prone to ask, "Are you saved?" focuses too narrowly. The biblical language, and hence the Christian language, is quite properly ambiguous. It says we *have been saved* by the life, death, and resurrection of Jesus; we *are being saved* by the ongoing processes of God's Conversation working within the church, in each member, and elsewhere in the world; and *we will be saved* eventually when God's work of reconciling His whole creation to His loving faithfulness, "the Kingdom of God," is finally accomplished. No theory can deal satisfactorily with all three: the mysteries of past history, present indeterminacy, and eschatological fulfillment. Our human language is simply inadequate. To speak of salvation in any lesser terms is to fail to have an adequate idea of it or of the depth of evil that requires it.

Just as the biblical language indicates, Christian experience involves the discovery that the limitless past of the Conversation led toward the saving of the world in the death and resurrection of the Christ. It also involves the awareness that our present lives are being saved by the Conversation's presence, which we are moved to call the Christ's presence in both the church and the world, and, further, the confident hope that looks forward to the completion of God's undertaking of saving His creation from its corruptions of its own freedom.

So I accept none of the theories "explaining" the cross.[26] I simply trust that what happened there contains the crux of our own existence, that the resurrection indicates the future's highest promise, and together they present an inexhaustible challenge to our thinking about nearly everything important a challenge we have to respond to in whatever way we find we ought.

Let me quote once more, as an appreciative Protestant, an important modern Catholic theologian, this time on the crucifixion:

> Christ's death . . . was not a liturgical flight from the world, but in the deepest sense, his immersion to the very depths of his being as a person in the human life in the world, a radical love for men, only intelligible in its completely radical character in the light of the love of God himself for men.[27]

Jesus' cry on the cross, "My God, why hast thou forsaken me?" is for me not only the climax of the poetic (but historically true in important ways) drama of the life of Jesus, but the sign of what is wrong with us, requiring the Resurrection to be the true signpost to the future. My Christian intuition hears that cry as the other side of God's identification with those who were crucifying him.

That cry shows that The Father's solidarity with Jesus' identification with humanity included His solidarity with Caiaphas, the Sanhedrin and

26. A profound but troubling interpretation is found in Zizek, *The Puppet*, 16, and here and there following.

27. Schillebeeckx, in Schreiter, *Schhillebeeckx Reader*, 250.

Pilate, with the mob, the Roman soldiers, Judas, and hence with all of us. "This is the way God loved the cosmos—and ALL in it: He gave his Son." But God did not consider those who slew Jesus as "them," but just as much "us" as Jesus himself. And that calls us to crawl out of our isolating and self-justifying shells into trusting the One who could do what we cannot.

Also, and this we love to forget, Jesus' cry from the cross was his recognition that doing God's will is to be confronted by the *terrifying awfulness* of God, what Rudolph Otto called "the negative Divine," God not merely "fascinating," saving, but "tremendous," frightening. "Our God is a consuming fire!" "He can create, and He can destroy!" To obey God is to face being destroyed. Jesus said, "Take up your cross," the most frightening death he or his hearers knew. A merely "gentle Jesus" cannot be a fit revelation of the overwhelming "zeal" of God.

To me, the gospel story, with its background and historical consequences, is the greatest and the truest of all poems, even if it's not philosophy. The philosopher, being human, can only kneel before the Cross and Resurrection. But then, he can rise to "Rejoice evermore; pray without ceasing; in everything give thanks" (1 Thess 4:16–18a).

That is the appropriate behavior of one who has been freed from the guilt of conventional self-defined humanity and is constantly (though far too slowly and too inconsistently) being remade into a more and more truly free and loving human person, living at least the promise of the eventual humanity of "the Kingdom of God" that Jesus announced and the church proclaims.

So about Jesus I can frame no unique theory. I am reduced to admitting that he has confronted us not physically, as the man from Nazareth, but as someone who causes us to stop, listen with the "third ear," trust, love, and obey. As he shapes our inner life, he reshapes our life with others, and eventually our perception of the world.

But this can't be stated in clear concepts. Those who have been, and still are, there—and are profoundly humbled—are the only ones who can testify to it.

19

Conclusion

Thou canst not think a mere barbarian Jew,
As Paulus proves to be, one circumcised,
Hath access to a secret shut from us?
Thou wrongest our philosophy, O king, . . .
Oh, the Jew findeth scholars! Certain slaves
Who touched on this same isle, preached him and Christ;
And (as I gathered from a bystander)
Their doctrines could be held by no sane man.

—Browning, *Cleon* 1

So FAR, THE VARIOUS themes promised in the Introduction have been dealt with, including the relation of philosophy to theology, and our problems with the sources telling of the stories of his birth, his miracles, his aims, his death, and his resurrection. We have also touched upon some modern problems for belief.

Before reviewing what has been done so far, the underlying theme of the whole book needs restating: the Enlightenment's commitment to clear, conceptual language led Deists like Jefferson to concentrate on Jesus' moral teachings as an escape from having to deal with the Resurrection. So Jesus' words became the center of attention. But Jesus' importance, as shown by both the whole New Testament and the history of the church, lay with his crucifixion and resurrection and his charge to the apostles to preach the latter, not primarily his teachings.

Further, the politicization of Christianity by Constantine tied the gospel to power, so that "faith" became submission and admission, rather

1. Browning, *Poems*, 246–47.

than response to the Christ. The Enlightenment was a huge rebellion against submission, which has lasted well into our own times.

Cleon's plaint in Browning's poem thus is not outmoded. One can hardly immerse oneself in today's philosophizing without recognizing that many doctrines the church has taught in the past can now "be held by no sane man," in some of the forms they have taken in the past.

But, as suggested, there are great poems some can't understand, and which others try to read as if they were prose and find them foolish. There is also great music that is little but organized noise for those with a "tin ear." We allow to some poetic gifts and to others musical gifts, but we don't want to say they know "truths" we can't know. And yet serious distinctions are made between "real" poetry and doggerel, and between "real" music and what is just "turned out," not "inspired." "Poetic truth" is widely recognized outside those circles like science, law, and much philosophy, which are enslaved to literal prose.

Why isn't that same allowance made for religious judgments? Because they claim to be some sort of norm for any human, giving God's measure of humanity, not just that of those piously bent. A "tin ear" for poetry or music isn't taken to limit a person's humanity or ultimate worth the way religious folks take unbelief to do.

Religion claims it has *knowledge* basic to understanding one's self, others, history, and even the cosmos; knowledge that can be transmitted though not prosaically. If it doesn't make that claim, it's not religion.

Part of the problem is that what it means for each of us *to be a human being* can't be put into prose. To quote Jacques Ranciere,

> teaching is first of all the exercise of our intelligence's leading virtue: the poetic virtue. The impossibility of our *saying* the truth, even when we *feel* it, makes us speak as poets, makes us tell the story of our mind's adventures and verify that they are understood by other adventurers . . .[2]

There is a sense that each believer has a unique religion, because genuine religion is so deeply part of us that it reflects the unique elements in our individuality. Or, as a Christian might put it, God calls us as free individuals into being still more deeply free individuals.

Anyone who has wrestled with the branch of "philosophy of religion" called "theory of religious knowledge" knows that works in that field are

2. Quoted by Arthur Dewey in Cameron and Miller, *Redescribing*, 109.

either full of problems or contain logical "stumbling blocks." Yet authors still write books about it. My library has quite a number of them. And they do so because the serious religious philosopher knows two things: there are people who *do* know something very deep and very religious, and *not one of them* talks logically satisfactory language about what they know. So they can't be "reasonable" about it, in any prosaic and public sense of "reasonable," let alone in a technical academic philosophical one. Yet what they have can be taught, if also caught.

What Cleon said of Christianity is often echoed. According to many contemporaries, doctrines the church has taught in the past can be "held by no sane man," especially in the form they were once held. But doctrines are particular formulations of the basic faith, which, due to the limits of every human language, may receive many differing formulations. Hence, any set of doctrines represents how the religious body happens to be teaching the faith in a certain age and culture, marked by their thought forms. Which means, they may be derivative, they may be modifiable.

Doctrines are but static plaster casts of once-living moments in the Conversation. It is a shame they have so often been taken as some final pattern of the Word, which, since it is the Living Word, escapes any static formulation.

That is particularly true of dogmas, which are those doctrines claimed by authorities to define the strict fundamentals of the faith, though the Conversation, which has "shone in the darkness" for centuries, and has promised to "lead us into all truth," tends to outstrip any such strict formulation.

Some of the popular difficulties many have in believing arise from time lag. Important statements of belief that were formulated in the fourth, fifth, thirteenth, sixteenth, or seventeenth centuries are still recited in the churches, though rarely carefully analyzed except by technical theologians for other theologians. And criticisms of Christianity that were cogent in the second or fourth centuries, or the seventeenth or eighteenth, though no longer having the same immediate relevance today, still hang on in other folks' minds, equally unanalyzed.

Our ideas of what being a human means vary from age to age, just as from culture to culture. When one's knowledge of himself is confronted by someone's testimony to Jesus, he is faced with the problem of a bridge or chess player who has to take over someone else's game. The starting point for each of us is different, even if the game has closely followed some traditional lines.

Each person, each age, and each culture finds itself meeting Jesus in a way appropriate to both its background and its peculiar bents.

One present problem is that crucial developments in Christian thought that developed in the nineteenth and twentieth centuries are popularly unknown. They have insufficiently trickled down into the pews. This is in part because, as noted in our discussion of language, religious language is inherently unclear. It should be qualitatively and practically ("pragmatically") as rational as possible, but it can't be quantitatively rational, and hence precise.

But it is also due to the fact that pastors are so busy running churches they don't have the time, the skills, or the inclination for much genuine philosophical or theological thinking—or the stomach for the controversy within the congregation that honestly airing one's own informed questions would stir up. As an especially effective pastor put it to me, "It is very difficult to raise problems for people you love."

Another part of the difficulty lies in one of the few weaknesses of our democratic thinking: if the judgment of the ordinary person, "the majority," is to rule, then the truth should be what "everybody" thinks. To be that, it must be simple and easily stated, something one can readily grasp and quickly reach agreement about, preferably, something one was taught long ago, that one needs to learn nothing new about. It is even better if it is couched in high-sounding words one doesn't really understand, but that nevertheless feel comfortingly familiar. Far too many congregations don't want to hear any theology that requires harder thinking, deeper experience, or more strenuous self-examination than they are accustomed to. Many don't want to hear any philosophy at all. Indeed, "true" in religion often just means "familiar," what I am comfortable with.

But equally part of the problem is the fact that most Christians know only their own small part of the immense Christian tradition, which spread eastward very early to India and reached China in 605, spread southwards to Africa (Ethiopia) and westward to both sides of the Strait of Gibraltar, and northward to the British Isles, Scandinavia, and Russia a thousand years ago or more, developing distinctive emphases and accents in each area. And usually only a small sliver of their own fraction is known. The more widely one knows the tradition, the more grounding he has for making intelligent decisions about meanings and relevancies. And the more problems he may also become aware of.

I have touched on some of these problems. First, are our records of Jesus reliable? The gospels, our only real sources for his story were discussed, with very mixed conclusions. They are not to be read as strictly history, but as presentations of traditions about Jesus, organized and worded in light of each evangelist's aims. Yet they were earnest efforts to present the meaning of Jesus as understood by some who sincerely accepted his authority, and they provide us with the only resources we can draw on.

My discussion granted Mark the most credence, as he was earliest, but he must be read in terms of his theological insights. His reports of fact that Jesus began to spread the Baptist's news of pending divine judgment to be followed by a new world-system, that he was popular as a healer and exorcist, that he chose and trained twelve followers, that he was opposed by Pharisees and temple authorities, and that he was crucified, are practically indisputable. These, plus his rising again, are widely shared in the Christian community.

Other teachings of Mark, such as the significance of Jesus' title "Son of man" and the difficulty and obscurity of the title "Son of God," were not clearly grasped, as evidenced by Mark's copiers and expanders, by Luke and then Matthew, nor probably by most Christians. And they still aren't.

Material not found in Mark that appears in the other gospels may be questioned, but not all is to be discounted, since some of it may well go back to Jesus. Deciding which does is difficult.[3]

As for the birth *stories* (not Jesus' birth), I also pointed out that neither of them was history. Emphasis on the "virgin birth" that developed should be seen as a consequence of Christians disputing Jewish critics, who preferred the Hebrew reading of an Isaiah passage to the Greek translation.

With the exception of the Resurrection, which requires special treatment, miracle stories, as I pointed out, need not be accepted wholesale, or even at all. I granted the *possibility* of miracles occurring, but agreed with Hume's point that miracle *stories* lack evidential value.

Jesus' role was to be a prophet of God's bringing in a new order; his task was to prepare a "New Israel" to await God's action, his expectation was to die, as a prophet, in Jerusalem, a victim of "the Beast," the world's

---

3. This not to say it has no authority at all over Christians. Tradition may be edifying, early tradition as well as later tradition.

(and the devil's) system of power. His hope was in God's future vindication, whatever that might turn out to be.

His resurrection occurred but is beyond description. His body was disposed of; and played no part in the resurrection, which nevertheless left him in some way recognizable. His "appearance stories" are more instruments of later controversy than historic accounts. He appeared to "apostles" in ways we can't know, but commissioned them to preach of God's appointing him to authority.

That summarizes my arguments so far. I return to the discussion of present barriers to belief.

A difficulty even more basic than those mentioned earlier is harder to speak of clearly. It is that "thinking of Jesus" has often been more "being a spectator toward Jesus," thinking "at Jesus." The reality, to put it in a clumsy but better way, is thinking "in the presence of Jesus." In the statement heading an earlier chapter Albert Schweitzer said: "He commands . . . And to those who obey him . . . he will reveal himself."

Thinking about Jesus is not simply juggling relevant concepts. Nor is it mooning over pleasing emotional responses. Nor is it just doing what I also have done, cooking up imaginary supplements to the gospels. It is letting him transform us, but not so we can brag about being "saved," or "orthodox," or "conformist." It is so that we can find who we really are, and what our deepest situation is. Jesus gets "under our skin."

Paul experienced this as "dying with Christ." That's a puzzling and confusing description, and hence, one quite appropriate to the way Jesus puzzles and confuses. Our humanity is in itself puzzling and confusing, and his is more so. Every philosopher knows that "God" is puzzling and confusing, so facing Jesus' Sonship must be so too.

Further, I pointed out that the sources of our knowledge of Jesus must themselves be criticized, as not firsthand, as tendentious, as unclear, as appearing with textual variations, as permitting various interpretations. These problems have been studied and argued about for centuries. Given such materials, we must do the best we can. (It must be pointed out, however, that the manuscript sources about Jesus are far older and much more extensive than those for Plato, Aristotle, or any other ancient philosopher). There is more than enough for careful study and defensible conclusions regarding Jesus. My conclusions, and the reasons for most of them, were given.

The introduction said we must make assumptions about Jesus' early years. In the stories, I assumed a number of things: his education, marriage, immersion in the Hebrew Scriptures, and his deep influence by Jonah and Daniel. Those assumptions are reflected in the discussions of his aims first, to be the announcer of the coming Kingdom, and then to form, or finally to be, the true Israel, the "Son of man." They would be overcome by the powers that be, the "Beast," but then would be eventually vindicated by an act of God. That act, I affirmed, began with the Resurrection, but it continues to unfold within that part of the church that participates in "the Conversation" which was offered as the meaning of John's "Word." God can take as long as he chooses.

The Resurrection was (and is) an event frustrating description or analysis. It is a given that we inherit from those few "apostles" whom Jesus confronted and addressed some time after his burial, and who supplied content for the Conversation.

That Conversation is the ocean we thrash about in, its subsequent tradition the water in which we frantically tread to stay afloat. Those on the equally puzzling and confusing but less-than-secure shore of secularism may wonder what it's worth for us to swim, over what Kierkegaard called "eight thousand fathoms." They don't see that we are supported by Him who is both the tide of God's history and the pulse of our livingness.

John's prologue reminds us that:

1. It is "the Conversation" that God is concerned with.

2. The "Conversation" is our clue to "what it means for God to be our 'God.'"

3. That "Conversation" was "from the beginning."

4. It "was shining in the darkness" through all of history and in all places, especially in the Jewish scriptures.

5. It "became an embodied part of human history" in Jesus of Nazareth.

6. Those who have "beheld its glory" know it to be "full of gracious truth."

A fundamental issue, then, is "where do we find an ongoing current of 'gracious truth' running through history?" Where do we "behold its glory"? The answer can only be, "Where we in fact do find gracious truth, and where we do behold its glory." It is a matter of seeing, based on hearing, not on argument.

But no matter how gracious the truth is, since the light "shines in the darkness" and every human culture is part of that darkness, the light comes as subverting the comfortable pretensions of the institutions of civility, and its glory points beyond and shames our habitual expectations.

The light may surprise us by breaking in upon us, but more likely we need to look for it. But when we find it, even though it be in the form of a "stumbling block" or "foolishness" that "can be held by no sane man," it will be an invitation we refuse at tremendous risk. It is also as an invitation we accept at a great risk of a different sort. It may revise our "sanity."

The problem is that the "Conversation" is corporate as well as individual. Conversation always involves two or more. When "gracious truth" is seen, it is communicated, and becomes part of multiple conversations. People perceive the truth of the conversation in different ways. These may congeal into "doctrines," and, where there is ecclesiastical authority, some are sorted out as "dogmas." Then "belief" may become defined in terms of the dogmas, rather than the "gracious-ness" of the "truth," excluding the freedom and the honesty it normally would provoke.

This book is not intended to be a book about doctrines, but about Jesus. Yet, as we have insisted, Jesus is important only as the Christ. And the core of the gospel, from which Christianity springs, and hence from which all doctrines should spring, is the proclamation that Jesus indeed *is* the Christ. But that is not a self-explanatory saying, so its explication has to be in terms of language meaningful for those to whom it is proclaimed. Where do the standards come from that such explication must meet to be true to the gospel?

As pointed out in the remarks on language, when an existing prosaic language, a denuded language, is inadequate for expressing what is seen in human life, we turn to metaphor, poetry, and narrative—and even ceremony and ritual—to express what is really the case. Such things may be stumbling blocks or empty words to the logician, the grammarian, the scientist, or the Philistine.

Critical history tries to encapsulate Jesus into academically respectable prose, but the significance of Jesus, and any reason at all for taking him seriously, emerges only out of reading the records of him and of those who have thought about him as echoes of a profound poem, part of the ongoing Conversation which is God-for-us. (We cannot know God-for-himself; we can only know God-for-us, and be thankful he is *for* us!)[4]

Musing about Jesus lures us into seeing his identity with us in his identification with all the sorts of folk he found around him, and in finding ourselves appearing as characters in the stories about him or the stories he told. Whatever else he was, he was one of us, perhaps more us than we ourselves are.

In doing this, he alters our perception of both God and us at the same time. As the man confronting us with "God's humanity," he gives us at the same time what it means for God to be God-for-us.

In the process, the contrast between our half-heartedness and Jesus' complete dedication both to God and to others confronts us with a challenge to our understanding of what it means to speak of humans as "in the image of God." We modern Christian European humans have been proud to claim that for ourselves, while enslaving, oppressing, exploiting, and decimating non-European peoples. At the same time we have criticized them for their inhuman treatment of one another, while often treating them inhumanly ourselves. Jesus stops us short by presenting us with an image of the humanity of God beyond any that we can justly claim for ourselves.

To follow Jesus is to accept the risk of seeing both history and cosmos in terms of his background, his faithfulness to being "the best Jew possible," his vision of what it means "to love the Lord thy God with all thy everything," and the compassionate goodness of God as revealed in his death and resurrection.

That may mean to share, in some way relevant to our lives and our place in the world, his suffering and even death, and to be personally identified with him in his resurrection. It also means sorting through what those who have followed him before us have suffered, while yet "beholding" the "glory" of the "gracious truth" offered in living in "the Conversation."

---

4. Compare the comment of Schadewaldt, a professor of Classical Languages: "There are circumstances which can only be expressed adequately in the form of a revelation which conceals . . . not because the one who talks . . . wants to make a mystery out of something . . . but because the nature of those circumstances does not allow any other kind of language as an adequate expression." (In his article in Hengel, *Studies*, 96.) See my comments in Appendix D.

That of course, is unbelievable if taken literally, but it is "the way things are" when seen in what the strange language points to. Everything in life becomes the Conversation when we seriously "take up the cross."

The problem immediately arises: much "poetic language" presents no truth, or little truth, or unimportant truth. What useful standard do we have to distinguish important truth from unimportant?

The answer is: the same basic method useful in science, business, common sense, in life. What can be lived, and how it can be lived, is the test, coupled with the continuing conversation of those who are living it.

Jesus gives us no rule book, only invitations, puzzles, and insights. He gives no plan of "the Kingdom" for us to implement. He gives us seed to sow, knowing that some of it will bear abundant fruit. He offers a new level of being human, and he also makes that new way possible for his followers.

By telling each of us to "take up his cross" and face our own crucifixion,[5] he promises us we will participate in the world's pain and sorrow, but by so doing identify with all sorts and conditions of men, and thus serve freedom. He calls us to *care, to be responsive, to reach out*. Above all, to be defenseless against the truth, however it confronts us. And to those who obey, and converse, and listen, truth will emerge.

This isn't philosophy. Philosophy too often seeks to engineer truth in the name of loving it. To love truth is to accept that The Truth loves us. And to notice The Loving Truth wherever it shows itself, even when it shows us up.

Something more follows. Jesus not only defines for us the past and present, he also colors the future. Not that he gives a particular social or economic program, but he indicates standards to apply to any such program, standards more like those of art criticism than like laws. He calls us to love the whole creation with profound and open sensitivities. He calls us to be faithful to whatever light we have.

Above all, he calls us to hope, as he had hope. The German theologian Moltmann has pointed out that Jesus did not come to establish a new

5. In a review of the recently-published *World Christian Encyclopedia*, Professor Michael McClymond reports that "the most surprising figure given in the *WCE* is the total number of Christian martyrs during the twentieth century—45 million . . . 'believers in Christ who have lost their lives prematurely, in situations of witness, as a result of human hostility.'" "Making sense of the census," 884. The "blood of the martyrs" has indeed been "the seed of the church," but only along with the blood, sweat, and tears of a multitude of lesser followers, including many not called to any heroics.

religion, but to bring hope, peace, joy, life all *shared*, none of which we are as yet fully able to characterize or appreciate, but must find ourselves on the way toward fuller awareness of them.

That Jesus did not come to establish a new religion is relevant to a problem mentioned in the Introduction: what of all the other religions in the world? They have their ways, their standards, their rituals, their literatures, and their theologies. Their adherents are just as much objects of God's love and compassion as are Christians. If we, made in God's image, are to be "sons," Jesus' "younger brothers," we cannot be patronizing toward them as the Pharisees and Sadducees patronized Jesus.

The Syrophoenecian woman noted that crumbs of the family's bread fall from every family's table, for others, even those we think of as dogs, to pick up. We are to be hospitable to all; if they find our crumbs nourishing, we should rejoice; and we should not despise their crumbs. How they hear the Conversation, which is what God can be for us, is between them and God, but Jesus' hospitality requires us to invite them to our table and to participate in the Conversation. And we can respect their attempts at conversation while acknowledging that we do not have the role of being their judges. If the Christ brings New Being, he offers it to them on his terms, not ours. We can only testify to what we have found to be true, and listen to them as part of our listening to The Conversation.

Hope, peace, joy, life, New Being. That sort of thing is expressed in poetry, in song. Poetic evidence is not scientific evidence, nor is it logical evidence or evidence of the sort honored by any typical empiricist philosophy. Evidence that is not self-involving cannot be evidence for *God*, since evidence for what is ultimately and inescapably self-involving, community-involving, and even cosmos-involving can only be self-involving, community-involving, and even cosmos-involving evidence.

That deep Christian thinker Schillebeecx has said,

> Detached from a life-style in conformity with the kingdom of God, the Christian confession becomes innocuous and *a priori* incredible. The living community is the only real reliquary of Jesus. . . . It is in Christian living that one sees who really believes in the risen Jesus, the future of a more hallowed world[6]

If evidence comes only from believing with the community of believers and living the appropriate form of life along with the community

6. In Schreiter, *Schillebeeckx Reader*, 187.

of that form of life, the meaning of Jesus for one's self and for one's place in history will appear, but only within the context of such serious living, noticing, and thinking within a believing community, a community of "the Conversation" which is the Logos. And this book has been an attempt at a serious contribution to that Conversation.

Does speaking of "The Conversation" claim "revelation"? In terms of whose account? There can be no "revelations" in the general terms philosophy deals in, as there are no criteria by which to identify one. I pointed out that our "reason" is a purely human and largely cultural thing, based on our habits of thought, developed through the evolution of humans and their cultures. The revelation of anything genuinely new may very well disrupt those well-established ruts in our minds. "Revelation" that is not in some sense "revolution" should be suspect.

"Revelation" is a theological term, which, as theological, has its anchorage in the judgments regulating the form of life of an already-existing believing community. That "form of life" gives meaning to life, since the meaning of life derives from some answer to the question, "What is required of me, as a human?" Outside of a community defined by an answer to that question—that is, outside a community of faith—true "revelation" is "contentless," except for some possible rhetorical function as a power claim.[7]

Within such a community, "revelation" simply means that the gospel has come to us, that it has confronted us and captured what is most central and best in us. God has not so much informed us as *called* us through the gospel. It is not a conclusion drawn from our living a form of life, but it is the foundation and illumination of that form of life, the certificate of its newly authenticated possibilities.[8]

7. It is a deep shame how often claims of "revelation" have served those who hold or desire power.

8. The Conversation, as described by an experienced pastor: "It is in local congregations that values are weighed in the presence of Word and Sacrament. It is in local congregations that private opinions and public policy are brought to the tribunal of biblical evidence and confessional history. It is in local congregations that a pastor whispers the gospel and preaches to the deepest hungers of the soul. And it is there, in the midst of the people, that love is tested in intimate struggles and one's own faith is nurtured by the example and rebuke of folk who support and cajole and inspire the pastor. . . . Is there another institution more focused on human priorities? More in touch with the crucial moments in life? More connected to the full range of the human condition? Better suited to question personal behavior and social patterns? To preach good news?" Creevey, *Seminary Chimes*, 13.

As has been maintained throughout, it is the gospel that gives meaning to the living of the form of life, which then gives meaning to the religious speech, which then in turn bestows meaning upon the theological language. The intellectual "empirical anchorage" of the basic language of faith is simply that we have found the gospel to draw forth a more compelling conspectus of what we are as humans, what our milieu really is, what past history means, where our most authentic possibilities lie, and that it constrains us to live in its terms.

The central gospel poem, Jesus, has a long sequel—the Christian tradition—but the two together are but part of the larger biblical poem. That is part, though a distinctive part, of the larger poem of human history generally, which is part of the still larger cosmic poem. And they are all part of The Conversation, which, as John's preamble points out, is what the word "God" means. We need to see all of them as the one Poem, embracing all there is.

If evidence comes only from living the appropriate form of life along with the community of that form of life, the word "God," lived with seriously, may therein provide its own evidence.

Poet William Cowper said,

> Blind unbelief is sure to err, And scan His works in vain;
> God is His own interpreter And He will make it plain.[9]

But since unbelief need not be blind, it may, seeking seriously, humbly, and communally enough, glimpse some "interpreting," eventually even something "plain."

Nothing I have said in these chapters constitutes any disproof of unbelief. I do not believe there is any such disproof. Thus those who dare the believer to show that it is irrational *not* to believe are making a safe bet, especially when "rational" is already defined on the basis of unbelief. Everything I have tried to call to readers' notice, every rhetorical question raised, everything that I have affirmed or to which I have testified, all added together, do not constitute an argument that believers are *objectively right* and unbelievers *objectively wrong*. Objectivity leads to prose; only gospel leads to faith, and gospel is not prosaic, because the fundamental truths about being human are not prosaic.

The language of faith is the language of life, of openness and freedom, not of objectivity and death. But it is also at odds with the intellectually

9. Cowper, *The Poetical Works*, 100.

responsible language of secular culture. Since Christianity is not some se-cret mystical cult, but an offer of life and freedom to the whole world, the believing philosopher must straddle two incompatible modes of speech in trying to speak of his faith to the world outside the church.

This discomfort was well put some sixty years ago by a Swiss scholar:

> To be a Christian means to stand in a clash of two languages. . . . Christian speech is canonical language at the borders of the world. . . . It is an illusion to believe in a Christian language free from apologetics, which is the point of contact with the world; but it is also foolish to deny that this very apologetics is bound to fail. . . . We try to use the speech of Athens in proclaiming the gospel there—but if this gospel falls on fertile soil, it is despite the method and not because of it. . . . And therefore we shall not be intimidated by the fear of using the wrong language as long as we stand in the biblical word and struggle for relevance in the contemporary one.[10]

Thus the language of faith is a language of fallibility, even when also of assurance within fallibility. The fallibility is both ours and secular culture's; God's faithfulness is the assurance.

To believe is, in large part, to locate rightness in God and His future rather than in oneself or in one's formulations based upon some prosaic account of the past. It is the complete acceptance of our "creaturehood," our finitude, what is required of us. As has been implied all along, faith does not need support, certainly not approval, from philosophy. Since it has an independent base, it just needs intellectual room in which to stand on its own feet, to make its own responsible interpretation of experience. Philosophy may go on from there.

I have tried to show that there is such room. Resolution can come only in the perceptions that arise out of appropriate forms of life. If the church cannot impress the world that it does indeed have something true to say, it should look to how well its form of life reveals what it proclaims, rather than to any form of argument.

Similarly, if a philosophy, or a whole culture, manifests to believers that it is, on its own presuppositions, quite deficient in its perception of what being truly human consists in, it, too, equally probably, should ask

---

10. Laeuchli, *The Language of Faith*, 238–40.

how its form of life answers the question, "What is required of me as a human?" This most basic issue is practical, not theoretical.

The gospel is the source of faith and of Christian language, but only God, not the gospel, is the Source and the Goal, the Alpha and the Omega. And, as known through any of the avenues of the Word, biblical or not, God is the beginning of obedience and the end of obedience. And obedience is the beginning and the end of fulfillment of the Shema', the beginning and the end of life, the beginning and the end of growing toward finding what it means to be a human in the full context in which we have been placed and the full range of authentic possibilities that lie before us.

The last word, therefore, must be in the language of faith, not that of philosophy. As the Beginning, God is the Inviter and the Giver; as the End, God is the ground upon which we look to being held responsible beyond anything we have ever known, to tasting the pain of existence, as we have not yet ever done. It also points to a fulfillment that embodies those authentic possibilities that are pointed to in the Christ, a fulfillment beyond any clear expectation.

Paul described this expectation as "to know him, and the power of his resurrection, and the fellowship of his sufferings" (Phil 3:10). For the cosmos it means whatever "a new heaven and a new earth" points toward.

Christians' language would say it is the Christ who lives in us, as we live in Him. Paul put it, "Christ in me, the hope of glory," but perhaps also, "your life is hid with Christ in God" (Col 3:3). He speaks many times of being "in Christ,"[11] and of Christ being "in" believers.[12] Such language may sound meaningless, but it expresses something believers know firsthand in their life with one another, something involved in their love for the world and those in it, something immediately bound up with the truth of the Resurrection, something much more than just an imaginative image. It is a poetic figure that could not be replaced by any other.

Jesus, known as the Christ, can take over one's whole horizon, one's orientation towards life. One is repeatedly surprised suddenly to see his relevance to some part of life one had never before associated with him.

To the strong, the athletic, he shows himself as Tennyson's

Strong Son of God, Immortal Love, . . .
Thou seemest human and divine,

11. Rom 8:1, 12:5, 16:3; 1 Cor 3:1, 15:18; 2 Cor 5:17; Gal 3:28; Col 2:6, etc.
12. Rom 8:10; Gal 2:20; Col 2:27, 3:11.

The highest, holiest manhood thou.
Our wills are ours, we know not how,
Our wills are ours, to make them thine.[13]

The tender, the ardent, would report their experience as

And what to those who find? Ah this
No tongue nor pen can show
The love of Jesus; what it is
None but his loved ones know.[14]

As another poet has put the sense of Christ's complete envelopment of the meaning of being human,

Yea, through life and death, through sorrow and through sinning,
He shall suffice me, for he hath sufficed.
Christ is the end, as Christ was the beginning;
Christ the beginning, for the end is Christ.[15]

In the Christian's "form of life," *that* is the end-point of believing, the final context within which both the questions of our "humanity" and our "rationality" are to be faced. It is the new song, sung in every garden within which the Great Hedgehog indicates his Elusive Presence, perhaps even to the philosopher. And if he is willing to notice it, to awaken to it, to live with it, she may eventually even say "Amen!"

Where, then, do we end up in this discussion of philosophy and Jesus? First, if treated as on an equal plane, they are irrelevant to each other. If philosophy is made triumphant, Jesus is still irrelevant. If Jesus is acknowledged as Risen Lord, philosophy, though somewhat demoted, is not at all debased. It is given a new and very comfortable context within which to do all its appropriate work quite respectably.

Second, philosophy still rules over conceptual thinking, and therefore wherever theology uses concepts, it must accept philosophy's logical guidance. But at the same time, philosophy must remember that there is language, and serious and responsible thinking, which deal with areas wherein strict concepts, because of the narrowness precision requires, would breed blindness and paralysis of mind and life. In such cases, truth comes through insightful and truth-loving conversation. As Paul pointed

13. Tennyson, "In Memoriam."
14. *Dulcis Jesu Memoria*, Bernard of Clairvaux, 1150(?) trans. Edward Caswell, 1849.
15. Myers, "Hark, what a Sound," *The Hymnal*, 110.

out, faith comes through hearing—if the other party in conversation also loves truth.

In the third place, truthful conversation requires a community that draws on confirmed past truth, presents current truth, and discovers and relevantly applies further truth, grows in it, and lives disciplined by it.

And fourth and most crucial, the Resurrection, though indescribable, did in fact happen, whatever it was. Despite the likely fact that none of the "appearance stories" come from witnesses, they were probably imaginative constructions created in later controversy.[16] To believe the Resurrection is to respond to the testimony of the earliest recorded eyewitness to the risen Christ, Paul, made more evidently reliable by his manifest reticence as to details and its effects on him, and his floundering around for language to argue from it (in 1 Corinthians 15, especially), and that testimony carried on through the church. He is the author closest to the event, and his acceptance of and relating of appearances to Peter, the twelve, and James is not easy to set aside.

So, when the church lives truly as the Conversation, it is the present witness for the Resurrection. Jesus is then believable, and relevant both intellectually and existentially. When (or if) the church functions in our world the way Jesus functioned in his, the power, and hence the fact, of the Resurrection is presented to the world. If it seeks not its own, as he did not seek to save himself, then its testimony to him is worthy of credence. If the Christian's life is a song, and the church an accompanying chorus, Jesus becomes evident as the Conversation. But theories about him, including my own, are only theories. And a church interested only in its own survival is no church at all.

If the gospel that Jesus is the Christ rings out as sublime music and beautiful poetry, the Conversation is present. I repeat again what Pascal said in his own way, that poetry presents truth that prose cannot handle.[17]

16. Luke's Emmaus story (24:13ff.) may have drawn on some earlier account, but has been so adapted by Luke for expounding his theology of history that it can hardly be viewed as evidence.

17. Pascal's "the heart has reasons that the intellect cannot know" does not use "heart" to mean "emotions," but in the biblical sense, wherein "Love the Lord with all your heart" means "with all your thinking processes, sensibilities, and interests." These go beyond conceptual formulation.

Conclusion

I close with the words of a Quaker saint who spent his life serving others, in which he describes his Christian experience as an invitation to ours. It is worth thinking about as possibly a dim echo of Jesus' own experience:

> The energizing, dynamic center is not in us but in the Divine Presence in which we share. Religion is not *our* concern; it is God's concern. The sooner we stop thinking *we* are the energetic operators of religion and discover that God is at work, as the Aggressor, the Invader, the Initiator, so much the sooner do we discover that our task is to call men to *be still and know*, listen, hearken in quiet invitation to the subtle promptings of the Divine.
>
> But the main point is not that a *new song* is put into our mouths; that point is that a new song *is put into* our mouths. We sing, yet not we, but the Eternal sings in us . . . The song *is put into* our mouths, for the singer of all songs is singing within us. It is not we that sing; it is the Eternal Song of the Other, who sings in us, who sings unto us, and through us to the world.[18]

Jesus the Christ is God's act, not ours. Not our projection, but God initiating our participation in the Conversation. It is a song sung to us, a song within us, a song put into us.

And as already said, true conversation, and The Conversation, are more like song than like prose.

The outcome of musing seriously about Jesus, even for a philosopher, is a song.

18. Kelly, *A Testament of Devotion*, 96–98 (italics in the original).

THE FELLOWSHIP OF HIS SUFFERINGS

I come to the garden alone
To greet the dew and to smell the roses.
There are thorns there, but no roses;
There are tears there, but no dew.
The garden seems a desert.

And He walks with me, and He talks with me.
But we are not alone,
For there is there a great multitude
Whom no one can number:
From the East and from the West,
From the North and from the South,
From every nation, tongue and kindred.
When He shares their thorns He shares mine;
When He shares their tears He shares mine.

Roses will not bloom in that garden,
Nor will they sparkle with dew,
Until the Sun of Righteousness rises in His glory.

That may take a long time.
But it is taking me a long time,
Walking and talking with Him,
To learn to share His thorns and His tears.
And theirs.

APPENDIX A

Was Jesus Married?

IN OUR IMAGINARY NARRATIVE, Jesus married. Many have assumed he never did. Thus Sullivan says bluntly, "Jesus was not married. . . . He viewed sexual attraction . . . as lust . . . Jesus approved of castration if performed for the kingdom of God." Sullivan is very tendentious. Every text he draws on as evidence can not only easily, but probably more correctly, be understood differently.

In Christian history one can find suggestions, recently exploited by the bestseller *The Da Vinci code*, that Jesus was married to Mary Magdalene. That book is effective fiction, but full of bad history, uncritical use of sources, and questionable theology. One can indeed read John 20:13 as Mary saying "they have taken away my husband," if ancient women could refer publicly to their husbands as "lord," but there is no supporting biblical evidence for such a reading. Similarly, an older Mormon tradition claimed Jesus was married to sisters Mary and Martha, justifying polygamy. None of these suggestions find serious support.

Yet, Jesus probably was married. Marriage was considered normal, indeed, more or less obligatory. Here we have a problem whose decision comes much more out of our sense of ourselves than from evidence, because we have none.

As a student, I was shocked to read theologian Emil Brunner's remark that he "couldn't think of Jesus as married." I must admit to the opposite reaction: I find it hard to believe he never was. His quoted saying, "There are some who have made themselves eunuchs for the kingdom of God" (Matt 19:12) is often taken to mean he forswore marriage. Yet, even if he was speaking of himself, and there is no direct implication that he was doing so, it says nothing about when, why, or how he "made himself a eunuch." That doesn't mean he castrated himself, though the church father Origen may have taken it that way. It would simply have meant he was abstaining from marriage or remarriage, and that meant all sexual activity, for the sake of "the kingdom of God," his calling.

The passage in Matthew appears in no other gospel, so it may have been a defense of Jesus against some criticism. It was certainly used later to encourage monasticism. But instead it may have been a genuine report in the tradition requiring us to interpret it in terms of our understanding of Jesus, rather than of Matthew and his situation. Jesus was certainly a person of great self-discipline.

On the contrary, his remark that marriage was God-ordained (Mark 10:6–9) and that divorce led to adultery are both more likely to be genuine. Jesus' strictness about marriage was not without precedent. The Essene *Damascus Document*, more than a century earlier, spoke of David as "caught in fornication twice by taking a second wife while the first is alive, whereas the principle of creation is, *Male and female created He them*. Also, those who entered the Ark went in two by two."

His views on marriage may well have arisen out of his own experience of becoming a childless widower, whether his wife died from disease or in childbirth, or, in those brutal times, was raped and killed or kidnapped and sold as a slave. Or he was most influenced by the beauty of his own marriage, as I believe. Biblical scholar Samuel Terrien puts such beauty well in his *Till the heart sings*:

> theologians . . . who look reflectively on the mystery of God—inevitably borrow from the language of true lovers . . . When creatureliness discovers its authentic humanity through a liberation from existential solitude, it ushers in adoration . . . Humanity transfigured by love mirrors divinity.

In any case, it is just as well Jesus left no children; there could have been a succession problem if he had (as it was, his brother Jacob "James" became leader of the church in Jerusalem, and a cousin followed him).

Late in his career he was challenged by the Sadducees with the tale of a childless widow who was handed down from one brother-in-law to another in six progressive attempts to get her pregnant with a son to inherit her original husband's estate (Mark 12:18–25). They asked, "In the resurrection, whose woman will she be?" Jesus' answer was, "When they rise from the dead, they neither marry nor are given in marriage, but are like the angels in heaven."

This has often been taken to be his denial that sex has any place in heaven, something we really know nothing about, nor do I think Jesus was making any such assertion.

Since Jesus undoubtedly knew of the account in Genesis of angels seducing human girls (Gen. 6:1–2), I read His saying with a quite different emphasis. He was insisting on the equality of worth of the sexes, by denying the inequality underlying the difference between "marrying," which a man was free to do, and "being given in marriage," which made a woman into a possession to be handed over.

The Sadducee's question was not primarily about sex, but about ownership. Their question was, "In the resurrection, whose will she be, for all seven owned her." In the heaven of the God who frees from oppression, there could be no slavery, no patriarchy, no ownership of persons by anyone but God.

Further, with the great stress in Judaism on the family, sex was considered primarily God's provision for the continuation of the human race. The "levirate law" to which the Sadducees appealed in their challenge was strictly to prevent inherited property being lost to a family by the childless death of its owner. By the law of inheritance, male children were required as heirs for property. Daughters should not of themselves inherit. A family would be left bereft of resources if the property passed to another.

In terms of those two functions, therefore, there would be no need for sex as procreation after the general resurrection, for there would neither be death or property transfers. However, our sense of population problems and overcrowding, our wide use of contraception, our multiplication of sex manuals hardly celebrating the production of offspring, coupled with the media's fascination with (and advertising's exploitation of) "recreational sex," gives to any concern about "will there be sex in heaven?" quite a different coloration.

I admit my bent here may be idiosyncratic. It apparently arises from my deep feeling that Jesus represents humanity, and, to me, on the basis of my own experience, being fully human means being married. Jesus certainly was much farther from being a "patronizing male chauvinist pig" than even his disciples. Women trusted him and followed him, and he was, for his times, very gentle and respectful toward them.

This may say something about his mother and sisters, but it also seems to me quite appropriate to his pattern of life for him to have deeply loved and lost, and yet to have remained faithful not only to his calling but to his spousal commitment. After all, he also said, of husband and wife, that they "become one flesh" in a way that forbids being set aside.

And there is an old tradition in the Eastern Church that a married priest whose wife dies cannot remarry.

His concern with and respect for women would imply at least that he did not relegate them just to being servants and breeding animals. In any case, there would be no room in his idea of the Kingdom of Heaven for any area subject to sin, and some ways in which women were treated were certainly sin.

Thus I don't feel eccentric in believing his answer to the Sadducees should not lead us to conclusions about his beliefs about sex or to a belief he must never have married. The idea of Jesus as a widower seems very congenial. He spoke of the disciples "leaving wives" for the sake of proclaiming the gospel. So I conclude he did without a second wife for the same reason.

APPENDIX B

The Son of Man

JESUS' USE, OR USES, of "Son of man" is a problem. In Mark it appears as an alternative to the "son of David" Messiah expected by Jesus' followers, where Luke and Matthew seem to use it simply as an alternative for Jesus himself. But in sayings ascribed to Jesus in Mark 13, it clearly refers to a divine figure sometime to invade human affairs.

"Son of man" as a figure "coming in the clouds" appears to have been interpreted by some first-century apocalyptics as a superior being about to come from heaven in judgment, ending the Present Age. Gospel references to such a being raise some historical problems. But Jesus' uses of the phrase that appear to be self-referential are the center of wide debate.

Despite the debate, it is a topic I believe to be so important that my interpretation requires more, and unfortunately stodgier, defense than makes for good reading.

There are two main sources claimed for the phrase in Jesus' usage. It is either an ordinary Aramaic substitute for "anyone" or "I," perhaps indicating some special function in oneself, or it derives from Daniel 7:13, where, in one of Daniel's "visions" he saw "one like a son of man (a human being) coming in the clouds of heaven" to stand before "the Ancient of Days." In the LXX translation, it is clearly "a son of man," but in the gospels it always appears with the definite article, "*the* Son of man." (Some have traced it to the book known as "Enoch," but there is no evidence of that work having influenced Jesus,[1] though it may show that the phrase had also caught others' interest.) As Fitzmyer remarks,[2] "there is no other or more plausible starting-point for the titular use of the phrase than Daniel 7:13."

Those who insist that the phrase is not a distinctive title seem to ignore the significance of the definite article in the gospels (Daniel says

1. Not one of twenty Dead Sea Scrolls from *Enoch* contains the section on the "Son of man." See Abegge et al., *Dead Sea Scrolls*, 481. There are reasons for considering that section to be a later Christian insertion, replacing a chapter on "giants."

2. Fitzmyer, *A Wandering Aramean*, 155.

"one like a son of man"; Jesus is quoted as always saying "*the* Son of Man," which implies "the aforementioned" or "the familiar"). Further, the Daniel passage makes it clear that the "a son of man" figure represents a group, "the saints of the Most High," a distinctive emblem for a special historically significant body of devout individuals.[3] Thus translations as "a human being" or "son of Adam" seem excluded, and the possibility is suggested that by it Jesus meant a group, "the true Israel," such as he called his disciples to be.[4]

The phrase occurs in the New Testament some 80 times, but so many of these are repeat quotations that they amount to 44 different utterances. Two (?) of them occur outside the gospels (Acts 7:56 and (?) Rev 1:13), and, though they refer to the Christ, they are in passages relating matters too late to apply to Jesus' earthly life, so we ignore them.

Twelve occur in John, all quoted as spoken by Jesus about himself, but they resemble each other so closely and differ so much from most of the other instances that we can assume they do not reflect Jesus' use of the phrase but rather what the phrase had become in Johannine usage: a particularly impressive title by which Jesus is represented as referring to himself.[5] I can't assume that John's use had no connection at all with Jesus' use, but can't argue that John reveals how Jesus himself used the term, or even that he did.

Most discussions tend to link uses in the three synoptic gospels together. This I question, since I find clear indications of a difference between Mark's usage and Matthew's, even in material not derived from Mark—and alteration in what Luke derives from Mark.

Even when copying Mark, Matthew shows a difference in understanding. See particularly Mark 8:27–31 = Matthew 16:13–21, where Mark quotes Jesus as asking, "Who do you say I am?" and then tells his

3. Aramaic *qaddishei 'elyonin*, Greek *hagioi hupistou*. "Holy ones" in the Hebrew Bible often means "angels," but by Mark's time, Christians were called "saints," that is, "holy ones," and that title may have had its primal source in Jesus' use of "The Son of Man."

4. Marcus (*Mark 1–8*) does not fully agree that the phrase refers to Jesus' body of disciples, but he admits (246) "even though the "Son of Man" figure is not *identical* to the elect people in Daniel 7 . . . he is still strongly linked with them, and this linkage carries over to the New Testament usages of the term."

5. Black, *An Aramaic Approach to the Gospels*, 329: "Although the saying in Aramaic is ambiguous, there is no doubt that the Evangelists were right in interpreting it as Messianic: Jesus intended the veiled allusion to His own identity as Son of Man." I do not believe one can lump "the Evangelists" together on this point.

disciples that "the Son of man" must suffer. Luke follows Mark in this but Matthew reverses Jesus' distinction, having Jesus ask about "the Son of Man" and then say that he (Jesus) must suffer. As long as an early date for Matthew was assumed, this difference seems to have been passed over. A later dating for Matthew makes it stand out.

This loss of Jesus' use of "Son of Man" can be attributed to the fact that after the crucifixion, the title no longer had the pointed future reference it had for Jesus (except for references to the one "coming in the clouds," which was itself a sort of Christian transformation of "Son of David" apocalypticism). Therefore it became a mere additional label for the Christ. It obviously had become a convention by the time of John.

As John's use doesn't tell us what *Jesus* meant when he used the phrase, what of the other three gospels? The phrase appears 13 times in Mark; nine of these reappear in both Matthew and Luke, the other four in either Matthew or Luke, so both those authors were quite accepting of Mark's language, though that doesn't mean they shared Mark's understanding of the phrase (or that of Mark's sources). Ten occasions appear in both the later synoptics, but not in Mark. In both: Luke 7:34 = Matt 11:19; Luke 9:58 = Matt 8:20; Luke 11:30 =Matt 12:40; Luke 12:40 = Matt 24:44; Luke 17:24–26 = Matt 24:37–39; and Luke 12:10 = Matt 12:32 (cf. Mark 3:28–29). If, as I hold, Matthew drew on Luke, we can't automatically attribute these to some Q, though Luke may have gotten them from some earlier source.

So we have 63 instances of 23 sayings to rely on, occurring in the primary sources other than John.

Five different sayings (eleven appearances) occur in the three versions of "the little apocalypse" (Mark 13, Matthew 24, Luke 17 and 21), passages in which it is difficult to decide what sayings, if any, go back to Jesus himself, though some may. These apparently had enough currency to appear in more than one place, but one can hardly argue from them.

(I believe that internal inconsistencies show that the most we can credit Jesus with is only Mark 13:32–37, and perhaps verse 5. No "Son of man" sayings appear therein.)

Difficult to evaluate are the fourteen sayings that occur in only the first or the third gospel—eight in Matthew, six in Luke. Three of the Matthew uses appear to be the author's editorial comments or additions, one of them (12:40) in a clearly Matthean addition to what follows (that last appears also in Luke) and comparison of the others (13:37; 26:2) with the Mark parallels shows them also to be Matthew's additions.

The same seems often true of Luke. I take them to represent later usage that had lost the point of Jesus' own use. The more reliable approach would thus seem to be to limit one's consideration to the occurrences in Mark and perhaps the "Q" material, omitting those in the "little apocalypses" and those that are obviously editorial comments. That leaves 11 sayings in Mark, and 4 "Q" sayings (Luke 6:22, 9:58 and 7:34 and 11:30ff = Matt 5:11, 8:20 and 11:19 and Matt 12:40ff).

Two of the entries in Mark would then be set aside, one, 13:26, "they will see the Son of man coming in clouds" occurring in the "little apocalypse," and 9:9, "he charged them to tell no one what they had seen, until the Son of man should have risen from the dead," since its wording may be ascribed to Mark rather than to Jesus. That whole section—the Trans-figuration—presents huge problems sometimes met by treating it as a "misplaced resurrection appearance." (There are other suggestions, no more satisfactory.)

Three entries in Mark characterize the Son of man: he "has authority to forgive sins" (2:10), he is "lord even of the Sabbath" (2:28), and he "came not to be served, but to serve" (10:45). Of these, despite some doubts, I accept the first as from Jesus. The second, though possibly authentic, I suspect to be a theological comment directed toward disputes in the Roman congregation, but nevertheless take it as presenting Mark's probably correct understanding of Jesus' usage.

The third I also accept as from Jesus, though the clause following it may be Mark's addition.[6] Thus we have two attributable to Jesus, though their contexts show them to refer also to the disciples, or at least the twelve, rather than just to Jesus himself (Matt 16:18 and 18:18, and John 20:23 indicate that later writers affirmed the community's power to forgive sins). Attributing occurrences to Mark himself is not to say they do not reflect Jesus' own usage, though it may give room for doubt.

Two instances say prophecy predicts his suffering, "How is it written of the Son of man? That he should suffer" (9:12), and "The Son of man must suffer many things" (8:31). The first of these is presented in direct

---

6. The question here is, does the word "ransom" (*lutron*) mean "forgiveness," or does it mean "release from oppression." If the latter, it may very likely go back to Jesus. Jesus of course spoke of forgiveness, but promised it only to the paralytic, while his main promises were of freedom from oppression, freedom from want, etc.

discourse, as uttered by Jesus. The second is in Mark's summary of Jesus' teaching, but there is no reason to reject it. I accept the first as showing Jesus' usage, the second as showing Mark's, but, again, as at least presenting Jesus' own use.

Four reflect anticipation of that suffering, "The Son of man shall be delivered into the hands of men" (9:31), "The Son of man shall be delivered to the chief priests" so that all will be fulfilled (10:33), "the Son of man goes as it is written of him (14:21), and "The Son of man is betrayed into the hands of sinners" (14:41). Only the last of these is presented in direct discourse. The other three are introduced by *hoti*, but New Testament usage, and particularly that of Mark, often uses *hoti* in direct quotation.[7]

All nine of these can as well be taken as including the Twelve, or some larger body of disciples, in "the Son of man." All had been bidden "to take up their crosses," which would hardly have been meant figuratively in the situation.

The two Markan occurrences remaining may seem to raise difficulty: 8:38, "of him will the Son of man be ashamed, when he comes in glory," and 14:62, "you will see the Son of man sitting at the right hand of Power." It is still possible to read these as collective, though centuries of creedal recitation of "He shall come to judge the quick and the dead" as continuing the singular "crucified, dead and buried," sets such a reading in violation of very well-established habits of thought and speech. Yet a "Q" passage speaks of the Twelve as "seated on twelve thrones judging the twelve tribes of Israel" (Matt 19:28 = Luke 22:30), that would seem to include the Twelve in the judgment scene as at least involved with "the Son of Man," as does James and John asking for top secondary authority (over the other disciples) in the Kingdom (10:35 ff.). A collective reading of these passages still seems appropriate.

Other "Q" passages are also amenable to a collective interpretation. "The Son of man has nowhere to lay his head" (Matt 8:20 = Luke 9:58), spoken to one who wished to join *the group of disciples*, certainly, as also "the Son of man came eating and drinking" (Matt 11:19 = Luke 7:34), when put with the question of Jesus' *disciples* not fasting.

7. "The presence of *hoti* before a quotation is in the New Testament therefore not even presumptive evidence that the quotation is indirect." Burton, *Who Wrote*, 345. But neither is it evidence that it is direct. That it is indirect is certainly possible, and must be considered in these cases.

Disregarding again the occasions in the "little apocalypse," we have only two more Q instances. "Whoever says a word against the Son of man shall be forgiven" (Matt 12:32 = Luke 12:10) is amenable, but its use of "the Holy Spirit," not otherwise found in Jesus' sayings, is not found in the Markan original, and may suggest that is a later addition that does not go back to Jesus.[8] And Luke 11:30, "For as Jonah became a sign to the men of Nineveh, so will the Son of man be to this generation," contrasts with Matthew 12:40's "so will the Son of man be three days and three nights in the heart of the earth," both being introductory to the reference to the men of Nineveh and the Queen of Sheba and the "something greater" (not "someone greater") that was present. Scholars agree that Luke's use of "Son of man" here in Luke should be assigned to "Q," but one can hardly assign Matthew's to anyone but the evangelist, not to Jesus, though the references to Nineveh and the queen should be attributed to Jesus, since their rhetorical form makes them good candidates for accurate transmission. Luke's use here probably goes back to Jesus.

One appearance in Matthew is worth special note, Matthew 25:31: "When the Son of man comes in his glory" he will judge "the nations," which is read "the gentiles," separating the "sheep" from the "goats." But it is not the "Son of man" who pronounces judgment, but "the King"! The "twelve" may judge "the twelve tribes of Israel," and the "Son of man" judge "the nations," but "the King" renders the verdict.[9] That at least permits taking "Son of man" collectively, though no attempt known to me to unravel this seems satisfactory. It may be completely Matthew's offering.

That outlines the evidence for taking "Son of man" as a collective in Jesus' usage, which, since all the disciples had fled, became, after the Resurrection, a retrospective soubriquet for Jesus alone, as we find in John, with only Mark retaining identifiable overtones of Jesus' own usage, already fading in Luke and more so in Matthew.

Outside the gospels, it occurs in Stephen's speech in Acts 7:56 (Luke's own composition), but nowhere else (except possibly in the vision in Rev 1:13). That absence counts strongly against attempts to refer all "Son of man" sayings to the early church, rather than to Jesus.

8. Though the title does occur many times in the Old Testament.

9. Matthew's concern with Jesus as "son of David" may perhaps be appealed to in justifying taking the "King" to be the exalted Jesus. If so, it would be the only reference *of his own* outside ch. 1.

Apparently it dropped out of Christian usage more quickly than can be explained on the basis of adjustment to Greek thought patterns, being maintained only in the traditional material making up the gospels. That it appears in John at all may even mark early levels in the stretched-out formation of that gospel.

Though I find some exceptions to take to Teeple's methods, and more to some of his conclusions, he assigns eight, perhaps nine of the 12 "Son of man" references in John to his "proto-gnostic ex-pagan gentile" source G, whose treatment of Jesus, he suggests, was influenced by the "Son of man" image in the *Parables of 1 Enoch* rather than by the Daniel image we have referred to. (That the evidence of the Qumran scrolls undercuts arguments in favor of an *Enoch* source we have already pointed out. The quote from *Enoch* in Jude 14 and 15 is quite late, and doesn't fit Jesus' presentation of himself.) The other three, by Teeple's "editor" E, are less distinctive (see *The literary origin of the gospel of John*, 150–51). Since I do not see how John's uses of the phrase can go back to Jesus, Teeple's observations do not affect my thesis.

After much careful consideration of contrary arguments, I am convinced that the key to understanding Jesus' use must be found in Dan. 7:13–14, 21–22, 18, taken in that order.[10] Verse 21 is enough to explain Jesus' understanding that "it is written" that the Son of man, "the saints of the Most High," must go to Jerusalem and be killed, with an unspecified later vindicating judgment, indicated in verse 22, to be given by "The Ancient of Days."[11] He was not willing to speculate about the relation of the "Son of man" who would "come in glory" to the "Son of man" who would be killed. Both would be "the Saints of the Most High." He had a strong sense of the eschaton, but was too down-to-earth to dabble in

10. Brueggemann, *Introduction*, following Towner, says of vss. 13–14, "this promise for the future is made to a particular group of Jews with the urging that they should remain obedient, faithful, and trusting in the midst of adversity. It is, moreover, likely that this particular group of the pious is to be contrasted with the militant Zealots . . . who sought to establish an earthly kingdom of their own." Though he adds, "the meanings are not clear and likely not stable," his reading is similar to what I take Jesus' to have been.

11. France argues, "it is not in their suffering and defeat but in their victory that they are represented in Daniel's dream by the human figure." *The Gospel of Mark*, 334. This assumes that 7:19–27 is not an elucidation of the vision of 7:13. As I read the latter, it is just that. The "one like a son of man" becomes indeed the ultimately victorious group, *after they have suffered*. I do not see that later Jewish exegesis emphasizing the final triumph bears significantly on Jesus' quite independent use of the passage.

imaginative apocalyptic speculations that went beyond Scripture, as he read it—and he did not read it as supplying any detailed literal predictions of the future.

It is worth noting that nothing in the "Son of man" title in Mark bears in any way on the quite different title "Son of God." Mark makes no connection between them. He affirms both, the first openly, the second very sparingly.

Those who would like to consult writers more competent than I are referred to the following in the bibliography: Manson's *The Teaching*, 211–34; Allison, *Jesus*, note 242, p. 65–66; Vermes, in Black, *An Aramaic*, Appendix E; Hooker, *The Gospel . . . St. Mark*, 88–93; Schweizer, *Good News*, 166–71; Marcus, *Mark*, 528–32, or any other competent commentary on the gospels. For more technical linguistic argument, see Fitzmyer, *A Wandering*, chapter 6.[12] In those, one will find a variety of views presented. Most disagree with my understanding.[13]

12. "There is no other or more plausible starting-point for the titular use of the phrase for Jesus in the New Testament than Daniel 7:13 . . . Finally, the New Testament phrase must be so interpreted as to fit the varied uses made of it in different situations." *A Wandering*, 155. These state my two starting-points, though I go beyond his restrictions.

13. A position very like mine is laid out in Moule, *The Phenomenon*, 34–36. After this book was written, I obtained Dunn's *Christology in the Making*, with its excellent review of the relevant arguments and evidence, and was delighted at the extent his conclusions tallied with mine, except for my distinction among the gospels and taking the title to apply to the disciples—a possibility irrelevant to his aims and hence quite properly not discussed.

APPENDIX C

Translating John's Prologue

EARLY CHRISTIANS STRUGGLED TO develop satisfactory ways of talking about Jesus and his work as the Christ, and they left us what they did in words that they understood in their way. How are those words to be understood by us, in our quite different cultural situation? The translation offered here is an attempt at a more contemporary interpretive translation that is still a close reading of the actual words we are given.

> *At the very bottom of everything there was the Conversation, and that conversation was what God was concerned with, since "being God" meant that conversation.* (John 1:1)

"At the very bottom of things": the Greek *arche*, used in LXX to translate the Hebrew *bereshith*, "in the beginning" of Genesis 1:1, is clearly echoed here; but *arche* also means "ruling," as in mon*arch*, "early," as in *archae*ology, "fundamental," as in Aristotle's *archai*, and so on. We take the last meaning to be dominant here.

"The conversation": *logos* may originally have meant "list," but gained many uses. E. R. Hardy remarks, "The chief thing to remember about the word "logos" is that it means everything except a single word—speech, design, argument, reason—therefore God's thought, plan, utterance, and so on").[1] In the Jew Philo it is close to the Hebrew word for "wisdom"[2]; in the Greek Stoics it is better-translated "reason." Just how it first came to appear in Latin as "word" (*verbum*) I don't know. I take it as in dia*logue*, since in the ancient world "words" were *spoken in conversation, elements in an ongoing process.* Our familiarity with printed words, especially dictionaries, tempts us to forget that.

---

1. Hardy, *Early Christian Fathers*, 233.

2. The background for *logos* in the Hebrew Bible's Wisdom literature cannot be doubted. However, "There is no reason to believe that each person who contributed a poem about or a speech in the mouth of personified Wisdom had the same background image in mind." Lenzi, "Proverbs 8:22," 690). Nor is there any full agreement among contemporaries as to what that image should be.

APPENDIX C

Those who identify John's *logos* with Philo's should consider Wolfson's judgment:

> "two main characteristics of the Philonic Logos are missing in the Johannine Logos . . . There is no hint at all that the Logos of John . . . contains in itself the intelligible world of ideas and there is no clear statement that before its incarnation it had two stages of existence. . . . The two missing characteristics were supplied in the second century by those Church Fathers known as Apologists."[3]

I see no reason why the translator must follow later (and differently motivated) interpreters.

"What God was concerned with": *pros ton theon*. In Greek, *pros* followed by the name of a god could mean "what that god was concerned with"; *pros* could even mean "what is necessary for."

"'Being God' meant that conversation": Every reader of the Greek has noted that John says "a god was the *logos*," not "the Word was God," and every New Testament grammar claims to give some explanation of this strange way of speaking.[4] John presents Jesus as representing *how we know what God really is*; "the Word was God" would assume we already know what God is, but need to be told what the Word is. That would reverse the logical order of John's whole gospel, wherein Jesus is clearly subordinate to the higher mystery of "The Father," but "no one comes to The Father but by" Jesus. So Jesus draws us into the Conversation, the Word, which is the grounding of what we can know of the mystery of God. So *logos* is "what 'God' really means," preparing for the "No one has ever seen God . . . the Unique Son . . . Has made him known," which sums up the argument.

> *That Conversation was what God was concerned with at the very bottom of things. Everything that came about occurred because of that Conversation, and aside from it nothing came to be of all that did come to be.* (1:2, 3)

These follow from 1.

---

3. Wolfson, *Religious Philosophy*, 39.

4. We take "*theos*" to be the subject explained by the predicate *logos*. Taking "God" here as a predicate nominative and applying "Colwell's rule" to explain the lack of an article for *theos* ignores the "usually" in his rule (Moule, *Idiom, book* 115) and disrupts the style established in what precedes. I grant, however, that the reversed order might be interpreted as a Hebraism.

> *What did come to be in that case was a livingness, and that living-*
> *ness was the light of human living. And that light has kept on shining*
> *amidst the darkness, and the darkness couldn't do anything with it.*
> (1:4, 5)

"A livingness": rather than "life," just to escape the static concept that "life" may imply.

"Keeps on shining": *phainei's* present tense is taken as continuative.

"Can't do anything with it": taking *katelaben* as something like a gnomic aorist, with the preceding present, and avoiding decision among "overcome," "understand," "take over," and the other meanings of this ambiguous verb.

(Omit 6–8)

> *It was the genuine light that lights every human, a light that kept on*
> *coming into the world. It was present in the world, and the world*
> *came to be on its account, but the world did not realize it. It came*
> *to its own place, and its own lineage did not make it their own.*
> (1:9–11)

"Kept on coming": continuative participle, modifying "light" (hence "light" is repeated), rather than a periphrastic with "was" (*en*). The two words are admittedly rather far removed from each other: "Was" is the first word in the sentence, "coming" the ninth.

The shift from "it" to "him" is required because "word" and "conversation," which are both neuter in English, translate *logos*, which is masculine in Greek. Thus it is a question just where in the prologue *logos* should be represented by "it" and where by "him." If "person" in the Trinity is an interactive role rather than an isolated individual description, the decision as to when to use "it" and when "he" depends on a prior theological decision. That "God" represents an interactive role is basic to biblical language and to the language of prayer, and that "Jesus" represents an interactive human being is hardly deniable, but *logos*, taken as "conversation," represents the interaction itself, which did not become a definite empirical individual until Jesus. It seems best, then, to stick with "it" until the historical appearance of Jesus.

> *But to all who responded faithfully to him, he gave the status to*
> *become children of God, ones becoming so not by ancestry nor by*
> *human history nor by human choice, but from God.* (1:12, 13)

"Responded faithfully": John never speaks of "faith," only of "believing," and speaks of "*doing* the truth." Thus "believe" can be a misleading translation. The Greek verb *pisteuein* also means "to be faithful."

"Ancestry, human history, human choice": literally, "blood," "will of flesh," "will of a man" are terms given a variety of interpretations over the years. We take them to be protests against "the Jews'" reliance on being "children of Abraham," and on history ("for the sake of the Fathers"), and perhaps also against the individualism of mystery-cults and Stoicism. (Perhaps even the early appearance of gnostic interpreters of John that Irenaeus later criticized.) To take "will of a man" as John's acknowledgment of Mary's virginity seems far-fetched.

> *And that conversation became a particular fact of human history,*
> *and was our meeting-place-with-God-in-conversation; we have seen*
> *his imposing status, a status like that of a unique one originating*
> *from God, full of faithful loving-kindness.* (1:14)

"A particular fact of human history": literally "flesh," but the biblical background of "flesh" is complex. It often refers to the weakness and transience of humans—history exists because we die. The conversation that was "in the beginning" became subject to human misery, futility, and death, but by that fact became what the "tent of meeting" served as, in the Exodus story (and hence the Christ "destroyed" the tent's sequel, the Temple).

"Imposing status": a perfectly normal translation of *doxa*, "glory."

"A unique one": a proper translation of *monogenes*. "Only begotten" was used by the early English translators for *unigenitus*, which St. Jerome used in the Latin Vulgate when applied to the Christ; but which elsewhere (except in Hebrews 11:17) he translated as *unicus*, "unique" (Luke 7:12; 8:42; 9:39). To what extent *unigenitus* became, before Jerome, a standard Christian usage reflecting the "virgin-birth" stories rather than simply meaning "unique," I don't know, having no early Latin manuscripts available. Jerome, a monk, did stress the virginity of Mary.

> *And from his fullness we have all received favor replacing favor, for*
> *the teaching (Torah) was given through Moses, then faithful loving-*
> *kindness came through Jesus the Christ.* (1:16, 17)

"The teaching": "Torah" is usually translated "law," which is misleading. God's "righteousness" in the Torah was guidance for the good life rather than threats against evil living. Torah, for Paul, was grace, until "sin, finding opportunity in the commandment, deceived me" (Rom 7:11)—anything gracious can always be misappropriated and misused.

"Faithful lovingkindness," translating *he charis kai he aletheia,* "grace and truth," as a hendiadys, echoing the typical Old Testament characterization of God's salient attributes "loving mercy and faithfulness," *chesedh* and *'emeth,* in the Old Testament, or, as Paul reflects it in reverse order (with a different translation) in Romans 15:5, "steadfastness and encouragement." John teaches Torah as kindred precursor of Christ (John 5:45–46).

> No one has ever seen God. That one (Jesus the Christ), the unique
> Son, the one closest to the Father, has made Him known. (1:18)

"That One (Jesus the Christ)": Jesus the Christ" is not stated, but the Greek *ekeinos* specifies "the one previously mentioned," distinctly indicating Jesus.

"The unique Son": the evidence of ancient texts is definitely in favor of "the unique-divine," which makes a clumsy reading of the rest of the sentence. The alternative, as "the unique son" is less widely attested. The most interesting reading, just "the unique" (one), is attested quite early, though too poorly to demand acceptance (only a very few scholars do so). The question is, which reading is the original, and which the derived, and just how or why? It's not clear exactly what difference in interpretation hinges on the choice. Though academic conscience urges us to bow to the weight of textual evidence, I accept the alternative reading, which has both broad and early attestation and is not without expert support (see Brown, *John 1,* p. 17, or Wikgren in Metzger, *A Textual Commentary,* 198n).

Again, "only begotten" may suggest some obstetric concern, but John manifests no interest in such, which, in the New Testament, is evident only in Matthew and Luke, and is questionable in both. The emphasis here is on the uniqueness of what Jesus as the Christ accomplished: the manifestation of God as "faithful lovingkindness" conversing with us. In verse 1 it was said that "'being God' meant that Conversation." If Jesus is "the Conversation" with us, which is what "being God" can mean for us without God's violating our freedom, perhaps the distinctions among "the unique," "the unique son," and "the unique god," are merely verbal, and don't matter much.

APPENDIX D

Redescribing Christian Origins

READERS THAT HAVE A technical interest in Biblical Criticism or History of Religions will note that much in this book is at odds with one important trend in contemporary research into Jesus and the beginnings of the church. The trend is well represented in the SBL symposium *Redescribing Christian Origins*, edited by Cameron and Miller. For such readers I feel a responsibility to state briefly how I stand toward that and similar efforts.

Having taught and written for many years in the fields of Philosophy of Religion and History of Religions, I admire the perceptiveness, learning, wide research, and open-mindedness shown by the authors involved. Also, I recognize the importance of what they are doing for that discipline, a discipline that is, by its nature, entangled in and undercut by discussions of its relation to theology, a relation inevitable and probably irreconcilable. The various authors have pointed out a mass of demanding questions, many of which my own Bible study had already raised for me, some of them years ago. They make valiant efforts to answer those questions within the limits set by the responsible standards of the History of Religions discipline (formerly called "Comparative Religion").

How the first-century body (or bodies) of believers identified and distinguished themselves is an important question, including how Jesus came to be called "Christ," "Lord," "Savior," etc. Yet the temptation to use one promising new technique to explain everything questionable, rejecting, for the sake of method, long-standing explanations against which there is no real negative evidence but only intellectual preferences, seems no more reliable than accepting such evidence as we have merely on the basis of such preferences. Surely history is too complex to be illuminated by only one sort of theory!

Two aspects of their work I most basically question are:

1. While it is quite justifiable to refuse to grant to the biblical sources the full privilege commonly given them, is it proper to grant a similar privilege

to such sources as "Q" and *Thomas*? "Q" is admittedly a hypothesis, and even if there was such a document, what justifies taking it so seriously? Can we assume we have the whole work? Can we decide about its unity, its date, its authors and their aims, and hence its relevance, when all we have is our own construction, whose attributed completeness and hence character, seems to be a ghostly remnant of nineteenth-century hopes for Papias' now rejected "*logia*"?

And, similarly, *Thomas*, attested only by a fourth-century manuscript, a fragment from the Cairo Genizeh, and Greek and Coptic offerings from Oxyrhynchus? For date or origin, we have neither adequate internal evidence nor any external evidence at all. And are decisions about "the Jesus movement" based on them built on anything more than very hopeful sand? (It is understandable, however, that the questionable character of the biblical accounts can tempt any scholar into immoderate enthusiasm for some promising alternate source.)

Ever since Herbert of Cherbury, the History of Religions has shown many cases of such enthusiastically accepted new approaches, all of which either lost their attractiveness a generation or two later, or only survived in a severely chastened form.

2. As indicated throughout the book, I find that truth, as uncovered by the various sciences and outside the sciences, has a spectrum that ranges from mathematics to art criticism and theology. Mathematics contains nothing but formal, and hence empty, concepts. Physics and Chemistry add stable conceptual generalizations of concrete data, which can be handled and tested completely in literal language. In Biology, however, there are tensions between theoretical biologists and field researchers (not to mention Ecologists), something even more evident in the fields of Psychology and Sociology. Their data is less amenable to crisp categorization, more in need of a hermeneutic, and therefore "explanation" divides workers into "schools of thought" separated by reliance on differing standards for classifying data. Such standards differ in their recognition or denial of the centrality of studying individual cases in their uniqueness— something that demands imaginative, even intuitive, and hence poetical, language, rather than literal (since such can indicate truths unavailable to our conceptual generalizations, and in doing so shows up the claim that everything can be put *into classes useful for conceptual inquiry* (see the quote from Rescher, p. 135).

Further, the "human" sciences tend to involve the more human researchers in *therapeutic* interests, trying to change states of affairs instead of just describing them. Their results manifest imperative qualities. Thus Jesus' Resurrection as an indescribable event cannot be treated only by some purely descriptive discipline. It must be either accepted or denied as a unique datum, and, if the former, it contains a huge imperative. Intellectually, it resembles "the Big Bang," another unique event that the methods of Physics and Astronomy cannot describe, except negatively, and thus it is one that can't be classified in any scientifically useful way but it is one having no imperative content whatsoever (beyond that of curiosity).

It follows that the decision to "redescribe" Christianity's origins on the basis of any sociological theory must involve ignoring the Resurrection (though, of course, not ignoring the reports thereof). As an actual event, it can only be intellectually acknowledged as unique and hence surd, or denied. But Sociology, and History rooted in Sociology, can only interpret its consequences as occurrences classifiable with other sociological data. Thus, Crawford's claim in the mentioned volume, "Far from inviting scholarly study, such claims bring further inquiry to a halt"[1] has a measure of truth. But even if there is nothing more important at the time than 'inquiry,' must the Enlightenment premises of inquiry, historically conditioned as they are, determine its starting point? May we not be in the presence of items that, though beyond present inquiry themselves, provide opportunity for different sorts of inquiry?

The Resurrection, as an event, can only be accepted as an overwhelming imperative with a unique impact on our understanding of other things including our historical understanding of Christian origins. It is not available to our intellect for description, inquiry, or interpretive control. But then is any account of the "origins of Christianity" that denies the Resurrection any more than just an embodiment of some sociological theory? And does that not illustrate the intellectual futility of trying to extend "scientific method" into areas like religion that present a *humanly fundamental imperative*—that is, one that can be expressed only theologically? It can only proceed when based on the questionable Enlightenment theology of the ultimacy of the "epic human enterprise."

In short, isn't any quest for "a general theory of religion" as futile as one for a general theory of "beauty" or "freedom"?

---

1. Cameron and Miller, *Redescribing*, 339n15.

APPENDIX E

On Paul's "Conversion"[1]

I FIND CONFIRMATION OF the Resurrection in Paul's so-called "conversion" in the following way.

Paul's writings are the earliest and best attested of all first-century works. In Romans 1:3 he speaks of Christ "according to the flesh" as son of David, and in 2 Corinthians 5:16 (Weymouth trans.) says, "Even if we have known Christ as a man, yet now we do so no longer," leading to (Goodspeed trans.) "God . . . has commissioned me to proclaim . . . how God through Christ reconciled the world [including the Gentiles] to himself" (bracketed material added). The "Son-of-David Messiah," in whatever form he was widely anticipated in Jesus' time, especially among Jewish Christians, was expected either to convert the Gentiles to Judaism or else to destroy them. The former certainly did not envision them being reconciled "through Christ" apart from the culture demanded in Torah.

These passages, when taken together, seem to indicate that Paul, as a zealous Pharisee and rabbinical student,[2] had, whether tentatively or enthusiastically, accepted Jesus as the "Son-of-David Messiah" widely expected among the Jews.

If enthusiastically, he would have been desolated, as a strict Pharisee, when the crucifixion showed that God had rejected and "cursed" Jesus—a theme he alone among New Testament writers stresses. Neurotic disappointment at this could have caused him to persecute the church with the intensity Luke reports, and for which he takes individual and personal, even self-flagellating responsibility (Gal 1:14–15; Phil 3:5–6).

---

1. For the unsuitability of using the word "conversion," see Fredriksen, "Mandatory Retirement," 233: conversion "necessarily implies something about a person's environment as much as about his mental state: a convert goes from A to B. . . . But if B cannot be said to exist yet in any way that would distinguish it in telling ways from A, we have a problem . . . can we say [it] . . . of Luther? Does he "convert" to Protestantism?"

2. Especially if, as some have suggested, his use of Scripture shows he belonged to the Shammai school rather than that of Hillel. (In that case Luke's reference to Gamaliel in Acts 22:3 would present Luke's imagination, rather than some earlier source.)

He persecuted the church because it proclaimed that Jesus' resurrection validated Jesus as having a unique God-given status. Believing in Torah, he could not accept such preaching, that one "hung on a tree" was God-certified rather than God-despised. Such a proclamation enraged him, possibly stirring up a deep contradiction in himself. Unlike Christian believers, he could not accept the testimony of the apostles, but he still could not shake off the impressions that Jesus and the Christians' testimony had made on him. One of Luke's accounts of Paul's "conversion" quotes the divine voice saying, "It hurts you to kick against the goads" (Acts 26:14).

In Galatians he tells us, not of a "conversion," but that "God . . . saw fit to reveal his Son to me, so that I might preach the good news about him to the heathen" (Gal 1:13–14).

He experienced not just a change of Messianic ideas, but also a commission to spend his life proclaiming that same resurrection he had been so angrily denying. That experience, whatever it was, confronted him with the resurrected Christ, making him an "apostle." So he later rhetorically asked, "Am I not an apostle (a witness to the resurrection)? Have I not seen Jesus our Lord?" (1 Cor 9:1), and reported, "Christ . . . was raised . . . and . . . appeared to Cephas, . . . then to the Twelve, . . . to James . . . And last of all, . . . he appeared also to me (1 Cor 15:3–8)."

I cannot see how such evidence can be easily set aside unless one has already decided dogmatically that The Resurrection could not have occurred. That seems to exhibit more pride in our surely limited ordinary means of knowing than is justifiable.

Further, it appears that Paul was not "converted" *out of* Judaism, since he still boasted of his Jewish antecedents and record, made a Jewish oath, and religiously entered the temple. These facts possibly illuminate several distinctive emphases in Paul: his remarkable stress on Christ as crucified and as risen, on the cross as curse and as "stumbling block" (which it certainly had been for him), his claim of special authority as apostle, and his ambiguous treatment of "the law," the Torah. Though he says, "so the law is holy, and the commandment is holy and just and good" (Rom 7:12), he also says "no human being will be justified in his sight by works of the Law" (Rom 3:20). Also, "To (the Israelites) belong the sonship, the glory, the covenants, the giving of the Law . . . ," but "Israel who pursued the righteousness which is based on law . . . did not pursue it on faith, but as if it were based on works" (Rom 9:4, 31–32—a reflection of Shammai's legalism?).

By "works" he did not mean ritual law, as some modernists declared, but understanding Torah in terms of *Jewish culture and national identity* rather than as God's free graciousness—something pointedly illustrated by Jonah's anger over God's sparing Nineveh without in any way Judaizing its culture. But, as already pointed out, Paul was jolted out of the, at bottom, Son-of-David Messiahship expectation of either making the gentiles Jews or destroying them.

Incidentally, this same distinction underlies in some degree the emergence of Reform Judaism in the nineteenth century: just how much ancient Israelite *culture* is incumbent on today's Jews? How much of *traditional Jewish life* is essential to the Covenant?[3] Paul never denigrated the Covenant; he only questioned how much of his previous Pharisaic understanding of "the whole Torah" was included in the continuing Covenant.

Thus, Paul's witness to the Resurrection is not to be dismissed lightly.

---

3. A parallel problem appeared in Modern Israel when the aftermath of the wars of the 60s and 70s moved many Israelis from thinking of Israel as a secular state to a Messianic one, requiring expansion of Israel as well as perfect keeping of the Covenant.

Bibliography

Abbreviations Used

BAG   Arndt, William F. and F. Wilbur Gingrich, *A Greek-English Lexicon of the New Testament*, rev. ed. Chicago: University of Chicago Press, 1958.

BDB   *The New Brown, Driver, Briggs Hebrew and English Lexicon, Henderson Reprint*, copyright 1979.

LCC   *Library of Christian Classics, 26 vols.*, Philadelphia, 1954–1957.

JAAR   *Journal of the American Academy of Religion*

JBL   *Journal of Biblical Literature*

SR/SR   *Studies in Religion / Sciences Religieuses*

SM   *Sacramentum Mundi*, ed. Karl Rahner. 6 vols. New York, Herder and Herder, 1968.

I. Reference Works and Texts

Aland, Kurt, ed. *Synopsis Quattuor Evangeliorum*. 13th rev. ed. Stuttgart: Deutsche Bibelgeschaften, 1985.

The Apocryphal Books of the New Testament. [No author or editor indicated], Philadelphia: McKay, 1901.

Bettenson, Henry. *Documents of the Christian Church*. Oxford, 1963.

Brenton, Lancelot C. L. *The Septuagint with Apocrypha: Greek and English*. Grand Rapids: Zondervan, 1980.

Burnaby, John, ed. *Augustine: Later Writings*. LCC, VIII. Philadelphia: Westminster, 1963.

Burton, Ernest De Witt. *Syntax of the Moods and Tenses in New Testament Greek*. Edinburgh, 1976.

Cowper, William. *The Poetical Works of William Cowper*. New York: Rand McNally, n.d.

D'Ostervald, trans. *Le Nouveau Testament*. 1894 revision. Paris, 1942.

Funk, Robert W., and Roy W. Hoover. *The Five Gospels*. New York: Macmillan, 1993.

Goodspeed, Edgar J. "The New Testament," in *The Bible: An American Translation*. Chicago: Chicago University Press, 1943.

Hardy, Edward R., ed. *Early Christian Fathers*. LCC I, III. Philadelphia: Westminster, 1953.

Bibliography

JPS Hebrew-English Tanakh. Philadelphia: Jewish Publication Society, 1999.

Josephus. *Antiquities*. Whiston, trans. Hendrickson, 1987.

Miller, Robert J., ed. *The Complete Gospels*. Polebridge, 1994.

Moule, C. F. D. *An Idiom Book of New Testament Greek*. Cambridge, 1963.

Phillips, J. B. *Letters to Young Churches*. New York: Macmillan, 1957.

Rahner, Karl, ed. *Sacramentum Mundi*. 6 vols. Herder, 1969.

Robinson, James M., et al. *The Sayings Gospel Q in Greek and English*. Minneapolis: Fortress, 2002.

Schmoller, Alfred, ed. *Handkonkordanz zum Griechischen Neuen Testament*. Stuttgart: Deutsche Bibelgesellschaft, 1982.

Smith, J. M. Powis, and Edgar J. Goodspeed. *The Bible, An American Translation*. Chicago: Chicago University Press, 1943.

Stroker, William D. *Extracanonical Sayings of Jesus*. Atlanta: Scholars Press, 1989.

Suryanice incil ve mezmurlar (Syriac New Testament and Psalms). Stuttgart: United Bible Societies, 1986.

Vermes, Geza. *The Complete Dead Sea Scrolls in English*. Penguin, 1997.

Weymouth, Richard F., trans. *The New Testament in Modern Speech*. London: James Clarke, 1908.

II. Commentaries

Beare, Francis W. *The Epistle to the Philippians*. Harpers, 1957.

————. *The Gospel According to Matthew*. Hendrickson, 1986.

Bloom, Harold. *Jesus and Yahweh: The Names Divine*. New York, 2000.

Brown, Raymond E., S. S. *The Gospel According to John*. 2 vols. Doubleday, 1970, 1996.

France, W. T. *The Gospel of Mark*. Grand Rapids: Eerdmanns, 2002.

Hooker, Morna. *The Gospel According to Saint Mark*. London: A & C Black, 1991.

Lachs, Samuel Tobias. *A Rabbinic Commentary on the New Testament: The Gospels of Matthew, Mark and Luke*. Hoboken: KTAV, 1987.

Lightfoot, R. H. *St. John's Gospel*. Oxford, 1956.

Marcus, Joel. *Mark 1–8*. Anchor Bible, vol. 27. Doubleday, 1999.

Metzger, Bruce M. *A Textual Commentary on the Greek New Testament*. UBS, 1971.

Schweizer, Eduard. *The Good News According to Mark*. Atlanta: John Knox, 1970.

Williamson, Lamar, Jr. *Mark*. Interpretation Commentaries. Louisville: John Knox, 1983.

III. Other Books Cited or Referred to

Abbagnano, Nicola, *Critical Existentialism*. ed. and trans. Langiulli. Doubleday, 1969.

Abegg, Martin, Jr., et al. *The Dead Sea Scrolls Bible*. San Francisco: Harper, 1999.

Aland, Kurt, et al. *The Greek New Testament*. United Bible Societies, 1968.

Allison, Dale. *Jesus of Nazareth: Millenarian Prophet*. Minneapolis: Fortress, 1998.

Ashbrook, James, and Carol Rausch Albright. *The Humanizing Brain*. Cleveland: Pilgrim, 1997.

Barrett, C. K. *The New Testament Background*. New York: Harper Torchbooks, 1961.

Bibliography

Barzun, Jacques, in Michael, *A Jacques Barzun Reader*. San Francisco: Harper Collins, 2002.

Bauer, Henry H. *Scientific Literacy and the Myth of the Scientific Method*. University of Illinois Press, 1994.

Beker, J. Christiaan. *Paul The Apostle*. Philadelphia: Fortress, 1980.

Black, Matthew. *An Aramaic Approach to the Gospels and Acts*. Oxford, 1967.

Bloom, Harold. *Where Shall Wisdom Be Found?* New York: Riverhead, 2004.

Bonhoeffer, Dietrich. *Christ the Center*. Edwin H. Robertson, trans. San Francisco: Harper & Row, 1978.

Browning, Robert. *Poems by Robert Browning*. Alice Meynell, ed. London: Blackie, 1903.

Brueggemann, Walter. *An Introduction to the Old Testament*. Louisville: Westminster John Knox, 2003.

Cadbury, Henry. *The Peril of Modernizing Jesus*. Macmillan, 1937.

Cadoux, C. J. *The Life of Jesus*. Penguin Pelican, 1948.

Cameron, Ron, and Merrill P. Miller. *Redescribing Christian Origins*. Atlanta: SBL, 2004.

Carnes, John R. *Axiomatics and Dogmatics*. Oxford, 1982.

Chilton, Bruce. *Rabbi Jesus: An Intimate Biography*. Doubleday Image, 2000.

———, and Jacob Neusner, eds. *The Brother of Jesus*. Louisville: Westminster John Knox, 2001.

Confucius, *Lun Yu*. ("Analects") in *The Four Books*. Chinese and English, trans. Legge, reprint. Hong Kong: Hop Kuen, n.d.

Cooper, Rabbi David A. *God Is a Verb*. New York: Riverhead, 1997.

Cowper, William. *The Poetical Works of William Cowper*. Chicago: Rand, McNally, n.d.

Crossan, John Dominic. *The Birth of Christianity*. San Francisco: Harpers, 1998.

Croy, N. Martin. *The Mutilation of the Marcan Gospel*. Nashville: Abingdon, 2003.

Damascene, Hieromonk. *Christ the Eternal Tao*. Platina, CA: Valaam Books, 2002.

De Broglie, Louis. *Physics and Microphysics*. Martin Davidson, trans. Harper Torchbook, 1960 (Originally Pantheon, 1955).

Donfried, Karl E., ed. *The Romans Debate*. Rev. ed., Hendrickson, 1991.

Donne, John. *John Donne: Selections*. John Booty, ed. Classics of World Spirituality. New York: Paulist, 1990.

Dunkerley, Roger. *Beyond the Gospels*. Penguin Pelican, 1957.

Dunn, James D. G., ed. *Jews and Christians: The Parting of the Ways, A.D. 70 to 135*. Grand Rapids: Eerdmanns, 1998.

———. *Christology in the Making*. 2nd ed., Grand Rapids: Eerdmanns, 1996.

Enslin, Morton S. *Literature of the Christian Movement*. Pt. III, *Christian Beginnings*. Harper's, 1956 (first published 1938).

Eusebius. *The History of the Church*. G. Williamson, trans. Penguin, 1965.

Feigl, H. and G. Maxwell, eds. *Current Issues in the Philosophy of Science*. New York: Holt, Rinehart, 1961.

Feiler, Bruce. *Abraham: A Journey to the Heart of Three Faiths*. Harper Collins, 2002.

Fitzmyer, Joseph A., S. J. *The Semitic Background of the New Testament*. Vol. 2, *A Wandering Aramean: Collected Aramaic Essays*. Grand Rapids: Eerdmanns, 1997.

Flew, Anthony, and Alasdair Macintyre. *New Essays in Philosophical Theology*. SCM Press, 1955.

Fujita, Neil S. *Introducing the Bible*. New York: Paulist, 1981.

Bibliography

Geyer, Hans-George. "The Resurrection of Jesus Christ: A Survey of the Debate in Present Day Theology." In Moule, *The Significance of the Message of the Resurrection for Faith in Jesus Christ*. Studies in Biblical Theology, 2nd series, no. 8. Naperville, IL: Allenson, 1967.

Goguel, Maurice. *Jesus and the Origins of Christianity*. O. Wyon, Eng. trans. 2 vols. Harper Torchbooks, 1960 (French originally published 1932).

Golomb, D. M. *A Grammar of Targum Neofiti*. Harvard Semitic Monographs, bk. 34. Scholars Press, 1985.

Goodacre, Mark. *The Case Against Q*. Harrisburg: Trinity, 2002.

Goodman, in Dunn, James D. G., ed. *Jews and Christians: The Parting of the Ways*. Grand Rapids: Eerdmanns, 1998.

Goulder, Michael. *St. Paul Versus Peter*. Louisville: Westminster John Knox, 1994.

Hardy, Edward R., ed. *Early Christian Fathers*. LCC I. Philadelphia: Westminster, 1953.

Harris, Roy. *The Language Machine*. Cornell University Press, 1987.

Hengel, Martin. *The Four Gospels and the One Gospel of Jesus Christ*. John Bowden, trans. Trinity, 2000.

————. *Studies in the Gospel of Mark*. John Bowden, trans. Fortress, 1985.

————. "The Septuagint as a Collection of Writings Claimed by Christians," in *Jews and Christians*. James D. G. Dunn, ed. Grand Rapids: Eerdmanns, 1998.

Heschel, Abraham J. *The Prophets*. Hendrickson, 2001 reprint of Harper Collins, 1962.

————, *Who Is man?* The West memorial lectures for 1963. Stanford, 1965.

Horsley, Richard A., and John Hanson. *Bandits, Prophets and Messiahs*. Harper & Rowe, 1985.

————, and Jonathan Draper. *Whoever Hears You Hears Me*. Trinity, 1999.

Hume, David. *Selections*. C. W. Hendel, ed. Scribner's, 1927.

Jewett, Paul. *A Chronology of Paul's life*. Fortress, 1979.

Kasemann, Ernst. *Perspectives on Paul*. M. Kohl, trans. Philadelphia: Fortress, 1971.

Kellermann, Bill. *A Keeper of the Word: Selected Writings of William Stringfellow*. Grand Rapids: Eerdmanns, 1994.

Kelly, Thomas R. *A Testament of Devotion*. New York: Harper's, 1947.

Klinghoffer, David. *Why the Jews Rejected Jesus*. Doubleday, 2005.

Kloppenborg-Verbin, John S. *Excavating Q*. Fortress, 2000.

Laeuchli, Samuel. *The Language of Faith*. Abingdon, 1962.

Leon-Dufour, Xavier, S. J. *The Gospels and the Jesus of History*. Doubleday Image, 1970 (trans. McHugh from *Les Evangiles et l'histoire de Jesus*, 1963).

Ludemann, Gerd. *What Really Happened to Jesus?* Bowden, trans. Westminster, 1995.

Machle, Edward J. "A Plea for Euthyphro," in Lang et al. *The Philosopher in the Community*. American University Press, 1984.

Mack, Burton L. *Who Wrote the New Testament?* Harper San Francisco, 1995.

Macquarrie, John. *Twentieth-Century Religious Thought*. 4th ed. Trinity International, 1988.

Manson, Thomas W. *The Teaching of Jesus*. Cambridge: University Press, 1951 (2nd ed., 1935).

————. *The Servant Messiah*. Cambridge, 1961.

————. *Bulletin of the John Rylands Library* xxxii, 1951.

Marius, Richard. *Martin Luther*. Harvard, 1999.

Marsden, George M. *The Outrageous Idea of Christian Scholarship*. Oxford, 1997.

McHugh, John. "'In Him was Life': John's Gospel and the Parting of the Ways," in Dunn, *The Parting of the Ways*. Grand Rapids: Eerdmanns, 1998.

Bibliography

Miller, Dale. *The Adult Son: A Study of the Gospel of Mark*. Omaha: Wallace-Homestead, 1974.

Milosz, Ceslav. *The Witness of Poetry*. Harvard, 1941.

Minear, Paul S. *The Bible and the Historian*. Abingdon, 2002.

Moule, C. F. D. *The Phenomenon of the New Testament*. Studies in Biblical Theology, 2nd series, no. 1. Naperville, IL: Allenson, 1967.

————. *The Significance of the Message of the Resurrection for Faith in Jesus Christ*. Studies in Biblical Theology, 2nd series, no. 8. Naperville, IL: Allenson, 1967.

Murray, Michael. *A Jacques Barzun Reader*. Harper Collins, 2002.

Neusner, Jacob. *Judaism without Christianity*. KTAV, 1991.

————. *Judaism in the Beginning of Christianity*. Fortress, 1984.

Nielsen, Kai. *God, Skepticism and Modernity*. Ottawa: University of Ottawa Press, 1989.

Pelikan, Jaroslav. *Jesus Through the Centuries*. Yale, 1985.

Placher, William C. *Jesus the Savior*. Louisville: Westminster John Knox, 2001.

Pratt, James Bissett. *The Religious Consciousness*. Macmillan, 1930.

Reardon, Bernard M. G. *Religious Thought in the Nineteenth Century*. Cambridge, 1966.

Rescher, Nicolas. "On the Probability of Nonrecurring Events," in *Current Issues in the Philosophy of Science*. H. Feigl and G. Maxwell, eds. New York: Holt, Rinehart, 1961, 229–44.

Riesenfeld, Harald. *The Gospel Tradition*. Philadelphia; Fortress, 1970.

Rubenstein, Richard. *When Jesus Became God*. Harcourt Brace, 1999.

Schadewaldt, Wofgang. "The Reliability of the Synoptic Tradition," in Hengel, *Studies in the Gospel of Mark*. John Bowden, trans. Fortress, 1985.

Schillebeeckx, Edward, see Schreiter. *The Schillebeeckx Reader*. Crossroad, 1986.

Schottroff, Luise, see Soelle. *Jesus of Nazareth*. SPCK, 2000.

Schreiter, Robert J. *The Schillebeeckx Reader*. Crossroad, 1986.

Scott, C. A. Anderson. *Christianity According to St. Paul*. Cambridge, 1966.

Scott, William A. *Sources of Protestant Theology*. Bruce, 1971.

Silver, Abba Hillel. *A History of Messianic Speculation in Israel*. Beacon, 1959.

Sinclair, Scott G. *Jesus Christ According to Paul*. Berkeley, CA: Bibal, 1988.

Soelle, Dorothee and Luise Schottroff. *Jesus of Nazareth*. SPCK, 2000.

Spence, Jonathan D. *God's Chinese Son*. Norton, 1996.

Spong, John Shelby. *Why Christianity Must Change or Die*. Harper San Francisco, 1998.

Stroker, William D. *Extracanonical sayings of Jesus*. SBL, 1989.

Stuhlmacher, Peter. "The Understanding of Christ in the Pauline School: A Sketch," in James D. G. Dunn, ed. *Christology in the Making*. 2nd ed. Grand Rapids: Eerdmanns, 1996.

Sullivan. *Rescuing Jesus from the Christians*. Trinity Press, 2002.

Teeple, Howard M. *The Literary Origin of the Gospel of John*. Evanston: The Religion and Ethics Institute, 1974.

————. *How Did Christianity Really Begin?* Rev. ed. Evanston: The Religion and Ethics Institute, 1994.

Terrien, Samuel. *Till the Heart Sings*. Philadelphia: Fortress, 1985.

Theissen, Gerd, and Dagmar Winter. *The Quest for the Plausible Jesus*. Westminster John Knox, 2002.

Tillich, Paul. *Systematic Theology*. 3 vols. University of Chicago Press, 1951, 1957, 1963.

————. *Theology of Culture*. Oxford, 1959.

van Huyssteen, J. Wentzel. *Essays in Postfoundationalist Theology*. Eerdmanns, 1997.

Vermes, Geza. *The Religion of Jesus the Jew*. Minneapolis: Fortress, 1993.

Bibliography

Vidler, Alec R. *The Church in an Age of Revolution*. Pelican, 1961.

Wedderburn, A. J. M. *Beyond Resurrection*. SCM, 1999.

Whitehead, Alfred N. *Science and the Modern World*. Mentor edition, 1948.

Wickgren, Allen, see Metzger. *A Textual Commentary on the Greek New Testament*. United Bible Societies, 1971.

Wilckens, Ulrich. "The Tradition History of the Resurrection of Jesus" in Moule, *The Significance of the Message of the Resurrection for Faith in Jesus Christ*. Studies in Biblical Theology, 2nd series, no. 8. Naperville, IL: Allenson, 1967.

Williams, Bernard. "Tertullian's Paradox," in Flew and Macintyre, *New Essays in Philosophical Theology*. SCM Press, 1955.

Winter, Dagmar, see Theissen. *The Quest for the Plausible Jesus*. Westminster John Knox, 2002.

Wolfson, Harry Austyn. *Religious Philosophy: A Group of Essays*. Harvard: Atheneum, 1961.

Zizek, Slavoj. *The Puppet and the Dwarf*. MIT Press, 2003.

IV. Journal Articles and Poetry

Aray, Rami. "Hellenism in the Towns of Jesus—the Case of Bethsaida." *SBL 2004 International meeting announcement*. Atlanta: JBL, 2004.

Balagangadhara, S. N. "How to Speak for the Indian Traditions: An Agenda for the Future." *JAAR* 73,4 (2005), 988–1013.

Berkowitz, "Decapitation and the Discourse of Antisyncretism in the Babylonian Talmud." *JAAR* 70,4 (2000), 747–48.

Connolly, William E. "Realizing Agonistic Respect." *JAAR* 72,2 (2004), 509–10.

Creevey, W. H. *Seminary Chimes*. San Francisco Theological Seminary, Spring 1995.

Czachesz, Istvan. "The Transmission of Early Christian Thought: Toward a Cognitive Psychological Model." *SR/SR* 36,1 (2007).

Dourley, John P. "Towards a Salvageable Tillich: The Implications of His Late Confession of Provincialism." *SR/SR* 33,1 (2004), 3–26.

Dowd, Sharyn and Elizabeth Struthers-Malbon. "The Significance of Jesus' Death in Mark." JBL 125,2, Summer 2006, 271–97.

Fredriksen, Paula. "Mandatory Retirement: Ideas in the Study of Christian Origins whose Time Has Come to Go." *SR/SR* 35,2 (2006), 231–46.

Gillihan, Yonder Moynihan. "Jewish Laws on Illicit Marriage, the Defilement of Offspring, and the Holiness of the Temple: A New Halakic Interpretation of 1 Corinthians 7:14." JBL 121,4.

Gutstein, Morris A., Rabbi. "Gamaliel II," *Collier's Encyclopedia*, vol. 8, 558–59. New York, 1952.

Hawley, John S. "The Danger of Separation." *JAAR* 72,2 (June 2004), 375n.

The Hymnal of the Protestant Episcopal Church. New York: The Church Pension Fund, 1943.

Kaser, Harold K. Personal reminiscence recounted in *Monday Morning*. April 3, 2000.

Kloppenborg, John S. "*Evocatio deorum* and the Date of Mark." JBL 124,3 (Fall 2005).

Lenzi, Alan. "Proverbs 8:22–31: Three Perspectives on Its Composition." JBL 125,4 (Winter 2006).

Bibliography

Lowell, James Russell. "The Present Crisis," 1845, *The Pilgrim Hymnal*.

Marcus, Joel. "Crucifixion as Parodic Exaltation." JBL 125,1 (Spring 2006).

Martin, Michael Wade. "Defending the 'Western Non-Interpolations.'" JBL 124,2 (2005), 269–94.

Martin, Troy W. "Watch During the Watches." JBL 120,4 (2002), 685–701.

McClymond, Michael. "Making Sense of the Census." *JAAR* 70,4 (Dec 2002).

Miles, Margaret R. "Sex and the City of God." *JAAR* 73,2 (June 2005).

Moore, Michael E. H. "Demons and the Battle for Souls at Cluny." SR/SR 32,4 (2003), 485–97.

Myers, Frederick W. H. "Hark, what a Sound," 1843–1901, *The Hymnal*. Philadelphia: Presbyterian Board of Christian Education, 1933.

The Pilgrim Hymnal. Boston: Pilgrim Press, 1958.

Peter, Tom A. "Cultures Clash in U. S. Mosques." *Christian Science Monitor*, May 19, 2007, 12, 16.

"Praise the Lord, ye heavens, adore him." Author unknown. *Foundling Hospital Collection*, 1796.

Satlow, Michael L. "Defining Judaism in Accounting for 'Religions' in the Study of Religion." *JAAR* 74,4 (December 2006).

Schweitzer, Don, "The Dialectic of Understanding and Explanation in Answers to Questions of Theodicy." SR/SR 34,3 (2005), 251–68.

Segal, Eliezer, review of Paul Heger. "The Pluralistic Halakhah." SR/SR 32,4 (2003), 520.

Smith, D. Moody. "When Did the Gospels Become Scripture?" JBL 119,1 (2000), 485–97.

Sweet, William. "Religious Belief, Meaning and Argument." SR/SR 36,1 (2007), 41–64.

Tennyson, Alfred. "In Memoriam," 1850. Excerpted from *The Pilgrim Hymnal*. Boston, 1958.

www.ingramcontent.com/pod-product-compliance
Lightning Source LLC
Chambersburg PA
CBHW070910100426
42814CB00003B/119